*Jottings under Lamplight*

# Jottings under Lamplight

## Lu Xun

*Edited by Eileen J. Cheng
and Kirk A. Denton*

Harvard University Press

CAMBRIDGE, MASSACHUSETTS
LONDON, ENGLAND
2017

*Library of Congress Cataloging-in-Publication Data*
Names: Lu, Xun, 1881–1936, author. | Cheng, Eileen, 1969– editor. |
    Denton, Kirk A., 1955– editor.
Title: Jottings under lamplight / Lu Xun ; edited by Eileen J. Cheng and
    Kirk A. Denton.
Description: Cambridge, Massachusetts : Harvard University Press,
    2017. | Includes bibliographical references and index.
Identifiers: LCCN 2017007814 | ISBN 9780674744257 (alk. paper)
Subjects: LCSH: Lu, Xun, 1881–1936—Biography. | China—
    Civilization—1912–1949. | China—Social life and customs—
    1912–1949.
Classification: LCC PL2754.S5 A6 2017 | DDC 895.18/509—dc23
    LC record available at https://lccn.loc.gov/2017007814

# Contents

## Part 2: Reflections on Culture

*Jottings under Lamplight*

# Editors' Introduction

## Lu Xun, the In-Between Critic

It is now deep into the night as the year draws to a close, so deep that it seems the night itself is about to expire. My life, at least a portion of my life, has already been wasted on writing these pointless things. What I have received in return is the increasing desolation and hardening of my soul. But I'm not afraid of these things and don't wish to conceal them; in fact, I'm quite enamored of them, because they bear traces of the vicissitudinous life I have lived amid sandstorms.

Lu Xun, "Preface to *Inauspicious Star*"

Lu Xun (1881–1936) was born in the waning years of the Qing empire (1644–1911) and died less than a year before China became convulsed in war with Japan. Straddling the "imperial" and "modern" divide in Chinese history, his life exhibited many contradictions. Born into a well-to-do scholar-gentry family in Shaoxing, he was among the last generation of intellectuals in China to receive a classical education in his youth. At the same time, he was among the first groups of government-sponsored students to pursue a Western-style education: he spent his intellectually formative years (1902–1909) in Japan, where he acquired a broad understanding of Western ideas and world literature.

Inspired by the success of the Meiji reforms, during which Western medical science was introduced to Japan, Lu Xun aspired to become a doctor.[1] He wanted to cure patients like his father, who suffered (and eventually died) at the hands of what he came to see as quack practitioners of traditional Chinese medicine. Yet he notes in "Preface to *Outcry*" that he later abandoned his medical studies and embarked on a literary career after seeing an image on a projected slide while a student at the Sendai Medical Academy: the imminent decapitation of a Chinese man by a Japanese executioner, as some Chinese bystanders look on apathetically. This look of apathy—which to Lu Xun reflected a lack of compassion and fighting spirit in the Chinese—led him to believe that his people needed not a cure for their physical ailments, but a cure for their souls.

Lu Xun wielded his pen to effect that cure. He became a radical antitraditionalist and a supporter of the New Culture movement, which sought to liberate a society shackled to a moribund tradition through the adoption of Western values.[2] Yet he was troubled by some of the effects of this cultural appropriation, including the rampant misuse of foreign ideas and the transmission of colonial narratives. Committed to bringing about a new and humane society, he was, at the same time, wary of fully endorsing any political cause and doubtful of the prospects for transformative social change. Ever the pessimist, he likened China to an iron house with no windows or doors for escape, slowly suffocating its slumbering inhabitants ("Preface to *Outcry*").

Lu Xun's relationship to the past was no less ambivalent. Critical of aspects of tradition, he also saw how certain traditional mores and systems of belief could counteract some of the ills of modern society. Indeed, although Lu Xun was canonized posthumously as "the father of modern Chinese literature," his worldview and literary sensibilities were profoundly shaped by the traditional values and conventions he was taught as a youth. The classical literary universe provided a repository of models, allusions, and images, as well as a lexicon, that Lu Xun frequently drew on to make sense of the events he encountered. Writing in violent times, he drew comfort and inspiration from a lineage of frustrated scholars, in particular Sima Qian (145–86 BCE?) and the poet-minister Qu Yuan (340–278 BCE?).[3] Their strong sense of social responsibility and feelings of anguish and helplessness in the face of injustice resonated with Lu Xun, who in his own prefaces, several of which are included here, echoes their expressions of frustration with the times and their mission to record history for posterity.

The image of the writer in the epigraph to this chapter and in other self-portraits of the author jotting notes under lamplight[4] alludes to another familiar figure in the classical literary tradition: the lone poet composing meditative verse under moonlight. These depictions play with images of light and darkness and the shadows in between. This shadowy in-between fascinated Lu Xun. Conscious of the many contradictions that riddled his life, he referred to himself as an "intermediate form" (*zhongjian wu*, more literally rendered as a "thing in-between")—belonging neither wholly to the traditional society he was helping to overthrow nor to the new society he sought to bring about ("Afterword to *Graves*").

The sense of displacement and ambivalence he experienced as an "in-between" was a source of constant agony for Lu Xun. Yet his insistence on confronting head-on the contradictions of his life and times and his refusal to indulge in nostalgic views of the past or visions of a utopic future contributed to his greatest strengths as a writer and critic. His intimate familiarity with both traditional and modern culture and his assumption of the role of a detached observer allowed Lu Xun to chronicle one of the most cataclysmic transformations in Chinese history with a critical eye and brilliant insight.

## Lu Xun and the Miscellaneous Essay

Lu Xun's life was indelibly marked by the violence and injustice of the times in which he lived. By 1902, when he departed for Japan, Qing rulers had signed a series of unequal treaties after successive defeats at the hands of foreign imperialist powers. The Qing empire collapsed in 1911, just two years after his return to China. The democratically elected government that replaced it, however, did not last long. In 1915, Yuan Shikai (1859–1916), the once-powerful general of the Qing court named president of the republic, attempted to establish a new dynasty and declare himself emperor. When Yuan died the following year, the republic fell apart, ushering in a decade-long period of political fragmentation known as the warlord era (1916–1926).

After assuming a series of brief teaching posts in Hangzhou, Shaoxing, and Nanjing, Lu Xun settled in Beijing in 1912, where he experienced first-hand the chaos and violence of the warlord era. The Northern Expedition that swept from the south in the mid-1920s tenuously united the provinces under a new Nationalist regime. However, the arrest and execution of alleged communist sympathizers—which included his students, friends, and acquaintances—under the Nationalist "white terror" campaigns appalled Lu Xun. He excoriated the brutality of the government in his writings and was blacklisted as a result. After departing Beijing in 1926 and spending short stints in Xiamen and Guangzhou, he eventually settled in Shanghai, where he lived for the last decade of his life.

The cultural devastation left in the wake of these political events was an enduring theme in Lu Xun's works. The collision of the modern and the traditional not only informed the content of his writings, but also the highly experimental style, language, and forms he adopted.[5] His eclectic fusion of diverse literary techniques and conventions is in part responsible for the aesthetically innovative, if at times puzzling and uneven, nature of the five volumes of what Lu Xun dubbed his "creative works": two short story collections, *Outcry* (Nahan, 1923) and *Hesitation* (Panghuang, 1926); a volume of prose poems, *Weeds* (Yecao, 1927); a collection of autobiographical essays, *Morning Blossoms Plucked at Dusk* (Zhao hua xi shi, 1928); and a collection of revisionist rewrites of fables and myths, *Old Tales Retold* (Gushi xin bian, 1936).[6]

Although Lu Xun's literary reputation, especially outside China, hinges largely on his two slim volumes of short fiction, essays dominate his oeuvre: twelve anthologies were published during his lifetime and four posthumously. The importance of the essay form to Lu Xun's writing should not be measured purely in quantitative terms, however; in premodern literati culture, the essay was the literary vehicle most closely associated with the "conveyance of the Way"—the mainstream Confucian view that literature should reflect on and transmit ethical values.

In imperial times, the essay could take a variety of forms, each with its own particular function: scholarly treatises, tomb inscriptions, prefaces and colophons, letters, memorials, biographies, admonitions, eulogies, examination compositions, and travelogues, among others. These forms were used to expound on topics of relevance to governance and to delineate paragons of good and evil so as to sharpen ethical standards for society. The *biji* (written notes), a loose category of essays, emerged in the period following the end of the Han dynasty (206 BCE–220 CE) and matured in the Song (960–1279) and later in the Ming (1368–1644) dynasties. Usually short and concise, *biji* could be written on any manner of subjects, from the mundane and quotidian to grand issues of political and philosophical import.

Lu Xun was an inheritor of this long and heterogeneous tradition of essay writing. By writing in a variety of prose forms and using those forms to respond to the political and cultural events of the day, he was behaving much as a late-imperial literatus might. What is striking about his essays is their consistent use of irony and satire and their playful parodying of existing prose forms. In their thematic thrust, they also generally denounce the social and ethical values that were at the core of the Confucian tradition. In using prose for political, social, and ethical purposes, Lu Xun sought to "convey" a new "way."[7]

*Zawen* (miscellaneous prose) is often used as a label for Lu Xun's essays. The term usually refers to the more explicitly political and satirical essays he wrote in later life, what he called his "daggers and spears." These *zawen* contrasted with the *xiaopin wen* (small essays) popular in the day, which Lu Xun castigated as meaningless "curios" for the leisured class ("The Crisis of the Small Essay"). But "miscellaneous" also describes his prose writing, with its myriad themes and styles, from the beginning of his literary career. As a whole, his prose has an elastic quality that defies any attempt to neatly define its generic parameters. Lu Xun questioned single notions of truth and, as Gloria Davies has noted, underscored the complexity of human experience;[8] his experiments with a variety of styles and forms may thus be seen as attempts to capture that complexity in writing. He experimented widely, seldom retreating to the comfort of familiar forms as he searched for new modes of expression.

In Lu Xun's fiction, the authorial persona tends to be obscured by the complex layering of narrative voices. His open-ended stories, which employ multiple narrative frames and ambiguous symbols, may have provided him a means to convey, if not fully resolve, his ambivalent views and conflicting impulses. By the mid-1920s, however, Lu Xun was increasingly drawn to Marxist theories, both literary and political. Keenly aware that his political vacillation was not conducive to propelling a revolutionary movement, he began allying himself, at least outwardly, with the leftist cause. The sharp edge of "daggers and spears" delivered direct social criticism and political messages to readers, important considerations given his newfound political commitment and some of his concerns over readers' misinterpretations of his stories ("How 'The True Story of Ah Q' Came About"). By 1926, with the exception of a few works of short historical fiction, Lu Xun was writing almost exclusively in the essay form.

Lu Xun's essays can be categorized into a variety of subgenres of prose: treatises, letters, memorials, speeches, prefaces and afterwords, "impromptu reflections," aphorisms, and parodies, to name just a few. In tone, he could be mocking and derisive ("Impromptu Reflections No. 38") or deeply personal, such as in essays expressing frustration over the lack of change in China or sorrow over the violent deaths of students, friends, and colleagues ("In

Memory of Liu Hezhen"). Although he often vilified enemies in the cultural world—for which he has sometimes been criticized as petty and vindictive—his essays could be profoundly introspective and self-mocking ("Afterword to *Graves*").

Lu Xun's essays exhibit a wide range of linguistic registers. His late Qing essays, which are not included in this volume, were written in a difficult parallel style of classical Chinese; they tend to be longer and more expository and academic in style than his later essays.[9] At the other end of the linguistic spectrum, many of his essays were written in an accessible form of vernacular Chinese. More often than not, however, Lu Xun's prose melds the vernacular with elements from the classical register, giving his language a hybrid quality. His frequent use of classical literary terms, idioms, and allusions helped him capture modern realities in concise terms that would be meaningful to educated readers.

As David Pollard notes, Lu Xun also drew upon a variety of rhetorical strategies, from both the Chinese and Western prose traditions.[10] One common strategy is to open an essay by citing a text—a newspaper article or the words of a political or cultural adversary, for example—and then methodically pick apart its fallacies ("Why 'Fair Play' Should Be Deferred"). Or he might begin with an observation of something apparently insignificant, only to reveal its deeper implications as the essay proceeds ("Untitled," "Ah Jin"). On occasion, he introduces the insignificant into an essay on a profoundly tragic topic ("In Reply to Mr. Youheng"). His essays make frequent digressions that may at first seem irrelevant to the subject at hand but almost invariably turn out to be central to his main point. Some essays ("On Photography and Related Matters") present several ostensibly dissimilar topics, forcing the reader to actively forge thematic connections among them.

Lu Xun's prose writing differs starkly from the styles of prose popular among his contemporaries. In their forthright engagement with the urgent political, social, and cultural issues of the day, Lu Xun's essays stand apart, for example, from the humorous essays favored by Lin Yutang, the lyrical essay (often labeled *sanwen*) of Zhu Ziqing, the regional "nativist" consciousness of Li Guangtian, the dreamlike surrealism of He Qifang, and the "small essay" of Zhou Zuoren (Lu Xun's younger brother).[11] Lu Xun favored short essays because they could be written quickly and thus respond with urgency to the social and political issues of the day. Many of his essays were first published in literary journals and newspapers before being anthologized, and their appeal lay in their spontaneity, immediacy, and intimacy. Written in the moment, they convey, with emotion, personal reactions to external events: the death of a friend, a suicide, a massacre. Lu Xun described his essays as "signs of the times" (*shidai de meimu*),[12] contemporary chronicles of the fleeting and ephemeral events of history as they transpired; they give literary substance to a historical moment, making it immediate, tangible, and relevant to his readership.

## The Essays

The essays selected for this volume are intended to give general readers a broad sense of some of the recurring themes in Lu Xun's works. Included here are important autobiographical and biographical essays that shed light on formative experiences shaping his worldview and sensibilities, as well as critical essays that provide valuable insights into the cultural currents of Lu Xun's time. More than half of the essays are new renderings of essays previously translated, most of them by the renowned husband-wife team of Gladys Yang and Yang Xianyi.[13] The Yangs' four-volume collection *Selected Works of Lu Xun* (1956, 1980), which includes works of fiction and nonfiction, gave English-language readers unprecedented access to Lu Xun's writings and contains some of the finest translations of its time. The *Selected Works*, however, has not had a broad appeal to a nonspecialist readership.[14] Although it contains a large number of essays, those essays are often difficult for a general reader to wade through; ordered chronologically, many are not accessible to readers unfamiliar with the context at hand. The English is at times stilted, and some translations contain emendations to and omissions from the original. Our hope is that *Jottings under Lamplight* will provide lucid and accurate translations for specialists and allow a more general readership access to Lu Xun's works beyond his two short story collections. The thematic organization is designed to showcase some of the main threads in Lu Xun's thought and provide readers a context for making connections among the ideas presented.[15]

Part 1, "Self-Reflections," consists of two sections: Lu Xun's autobiographical essays, many of which are prefaces to his essay anthologies; and biographical essays, many of which are written in memoriam. Lu Xun's prefaces, often published first as stand-alone pieces in journals, largely follow traditional conventions of preface writing, revealing his intentions and giving readers a snapshot of the authorial mind. Indeed, much of what we know of Lu Xun's life and his motivations for writing come from these prefaces. Contrary to a popular image of Lu Xun as a literary warrior brandishing his pen, his self-portraits reveal a man plagued by doubt and riddled with contradictions. His writings are often a form of "merciless" self-dissection ("In Reply to Mr. Youheng"), exposing his own limitations and hypocrisy. In "Preface to *Outcry*," for example, he paints his early ambition to cure people's spirits through literature as little more than a delusion of grandeur. He depicts himself at midlife as an apathetic bystander to the New Culture movement, holed up in his room copying ancient inscriptions to while away the time.

Why this apathy? For one thing, in his autobiographical writings, Lu Xun at times anguishes over the violence of representation and the futility of writing to enact social change ("Preface to *Outcry*," "Preface to *Inauspicious Star*," "Preface to *Graves*," "Preface to *Self-Selected Works*," "Preface to *Essays from the Semi-Concessions*").[16] He was well aware that writing could be used to propagate false morality and legitimize hierarchies of power ("Preface to *Outcry*," "My Views on Chastity"). His disillusionment with creating a new form of writing and literature to bring about real change was also informed by his own early failures in publishing—his literary magazine *New Life* (Xin sheng) failed to launch, and his first volume of translations sold just a few copies ("Preface to *Outcry*," "Preface to *Self-Selected Works*"). The unremitting violence and political chaos of his times added to his pessimism. Attuned to the ills of society and the limitations of his fellow men, he decried the fact that change comes only when "a great whip lashes" a nation's "back" ("What Happens after Nora Walks Out").

On Lu Xun's autobiographical writings, a number of critics have noted inconsistencies and inaccuracies. One of the most prominent among these is the description of the photographic slide in "Preface to *Outcry*": depicted in the Preface as a beheading, the execution is described in Lu Xun's memoirs as being carried out by gunfire.[17] Efforts to find this slide have come to naught, leading some scholars to speculate that Lu Xun might have fabricated the incident.[18] Traditional autobiographical conventions offer a plausible explanation for Lu Xun's inclusion of possibly fictive details in his personal accounts.[19] Chinese historical and biographical writing—which differs widely from modern Western historiographic conventions—often adopted fictionalized elements; authors were less concerned with veracity than with conveying a moral message. Like Sima Qian in his magisterial *Records of the Grand Historian*, which incorporated fictionalized and dramatized scenes, Lu Xun may have been more concerned with achieving a particular effect than with accuracy per se.

Traditional conventions are also at work in Lu Xun's biographical essays, which echo the mission Sima Qian articulated in the biography section of *Records*: to ensure that worthy individuals who have gone unrecognized in their lifetime are given their just rewards. Biographical essays provided a venue through which Lu Xun could reflect on himself in relation or comparison to the person memorialized. He commemorated a wide range of figures, the more famous of which include the silent film actress Ruan Lingyu ("On 'Gossip Is a Fearful Thing'") and the philologist and radical revolutionary Zhang Taiyan ("A Few Matters regarding Mr. Zhang Taiyan," "A Few Matters Recalled in Connection with Mr. Zhang Taiyan"). Acutely aware of how biographical narratives can be manipulated, Lu Xun pays close attention to the ways the lives of the deceased are rendered in writing. In his tribute to Ruan Lingyu, he excoriates the sensational media portrayals of her tumultuous personal life and suicide at the age of twenty-four. He allows the actress to speak for herself in his haunting repetition of a phrase in Ruan's suicide note: "Gossip is a fearful thing." In his essays memorializing Zhang Taiyan, Lu Xun expresses consternation over depictions of Zhang as a conservative eccentric and a has-been revolutionary. Lu Xun recalls in vivid detail the radically iconoclastic gestures of the young Zhang and paints him in a culturally familiar guise—as a frustrated scholar whose ambitions were thwarted and whose true talents went unappreciated in his time.[20]

Some names would likely be unknown today were it not for Lu Xun's literary commemoration. They include his student Liu Hezhen ("In Memory of Liu Hezhen") and his friend Wei Suyuan ("In Memory of Wei Suyuan"). Besides paying homage to these individuals and leaving a written record of their deeds and personalities, writing these tributes may also have helped

Lu Xun to soldier on, despite the bouts of despair he experienced as he witnessed the deaths of public figures, friends, students, and fellow intellectuals in the political violence of his time.

Lu Xun's meditations on the state of Chinese art, literature, and culture are collected in Part 2, "Reflections on Culture." Many of the essays in the section "On Art and Literature" express his dissatisfaction with the state of the cultural field. Neither producers nor consumers of literary and artistic works are spared his censure. He decries the commercial state of the field, where writers churn out sensational and dramatic accounts to cater to vulgar tastes ("On 'Gossip Is a Fearful Thing,'" "A Glimpse at Shanghai Literature"). Evidence of this "vulgarity" can be found, for example, in the widespread adoration of the female impersonator Mei Lanfang ("The Most Artistic Country") and the popular appeal of adventure films set in Africa ("Lessons from the Movies").

On the whole, Lu Xun's assessment of the state of Chinese art and literature was negative. He went so far as to suggest to young readers "to read fewer Chinese books—if at all—and read more foreign books" ("Must-Read Books for Young People," "This Is What I Meant"). Yet, apart from in his early essays written in classical Chinese, he seldom offered concrete proposals for change. Some more general, sometimes tautological, prescriptions are to be found in his later polemical essays, after he emerged as a leading figure of the League of Left-Wing Writers (1930–1936), an underground organization set up by the Communist Party. Some of these essays were first delivered as speeches. Aware of the respect he commanded and perhaps as a sign of his self-skepticism, Lu Xun routinely offered disclaimers at the outset on his lack of qualification to speak on the issues at hand ("The Divergence of Art and Politics," "Before the Appearance of Geniuses"). Even in the 1930s, when he publicly advocated the writing of proletarian literature, Lu Xun continued to express his doubts over the efficacy of art and literature in forwarding a revolutionary cause ("Literature and Revolution: A Reply," "The Divergence of Art and Politics," "A Glimpse at Shanghai Literature," "The Most Artistic Country").

In the section "On Tradition" are essays attacking and mocking what Lu Xun saw as insidious traditional conventions and practices—from the cult of chastity to Confucian notions of filial piety ("My Views on Chastity," "On

Conducting Ourselves as Fathers Today"). He denounced what he saw as the "slave mentality" of the Chinese, long indoctrinated into a culture defined by strict social hierarchies and governed by principles of domination and submission ("Jottings under Lamplight," "Voiceless China," "The Evolution of Men"). In other essays, however, Lu Xun appears as both critic and defender of tradition, expressing consternation over what he regarded as deliberate distortions and misappropriations of tradition in modern times. He belittled, for example, some of his contemporaries' attempts to revive traditional literati practices, such as writing in the classical language. He saw such practices as a panacea for boredom and a means through which intellectuals flaunted their elite status ("Thinking of the Past Again"). He expressed a modicum of sympathy for the hard lot Confucius endured in his lifetime, and he pointed out how "Confucianism" only later gained prominence when those in power used his thoughts to legitimize their own rule ("Confucius in Modern China").

In "Afterword to *Graves*," Lu Xun laments the fact that he had been "poisoned" by the thought of ancient philosophers. Yet given his deliberate engagement with tradition throughout his life—reading classical texts, collecting old stationery and tombstone rubbings, and composing classical poetry, activities from which he derived obvious pleasure, meaning, and inspiration—such laments are difficult to take at face value. His intimate familiarity with traditional conventions and worldviews, in fact, gave him a unique lens through which to assess modern practices. He observed with amusement the uncanny coincidences of the "traditional" and the "modern," how so-called "modern" ways turned out, more often than not, to be perpetuations of practices of old ("Thinking of the Past Again").

In the essays in the section "On Modern Culture," Lu Xun often assumes the role of a bemused observer chronicling the curious interplay of the past and present, modern and traditional, Chinese and foreign, in the culture of his time ("On Photography and Related Matters," "Impromptu Reflections No. 38," "The Decline of the Western Suit"). Some essays speak with admiration of the practices of foreign cultures. For example, he notes how toys and books designed to stir children's imaginations, commonplace in some Western cultures, are absent in China ("Toys," "Shanghai Children"). Yet more often than not, his essays point to the superficial and indiscriminate appropriation of things Western ("Decline of the Western Suit," "Tablet"). He also wrote of the possible tragic consequences of promoting Western values to a society not yet prepared to accept them. For example, in "What Happens after Nora Walks Out," written in 1926, Lu Xun argues that promoting women's emancipation at that time would not only give Chinese women false hope, but could also lead to their ostracism or even death.

Residing in his later years in Shanghai's Japanese-controlled foreign concession, which afforded him some protection from the Nationalist "white terror," gave Lu Xun a firsthand view of the interplay between the foreign and the indigenous. Nine of the fourteen essays in this section were written after his move to Shanghai. Many of them speak to the subliminal effects of foreign technologies and media. Lu Xun displays a keen sensitivity to how media such as photography and film are used to disseminate narratives of white superiority and legitimize colonial domination; these messages, he feared, would be internalized by unwitting Chinese audiences ("Modern History," "Lessons from the Movies," "The Glory to Come"). With penetrating insight, he likens the colonized to the animals tamed in the popular Hagenbeck Circus, which toured China in 1933, noting how people are trained to act "civilized" and accept their lot as subordinates to their Western masters ("How to Train Wild Animals"). In a rare prescriptive piece, Lu Xun proposes that rather than passively accept things from abroad, the Chinese ought to think critically about how to actively "take" only that which would contribute to positive change ("Take-ism").

Given Lu Xun's ambivalence about writing and his pessimism concerning the possibilities for reform, what made him persist in his mission to use literature as a means for social transformation? Lu Xun writes that uncertainty brings with it the promise of that which has never come before. While the future might bear "the horror of annihilation," it might also hold "the hope of regeneration."[21] For Lu Xun, part of the key to a regenerative future lay in comprehending the present and learning from the past. In spite of his own skepticism, his writings are driven by a "radical hope":[22] that by chronicling the ills of his culture, new and old, for his contemporaries and

for posterity, he could stir his readers and help pave the way for a more humane society. As an "in-between" critic who often jotted notes under lamplight deep into the night, he hoped that he might be able to prop open the
"gate of darkness" so as to release the "children into a world of light" ("On
Conducting Ourselves as Fathers Today").

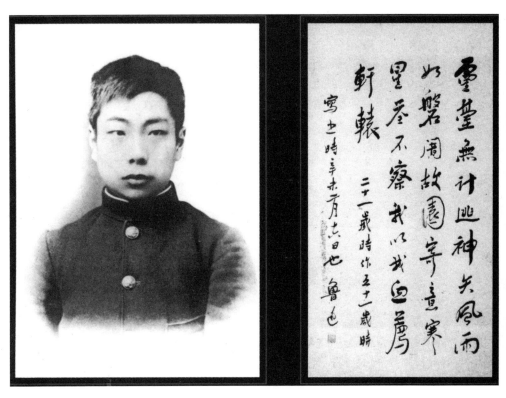

Lu Xun in Japan, 1903. Lu Xun had inscribed a patriotic verse on a copy of this photo sent to his friend Xu Shoushang. He recopied this verse in 1931 in the calligraphy on the right.

# PART 1

## Self-Reflections

# SECTION I

*Prefaces and Autobiographical Essays*

# Preface to *Outcry*
## 自序

When I was young, I, too, had many dreams, most of which I later came to forget, but in this I see nothing to regret. While the thing called memory can make one feel delight, there are also, ineluctably, times when it makes one feel lonely. What is the point of tying the loose threads of one's thoughts to those lonely bygone days? And yet, I am plagued by the inability to forget completely; some of the things I am unable to forget completely have now become the source for *Outcry*.

For a period of over four years, I often, almost daily, made my way in and out of the pawnshop and the apothecary. I no longer remember how old I was at the time, but the counter of the apothecary was just my height and the pawnshop's twice that. Up over the counter that was twice my height I would hand clothes or trinkets and take the money given to me under a scornful gaze; then I would go to the counter that was my height to purchase medicine for my chronically ill father. After returning home, I had other matters to occupy me, because the doctor prescribing the medicine was preeminent and the formulas he used especially bizarre: aloe root dug up in the winter, sugar cane that had endured three years of frost, crickets had to be original mates, ardisia in the seed-bearing stage . . . mostly things that were not easy to come by. But my father's illness worsened day by day until he finally died.

Those from comfortable circumstances who have slipped into poverty, I presume, are able to see people's true nature along the way. My desire to go to N and enroll in K Academy[1] seemed to have stemmed from a wish to strike a different path, to escape to a different locale, to seek out different kinds of people. My mother couldn't do anything about it, so she gave me eight *yuan* as travel fare, telling me to use it as I saw fit. She cried nonetheless, as was to be expected, because at the time studying the classics and

---

Published in the literary supplement to the *Morning Post* (Chen bao) on August 21, 1923, and in the story collection *Outcry* (Nahan, 1923, also translated as *Call to Arms*) released in the same month. Lu Xun, *Lu Xun quanji* (Complete works of Lu Xun) (Beijing: Renmin wenxue, 2005), 1: 437–443.

taking the examinations was regarded as the proper path. In the eyes of society, studying "Western learning" was only for the desperate who had no choice but to sell their souls to the foreign devils and therefore deserved to be doubly scorned and ostracized. Moreover, she would no longer be able to see her son. I, however, couldn't be bothered with all this and, in the end, went to N and enrolled in K Academy. It was at this academy that I first learned that such things as science, arithmetic, geography, history, drawing, and physical education existed. Physiology wasn't taught, but we did see some woodblock editions of texts such as *A New Treatise on Anatomy* and *On Chemistry and Hygiene*. I still remembered the theories and prescriptions of earlier doctors, and when I compared them to what I now knew, it gradually dawned on me that doctors of traditional Chinese medicine were nothing more than witting or unwitting charlatans. At that time, I also began to feel a great deal of sympathy for the patients and their family members who had been so deceived. Furthermore, from translated histories, I learned that the reforms in Japan largely came about with the introduction of Western medical science.

Such a naive understanding led me to pursue my studies at a medical academy in provincial Japan. My dream was a beautiful one: after graduation, I planned to return to cure the suffering of patients who, like my father, had been improperly treated; in times of war, I would serve as a military doctor and, at the same time, also strengthen my countrymen's faith in reform. I do not know what advances have been made in the methods used to teach microbiology nowadays, but at that time photographic slides were used to display the forms of microorganisms. Sometimes when we completed a section of the lecture materials before the period was over, instructors would show some slides of natural scenery or contemporary events to the students to while away the remaining time. Since this happened during the Russo-Japanese war, there were, naturally, many more war-related slides. In this particular lecture hall, I often had to go along with the clapping and cheering of my classmates. On one occasion, I unexpectedly encountered Chinese people, whom I hadn't seen in a long time, in a slide. There were many of them. One was bound in the middle and many others stood to his left and right, all physically strong bodies, yet displaying expressions of apathy. According to the explanatory caption, the one bound had served as a spy for the Russians and was about to be decapitated by a Japanese soldier, to serve as a public example to others. Surrounding him were people who had come to appreciate the grand spectacle.[2]

Before the academic term was over, I left for Tokyo, since from that moment on, I felt that studying medicine was not of foremost importance. Citizens of an ignorant and weak nation, no matter how healthy and sturdy their bodies, can serve as nothing more than subject matter for or spectators of meaningless public displays. That many of them die of disease is not, necessarily, something unfortunate. Our most important mission lies in transforming their spirits, and at the time I felt that the best way to transform their spirits was, of course, through literature, and so I wanted to promote a literary movement. Many of the Chinese students in Tokyo studied law, politics, physics, and chemistry, while some even majored in policing and industry, but no one studied literature or art. Amid this cheerless atmosphere, I was fortunate enough to find several comrades. Moreover, I was able to gather together a few crucial people, and after discussing it, we decided that the first step was, of course, to publish a magazine, the title of which was derived from the idea of creating "new life." Because we were inclined toward reviving the classics at the time, we called it *Vita Nova* (New life).

As the publication date of *New Life* drew near, several of the contributing writers disappeared, then some of the funds vanished; the result was that only three people, none with a penny to their names, remained. Since the launching had an inauspicious start, when things failed, there was of course nothing more to be said about the matter. Afterward, even these three remaining people, each driven by their own destinies, could no longer gather together to freely discuss their dreams for the future. Such was the fate of our aborted *New Life*.

After this, I felt an emptiness unlike any I had experienced before. At the time, I didn't understand the reason it came about. Later, it occurred to me that if a proposition is met with approval, it encourages you to go forward; if met with opposition, it encourages you to fight back. The real tragedy strikes when one raises one's voice among the living, only to elicit no response, be it approval or opposition, as if one were helplessly stranded in a boundless wasteland. It was then that I became aware of the feeling of loneliness.

This loneliness grew day by day, like a giant poisonous snake wrapping itself around my soul.

Yet despite my inexplicable dejection, I was not resentful, because the experience prompted me to self-reflect and see myself for who I was: that is, I was by no means a hero who could rally the masses with a battle cry and a raised fist.

But my loneliness had to be dispelled because it was more painful than I could bear. And so I used various methods to numb my soul, submerging myself among the people and returning to ancient times. Afterward, I either witnessed or experienced firsthand several events that made me feel even more lonely and dejected, things I no longer wish to recall and am happy to see perish, along with what was in my mind, into the dust. But my method of anesthetizing my soul appears to have had some success; I have never again experienced the impassioned fervor of my youth.

S hostel had three rooms. It was said that a long time ago a woman had hanged herself on the locust tree in the courtyard. The locust tree is now tall beyond reach, but the rooms remain unoccupied. For many years, I resided here, copying ancient inscriptions. Few guests came to visit, and in the ancient stone tablets there were few "problems" and "isms" to be encountered, so a portion of my life was thus quietly whiled away, which was my only wish at the time. In the summer evenings when there were a lot of mosquitoes, I would wave my palm leaf fan as I sat under the locust tree, catching glimpses of the specks of blue sky that appeared through the dense foliage. The late-emerging caterpillars would often drop and land icily onto my head and neck.

At the time, one of those who occasionally dropped by to chat was an old friend, Jin Xinyi.[3] He placed his big leather clutch bag on the dilapidated desk, took off his long robe, and sat down across from me. Because he was afraid of dogs, it seemed his heart was still pounding.

"What's the purpose of copying these things?" he asked me pointedly one evening as he leafed through the ancient inscriptions I had hand-copied.

"There isn't any purpose."

"Then, what's the point of you copying them?"

"There isn't any point."

"I'm thinking that you could write some essays . . ."

I understood what he meant. They were in the midst of launching *New Youth*, but it seemed that at the time not only did no one show approval, no one opposed it either. I felt they were probably feeling lonely, yet said:

"Suppose there is an iron house, without a single window or door and virtually indestructible. Inside are many inhabitants sleeping soundly, all about to suffocate to death. Since they would die in their sleep, they wouldn't feel the agony of death. Now if you were to call out, awakening those few who are dozing lightly, leading these unfortunate few to suffer the agony of facing a sure death, do you think you would be doing them any good?"

"But if a few people are awakened, you can't say that there's absolutely no hope of destroying the iron house."

Indeed, in spite of my own convictions, when it came to the matter of hope, I had no way of blotting out its existence. Because hope is something that lies in the future, I couldn't possibly use my conviction in its nonexistence as evidence to refute his belief in it. So in the end, I agreed to write something, which turned out to be my first piece, "Diary of a Madman." Once I started, I couldn't stop and often wrote some things resembling fiction as a way of humoring the requests of my friends. In the course of time, my writings accumulated to over ten pieces.

As for myself, I felt I was no longer someone with a pressing need to express himself. But perhaps because I hadn't yet been able to forget the grief from my past loneliness, I still couldn't help calling out now and then, to console, for the time being, those brave warriors charging on in loneliness so that they would have the courage to pave the way. Whether my cries were brave or sorrowful, hateful or ridiculous, was of no concern to me. But since I was crying out, I naturally had to obey the commander's orders. And so I seldom had qualms about resorting to sleights of the pen—making a garland of flowers appear out of nowhere on little Yu's grave in "Medicine," deliberately refraining to mention that Fourth Sister Shan in "Tomorrow" hadn't seen her son in her dreams after all—because the commanding generals at the time did not advocate pessimism. For my part, I also did not want to infect the young people who were dreaming beautiful dreams, just as I had at the time of my own youth, with the loneliness I have found so bitter. Seen in this light, one can well imagine how far my stories fall short of being true works of art. Regardless, that these things can be passed off as fiction and even be published as a volume is, indeed, fortunate. Though this stroke of luck makes me feel ill at ease, knowing that for the time being they still have some readers in the world makes me glad all the same.

So this was how I came to gather my short stories together and have them printed in one volume. For the reasons mentioned above, I have titled it *Outcry*.

December 3, 1922, recorded in Beijing

TRANSLATED BY EILEEN J. CHENG

# Preface to *Inauspicious Star*

《華蓋集》題記

Deep into the night as the year draws to a close, I have been organizing the miscellaneous essays I wrote this year. It turns out that there are even more essays than the ones I wrote over a four-year period and collected in *Hot Wind*. The opinions are still largely the same, although the attitude is no longer as straightforward; the expressions used are often roundabout, and the discussions often mired in a few trivial matters, all of which may seem ridiculous to the erudite. But there's nothing one can do about it. These happen to be the trivial matters I encountered this year, and I happen to have a temperament that dwells on the trivial.

I know great men have the penetrating vision to see through the past, present, and future and can apprehend all matters through contemplation because they have experienced great tribulations, tasted great happiness, and can awaken great compassion for all living beings. But I also know that this requires retreating deep into the mountains and forests, sitting under an ancient tree, quietly contemplating and reflecting, and opening one's divine eyes;[4] the farther one's distance from the secular world, the deeper and wider the expanse of one's knowledge of it. And so when one speaks, the words are loftier and have more impact, and one then becomes a "teacher of gods and humans." When I was young I dreamt of flying, but to this day I remain rooted to the ground. I still haven't managed to recover from the small inju-

---

First published in issue 2 of the journal *Wilderness* (Mangyuan) on January 25, 1926, and later anthologized in *Inauspicious Star* (Huagai ji, 1926). Lu Xun, *Lu Xun quanji* (Complete works of Lu Xun) (Beijing: Renmin wenxue, 2005), 3: 3–7.

ries I've sustained; how would I have the leisure to cultivate a magnanimous spirit and open mind and hold opinions that are fair, appropriate, righteous, and reasonable, like those of the "estimable gentlemen"?[5] Like a little bee that has gotten itself wet, I am just crawling back and forth in the mud and I dare not compare myself to the erudite men living in Western-style buildings. But I also have sorrows and frustrations of my own, which are by no means intelligible to the erudite men living in Western-style buildings.

The root of such suffering lies in the fact that I live in the human world and that I am an ordinary mortal, subject to "inauspicious fortune."

I have never in my life studied fortune-telling, but I have heard the elderly talk about how we are sometimes subject to "inauspicious (*huagai* 華蓋) fortune." The *huagai* they speak of has likely been mistakenly written as the characters 鑊蓋, so I'll make a correction here. When this luck lands on a monk, it is considered good fortune; a *huagai* star above is, naturally, a sign that one will attain Buddhahood or become a lineage patriarch. But this isn't the case with secular folks; when there's a *huagai* star about to hover over you, you're bound to run your head into a brick wall. When I started writing my miscellaneous thoughts this year, I ran into two such brick walls. One was on account of the essay "Obsessing over Words" and the other due to "Must-Read Books for Young People."[6] I received a whole bundle of letters, both signed and anonymous, from heroic men cursing me. To this day, the letters remain stuffed under my bookcase. Afterward, I suddenly encountered some so-called scholars, littérateurs, upstanding men, gentlemen, etc. purportedly talking about fair-mindedness and justice in the public interest and repudiating the idea of "allying with one's clique to attack those who are different."[7] What a pity I'm just too different from them, so I was also attacked by them several times. But naturally this was out of their sense of "public interest," which is altogether different from my case of "allying with one's clique to attack those who are different." Up until now there's been no resolution to our differences, so we can only "await the coming year."

There are also people who have urged me not to write these kinds of short criticism. For their good intentions, I'm very grateful; moreover, it isn't as if I'm unaware of how valuable original writings are. Yet when I am about to write such things—and I'm afraid I will still have to write such things—I feel that if there are such bothersome bans in the palace of art, one might as well not enter it at all. Might as well stand in the desert and watch the flurry of sand particles and sliding rocks, laughing heartily when happy, crying out loudly when sad, cursing vociferously when enraged. Frequently caressing the congealed blood on one's body and head, calloused and battered by the bombardment of grit, as if it were a decorative pattern is not necessarily any less pleasurable than the Chinese literary scholars' supping on bread with Shakespeare.[8]

Yet what a shame that my sights are so narrow; so many important events happened this year in China alone that I have yet to write about, it's almost as if they hadn't affected me at all. I have long wished that Chinese youths would step up without a shred of fear to criticize Chinese society and civilization. And so I edited and printed *Wilderness* as a platform for voicing such opinions, but a pity only a few spoke out. Other periodicals mostly attacked those who challenged convention, which really makes me afraid to imagine what lies ahead.

It is now deep into the night as the year draws to a close, so deep that it seems the night itself is about to expire. My life, at least a portion of my life, has already been wasted on writing these pointless things, and what I have received in return is the increasing desolation and hardening of my soul. But I'm not afraid of these things and don't wish to conceal them; in fact, I'm quite enamored of them because they bear traces of the vicissitudinous life I have led amid sandstorms. Those who feel that they, too, are living a vicissitudinous life amid sandstorms will understand the meaning of this.

When I edited *Hot Wind*, besides the essays I had forgotten to include, I also deliberately excluded several essays. This time it's a little different, and almost all the miscellaneous essays I wrote over a period of time have been collected here.

> Evening of December 31, 1925, recorded at the
> eastern wall of the Emerald Forest Bookstore

TRANSLATED BY EILEEN J. CHENG

# Preface to *Graves*

《墳》題記

The reason for taking things so completely disparate in form as these and gathering them into something like a book is not all that high-sounding once actually put into words. To begin with, I did it because I would from time to time look at several of these what we might call essays written almost twenty years ago and think: Did I write these? But reading through them it would seem that I actually did. These are the manuscripts submitted to the journal *Henan*;[9] because the editor had a peculiar temperament and wanted long essays, the longer they were, the higher the fee he paid. So the elements in pieces like "On Mara Poetry" were practically forced together. Had I written them in more recent times, it is likely that I would not have done it that way. I also favored odd phrases and archaic characters, something influenced by the journal *People's Paper*[10] of those years; now, however, for the convenience of the printers I have changed a few things, but the rest of them are left to their own devices. Were others to create such obdurate and awkward things, I probably would not be able to resist urging them to "kill their darlings," but for myself I invariably want to preserve them, if only to avoid thinking that "at age fifty I came to believe that everything from my first forty-nine years was in error"[11] and that I have progressed with age. There are a number of poets mentioned in the essays that no one speaks of any longer, which is another small reason I cannot bear to discard these old manuscripts. Back then, how their names filled me with passion! But with the coming of the Republic in 1912, I forgot all about them, although they have now unexpectedly begun to appear again before my eyes.

Secondly, of course, is that there are still people who wish to read them, but even more because there are others who hate my writing. When people despise what you say, it's still a happier circumstance than creating no effect at all. The world is full of people lacking comfort, and there are also those

First published in issue 106 of *Threads of Talk* (Yusi) on November 20, 1926, and later anthologized in *Graves* (Fen, 1927). Lu Xun, *Lu Xun quanji* (Complete works of Lu Xun) (Beijing: Renmin wenxue, 2005), 1: 3–7.

Owl illustration by Lu Xun, included in *Graves* (Fen)

intent on nothing other than creating a realm of comfort for themselves. This should not be so cheaply achieved, and we should thus place some odious things before them to afflict them with a bit of discomfort now and then so they may know that it is not possible to create their own perfect zone of comfort. When flies buzz about, they are not aware that people detest their buzzing; I, however, know it, but I will insist on buzzing as long as I am up to it. I am sometimes aware of my own obnoxiousness, so my giving up liquor and taking cod-liver oil to extend my life is not merely for the sake of those who love me, but is, in large part, for my enemies—let's give them a little credit and at least call them enemies—so as to leave a few imperfections in their perfect worlds. These estimable gentlemen say: Why don't you go after the warlords, who kill without blinking an eye? Failure to do this is base and cowardly! But I won't get taken in by traps like these. The scholar Jia Fuxi (1592–1674) had it right when he wrote, "Being hacked on the head for years on end with a soft knife, you don't feel you're going to die," and I want to thoroughly condemn those who call themselves "the gunless class" and who are actually demons wielding the soft knives. The words of the estimable gentlemen quoted above are just such a soft knife. And should you encounter catastrophe, do you think they will respect you as a martyr? No, they would simply come up with another line of derision. If you don't believe this, take a look at how they evaluated the young people who died in the March 18, 1926, massacre in Beijing.[12]

These reasons aside, these essays also contain some slight significance for myself, inasmuch as they are, after all, a partial record of my life. So although I am completely aware that the past has already passed, and that old states of mind cannot be tracked down, I just cannot make such a clean break, and I still wish to gather up the dregs to create a tiny new grave, partly for the sake of burial, partly for the sake of nostalgia. As for the grave being trodden flat in the near future, I have no mind to pay any attention to that, nor any way of paying it attention even if I wanted to.

I am thoroughly grateful to several of my friends who collected, copied out, proofed, and printed for me, each spending much precious time that can never be recovered. My repayment can only be the hope that when the book is printed and bound, it will elicit a smile of genuine satisfaction from each of them. I have no grander hope than this; at most I wish for the book to take its place among a stack of other books in a bookshop for a short time, much as the great clod of this earth must surely be able to accommodate another small clump of dirt. It would be somewhat out of line to take it a step further—that is, to place hopes on the fact that the thoughts and interests of the Chinese people have yet to be united with those whom I call the estimable gentlemen; for instance, some people pay homage to the imperial tombs, and others meditate on forsaken graves; anyway, and at any given time, there will likely always be people not worth a second thought. As long as things are thus, I will be quite satisfied, a satisfaction that one can say is no less than taking a fortune from a rich man.

The gusty evening of October 30, 1926; Lu Xun in Xiamen

TRANSLATED BY THEODORE HUTERS

# Afterword to *Graves*
## 寫在《墳》後面

Upon hearing that half of my collection of essays had been printed, I wrote a few prefatory lines and mailed them to Beijing. At the time I just wrote down what came to mind, and sent it off when I was done; that was not even twenty days ago, but I've long since forgotten what I said. Tonight the surroundings are very tranquil, with the faint light of a wildfire rising from the foot of the hill behind my room; they are putting on a marionette opera at the Nan Putuo Temple next door, and from time to time the sound of beating gongs is transmitted, making the intervals between seem even quieter. The electric lights are of course very bright, but for some inexplicable reason, I was suddenly overcome by a faint sense of melancholy, and I seem to be regretting the printing of my essays. I find my regret quite puzzling, as it is not something I encounter very often, and until now I'm still not completely clear what this thing called "regret" actually is. But the mood passed soon enough, and of course the essay collection was still going to be printed, but I just want to say a few words to drive away my present melancholy.

I recall having said that these essays are nothing more than a few traces of my life. If the things that have occurred in my past can be counted as actual living, then it can also be said that I have done some work. But ideas do not spout from me as from a fountain, nor are my essays great and resplendent,

First published in issue 108 of *Threads of Talk* (Yusi) on December 4, 1926, and later anthologized in *Graves* (Fen, 1927). Lu Xun, *Lu Xun quanji* (Complete works of Lu Xun) (Beijing: Renmin wenxue, 2005), 1: 298–304.

and since I have no ideology to promote, neither do I wish to begin any sort of movement. I have, however, found that disappointment, whether big or small, has a bitter flavor. So over the past several years when someone wanted me to write something, as long as our opinions were not too far apart and I had the strength to do it, I always strived to write a few things to give the tiniest bit of pleasure to the next generation. Life is full of hardship, and yet people sometimes find comfort remarkably easily; so why waste drops of ink on making people feel more of the sorrow of loneliness?

So, aside from stories and random thoughts, I gradually came to have a dozen or so essays, long and short. Among them, of course, were a few written for money, which have been mixed together here with the other writings. A portion of my life has been spent this way, that is, on doing this sort of work. Even now, however, I still do not understand just what I have been doing all this time. It is like someone who digs for a living, who keeps working and working without understanding whether he is building a platform or digging a hole. Even if he knew it was in fact a platform, it would be just something he can fall off from or display himself on as he dies of old age. If it were digging a hole, then of course it would be for no other reason than to bury himself. In short, things pass away and pass away, every and all things pass away quickly like time; they are passing away and will pass away—that is all there is to it, but I am perfectly content with it.

All this, however, is more or less just a passage of words. Yet, as long as I am still breathing, and as long as they are mine, I like gathering up the traces from the past from time to time, knowing full well they are worthless; yet I can't help feeling some attachment to them. So I've gathered my essays into one collection and called it "Graves," something that is in the end still a clever concealment. When Liu Ling of the Six Dynasties period would get so drunk he stank to high heaven, he would have someone carry a spade and follow him, saying: "Bury me if I die." And although he thought of himself as unconventional, in fact this could only fool those who were completely naive.

So the publishing of this book is nothing more than this to me. As for others, I recall that I have already said that I wish to give a bit of pleasure to those customers who are partial to my writing; and to make those who hate my writing retch—I know that I am not a person of magnanimity, so I am happy to make those who hate my writing retch. Apart from this, there is no other point. If we must find some other good things about them, those few poets that I introduced are perhaps worth a look; the final piece on "fair play"[13] can be taken as a reference, because although it was not written with my blood, it was written after having seen the blood of those of my own generation and people younger than myself.

Readers partial to my work sometimes offer the critique that my writing speaks the truth. This is an undeserved compliment, and it is owed to their partiality. It is of course not my intent to deceive people, but I have also never given full expression to my innermost feelings. I consider the job done when things look more or less acceptable and can be handed in. It is true that I often dissect others, but I dissect myself even more mercilessly, and when I publish a bit of this, those passionate about human warmth consider it quite callous; if I revealed my blood and flesh in its entirety, I don't know where it would lead. Sometimes I also want to use this to drive those around me away, but when I do and they still don't spurn me, even if they are monsters, they become my friends, and they are, in fact, my true friends. And if I lack even these, then being alone will still be all right. But now I am not alone, because I am not that brave, the reason being that I still want to live and be part of society. There is still another, more minor, reason, one that I have already enunciated a number of times, and that is that I am determined to have what I call the estimable gentlemen and their ilk suffer a few days of discomfort, so I have left a few pieces of armor on my body and will stand my ground, to add a few imperfections to their worlds, until I grow tired of it and want to take off the armor.

If one speaks of leading the way for others, that is even more difficult, inasmuch as I myself do not know which way to go. China more than likely has enough "elders" and "advisers" to the young, but I am not one of them, nor do I trust them. I know for a fact only one destination, and that is the grave. This is, however, something everyone knows, and no one is needed to lead the way. The issue lies in the path that takes one from here to there. There is, of course, more than one way, but I really don't know which way is best, though even now I still look for a path from time to time. In the midst of the search, however, I fear that my unripe fruit will poison those who are partial to it, while those who hate my work, like those I call the estimable gentlemen, end up, perversely, hale and hearty. So when I speak, I often can't avoid being equivocal and stopping midway, as I think to myself: Perhaps the best contribution I can give to those readers partial to me is simply "nothing."

The first edition of my collection of translations had an initial printing of a thousand copies, with another five hundred added later, and most recently another two to four thousand. I am quite happy with each new printing, because it means more money; but this feeling is also accompanied by grief, because I am afraid that it may be harmful to my readers. As a result, when I write, I am more often than not even more careful, more hesitant. There are those who think that I directly write out my feelings, which is, in fact, not entirely the case, as I have not a few misgivings. I have long been aware that I am by no means a warrior or a pioneer, and that I have all these misgivings and recollections. I remember that three or four years ago a student came up to me to buy my book, taking money out of his pocket to put into my hand, the money still warm. This warmth made a deep impression on me, and even today when I write I am often afraid of poisoning this sort of young person, causing me to hesitate as I set pen to paper. The days when I can speak with no misgivings whatsoever, I'm afraid, may never come again. But sometimes I also think that to speak with no misgivings at all is, in fact, the only way to do justice to this type of young person. But even now I still cannot commit myself to doing so.

That is all I want to write today, at least that which can be considered relatively truthful. Aside from this, there are a few things that remain to be said.

I recall that when the vernacular was first being advocated, it was fiercely attacked from all sides. Eventually, when the vernacular gradually came into common use and developed a momentum that could not be stopped, a few people abruptly changed their positions and took credit for it, giving it the high-sounding name of the New Culture movement. Then there were others who advocated that there was no harm in the vernacular being used for popular writing, and still others who said that to write the vernacular well, it was necessary to read old books. Those in the first group have already changed their positions twice and are now once again jeering at the "New Culture," while those in the latter two groups have been obliged to become mediators whose only hope is to keep a stiffened corpse around for a few more days; there are quite a few of these, and I have lashed out at them in the past in my random thoughts.

I have most recently come across a journal published in Shanghai that also says that in order to write good vernacular one must read good classical texts, and I was one of the examples they cited. This actually gave me the shivers. I can't speak for others, but as for myself I have in fact read many old books, and for the sake of teaching continue to read them. I have thus been unconsciously affected by them and they have influenced my vernacular writing, with certain words and patterns inevitably slipping into my prose. I am, however, pained by the fact that I cannot escape from these ancient specters I carry on my back, and often feel a depressing weight on myself. As for my thinking, I have often been poisoned by Zhuangzi and Hanfeizi, at times quite casually and at others quite vigorously. I read the Confucian books earliest and most thoroughly, but they for some reason seem to have little connection with me. But probably in large part out of laziness, I often take comfort in the fact that in all things as they change there are always a number of intermediate forms. There are intermediate forms between plant and animal life, and between invertebrates and vertebrates; actually, one can simply say that along the evolutionary chain, everything is an intermediate form. As writing begins to be reformed there will inevitably be three or four writers of dubious status—it can only be so and must necessarily be so. Their mission is to call out in a new voice once they achieve some awareness; in addition, because they come from the old fortress and see the situation relatively clearly, they can turn their weapons against their own side to more easily slay a powerful enemy. But they should still pass away like time itself, gradually wither away, to be at most a piece of timber or a stone that is part of a bridge, not some goal or model for the future. What is to emerge should be different, even if it is not some divinely gifted sage; and if as expected old customs cannot be extirpated all at once, what emerges should, at the very least, bring with it a new atmosphere. As for the written word, we need no longer seek our livelihood in old texts, but can, rather, take the language of living people as our source, moving writing even closer to speech, and make it ever more lively. And as for how to remedy the deficiencies and poverty of current popular speech and make it richer, that is a very large issue, and we should perhaps take some resources from the old writing and put them to use, but this is not within the scope of what I wish to speak of here, so I will leave it aside for now.

I believe that if I work at it hard enough, I can probably gather together enough from the spoken language to reform my writing. Because I am both lazy and quite busy, however, I have yet to do so. I often suspect that this is closely related to having read old books, because I feel that I share some of the loathsome ideas written by the ancients in their books, and I have no confidence as to whether I can get rid of them all at once by my own efforts. I often curse this thinking of mine and hope that it will no longer show up in the young people of the future. Last year I proposed that young people read fewer or simply not read any Chinese books at all, a truth hard won with a good deal of pain and absolutely not a passing fancy, a joke, or words spoken in indignation.[14] The ancients said that if you don't read, you will become a fool, which is of course not incorrect. The world, however, was created by fools, and clever people really cannot control it, particularly the clever people in China. Now, though, ideas aside, in the realm of letters many young writers pick out a few beautiful and quite hard-to-understand phrases from ancient prose and poetry to use as conjuring tricks to decorate their work. I don't know if this has any relationship to the advocacy of reading classical prose, but it is obvious that this is, in fact, a return to the ancients and a suicide attempt on the part of the new literature.

Unfortunately, my collection of writings, a mix of classical and vernacular pieces, happens to appear just at this moment, and it will perhaps do readers a certain amount of damage. But for myself, I cannot firmly and decisively destroy them, wishing for the time being to use them to observe the remaining traces from a life that has passed by. I only hope that readers partial to my work merely take this as a souvenir and know that within this small tumulus there is buried a body that was once alive. And after the passage of yet more time it, too, will transform into dust, the memories of it will also vanish from the human realm, and I will have accomplished what I set out to do. This morning I happened to be reading some classical Chinese and recalled a few lines that Lu Ji (261–303 CE) wrote in mourning of Cao Cao, which I will use to conclude this piece:

Casting back to antiquity, he discarded all encumbrance,
Believing in simple rites and setting little store in burial.
His fur coat and ribbon seal ended up who knows where,

leaving disgrace and derision to later kings.
I lament the persistence of attachment,
that, wise as he was, he could not disregard.
Deeply moved as I read the works he left behind,
I offer this piece as token of my sorrow.[15]

The evening of November 11, 1926

TRANSLATED BY THEODORE HUTERS

# How "The True Story of Ah Q" Came About

## 《阿Q正傳》的成因

In issue 251 of *Literary Weekly*, Mr. C. T.[16] undertook a discussion of *Outcry*, paying particular attention to "The True Story of Ah Q." For some reason this caused me to recall a few things, so I'd also like to take this opportunity to say something, partly so as to write an essay and submit it for publication and partly to give those who are interested something to read.

But first I'll quote a paragraph from Mr. C. T.'s essay:

It is not without reason that this piece has received the attention it has. But there are a few things about it that need further consideration. For instance, I thought there was something not quite right about the concluding "Grand Finale" scene when I first read it in the *Morning News*, and I still think this to be the case: it seems to me that the author's ending for Ah Q is too hasty—he didn't want to continue writing, so he quite casually gave him a "grand finale." For someone like Ah Q to end up joining the revolutionary party and to have an outcome like the one he received in the "grand finale" seems like something not even the author himself would have imagined when he began writing. At the very least, it seems as if there are two different personalities here.

First published in issue 18 of the journal *Beixin* on December 18, 1926, and later anthologized in *Sequel to Inauspicious Star* (Huagai ji xubian, 1927). Lu Xun, *Lu Xun quanji* (Complete works of Lu Xun) (Beijing: Renmin wenxue, 2005), 3: 394–403.

Whether Ah Q really wanted to be a revolutionary, or supposing that he did become a revolutionary, whether he seems to be two different personalities are things we shall leave aside for the moment. But the question of how the story came about is something that will take a good deal of effort to explain. I often say that my writing does not flow out of me, but is squeezed out. Those who hear me say this often mistake this as modesty, but it really is the case. I neither have anything to say nor anything I wish to write, but I have a self-destructive temperament that obliges me to utter a few outcries from time to time, wishing thereby to add a bit of bustle to the current scene. I'm like a weary old ox who is well aware that he no longer can be of any real use, but worthless things can still be of service, so when the Zhangs need me to plow a bit of ground, it's fine with me; or if the Lis want me to turn their millstone a few times, it's also fine; or when the Zhaos wish me to stand in front of their shop with an advertising placard on my back announcing that our modest enterprise has fat cows that produce superior pasteurized milk. Though I am fully aware of how emaciated I am, not to mention that I am a bull and am thus without milk, when you consider it from their standpoint of wanting to drum up business, it's understandable and I have no objections to raise so long as what they are selling is not poisonous. It won't do, however, if they use me to exhaustion; I still need to find grass to graze on and a bit of time to catch my breath. Neither would it do if I were declared to belong to someone in particular and kept in his cowshed, as I still might want to pull someone else's grindstone every so often. Should someone even wish to sell me as meat, that naturally would be even more unacceptable, the reasons being obvious and without need of further discussion. Were I to encounter any of these three aforementioned taboos, I would run off or simply vanish into the wilderness. Even if this were to mean that I would suddenly change from being profound to being shallow, from being a warrior to being a domesticated beast, or if they try to frighten me by comparing me to Kang Youwei or Liang Qichao, I simply wouldn't care and would still run away or hide out; I will absolutely not be fooled again, because I really am a bit too "sophisticated" by now.

*Outcry* has come to have numerous readers in recent years, something I never anticipated when I was writing it, in fact something I never even gave a thought to. I was simply going along with the wishes of some people I knew, and when they asked me to write something, I did. I wasn't terribly busy, since

Image of Ah Q, by Feng Zikai

few people knew that I was Lu Xun. I also had more than one penname: LS, Shenfei, Tang Si, A Certain Person, Xuezhi, Fengsheng, and a number from even before that: Zishu, Lingfei, Xunxing. "Lu Xun" in fact comes from "Xunxing," because the editors of New Youth at the time did not want authors to use words that resembled old-fashioned "courtesy names."

There are some people nowadays who think I want to be the leader of some sort of pack, which is truly pathetic, considering they have looked into the matter so many times and still do not understand. I have never, for instance, visited anyone sporting the banner of "Lu Xun"; that "Lu Xun is none other than Zhou Shuren" was uncovered by others. Of these people, there are four types: one consists of those who study fiction and thus wish to know an author's personal information; another is those who are simply curious; yet another is those who, because I write critical essays, make a point of trying to expose me and get me into trouble; the last is those who think that doing so will be useful to them and help them worm their way in.

At the time I was living in the western district of Beijing, it was probably only those associated with New Youth and New Tide who knew that I was Lu Xun; Sun Fuyuan was another. He was then editing the literary supplement to the Morning News. I don't know whose idea it was, but they suddenly planned to add a page called "Happy Talk" that was to appear once a week. He wanted me to write a little something for it.

The image of Ah Q seems actually to have been in my mind for a number of years, but I never had the slightest intention of writing him into existence. Having received this proposal, I suddenly thought of him and that evening wrote a bit, which turned out to be the first chapter: the Preface. Wishing to stay in keeping with the theme of "happy talk," I randomly added some utterly gratuitous levity that actually had nothing to do with the chapter as a whole. I signed it "Ba Ren," alluding to nothing more elegant than "country fellow." Who would have imagined that choosing this name would get me into trouble, although I only learned about it this year when I read Han Lu's (that is, Gao Yihan) "Idle Talk" in Modern Review. The story goes:

> I remember when "The True Story of Ah Q" was appearing serially section by section, there were any number of people who were in utter terror that any further obloquy would fall on their heads. I even had a friend who told me directly that one segment of yesterday's "The True Story of

Ah Q" was aimed directly at him, and that because of that he suspected that "Ah Q" was written by a certain person; and why did he think that? Because only that person knew about that personal matter of his. . . . From this point on, he became a bit paranoid, assuming that everything attacked in "The True Story of Ah Q" was in fact a reference to his personal matters; so anyone who contributed to the newspaper that published "Ah Q" became a suspect in his eyes! Only after he figured out the name of "Ah Q's" author did he realize that he and the author didn't know each other at all and suddenly became aware of his error, and subsequently told everyone he met that it wasn't directed at him. (vol. 4, no. 89)

I am truly apologetic to this "certain person," who had to endure many days of being a suspect because of me. Unfortunately, I don't know who it is, and because "Ba Ren" is easily taken as someone from Sichuan, it is perhaps someone from there. Right up to the time the piece was published as part of *Outcry*, people were still asking me: "Who were you in fact reproving?" My only recourse was to be indignant and to rue the fact that I was unable to make people see I am not quite as despicable as all that.

Following the appearance of the first chapter, "suffering" reared its head, as I had to produce a chapter every week. Although I wasn't particularly busy at the time, I was living the life of a displaced person, spending my nights sleeping in a room that was actually a passageway and that had only a single rear window and no real place to write, much less a place to think or meditate. Although Fuyuan was not as fat as he is now, he was already as jolly as could be and very talented at pressing me for copy. He would come by once a week, and as soon as he had the chance it would be: "My dear sir, 'Ah Q' . . . It has to go to print tomorrow." So I had to write, thinking all along, "The saying goes: 'beggars fear dogs and degree candidates fear their annual exam,' and although I am not a degree candidate, I still have to endure a weekly exam, which vexes me to no end." I would, however, eventually produce another chapter. But I seemed gradually to start to take it more seriously; Fuyuan also thought it not exactly "happy talk," so starting with the second chapter, it was moved to the "New Literature" section.

Week followed week in this way until eventually the question of whether Ah Q would join the revolution inevitably came up. It was my thinking that if there had been no revolution in China, Ah Q would not have become a revolutionary, but since there was a revolution, he would become one. My Ah Q's fate could only be thus, and it was not a question of him being two different characters. The first year of the Republic has long passed, and what's gone is gone, but if there is another revolution to come, I do believe that revolutionaries like Ah Q will reappear. I would much prefer that I had, as people have said, written only about a time before the present or about a certain period, but I fear that what I saw was not, in fact, a precursor of the present, but rather what is to come, or even what is to follow twenty or thirty years from now. This does not bring discredit to revolutionaries; Ah Q did, after all, roll up his queue with a chopstick. Fifteen years later did not Gao Changhong become a Chinese "Shevyrev" when "he entered the world of publishing"?[17]

After I had been writing "Ah Q" for about two months, I really wanted to finish it off; although my memory of it is no longer very clear, it seemed as if Fuyuan did not approve, or at least I suspected that if I finished it off, he would come over to protest. So I mentally sequestered the "grand finale," which meant that Ah Q was already on his path toward death. Had Fuyuan been around when it came to the final chapter, he would perhaps have suppressed it and demanded that I allow Ah Q to live for another couple of weeks. It just happened to work out, however, that Fuyuan returned home for a spell, with He Zuolin taking over for him, and since the latter had no predisposition in regard to Ah Q, I sent in the "grand finale" and he published it. By the time that Fuyuan returned to Beijing, it had already been over a month since Ah Q had met his end at the hands of a firing squad. Now no matter how practiced Fuyuan was at pressing me for copy, and no matter how jolly, he could no longer say, "My dear sir, 'The True Story of Ah Q' . . ." At this point I seemed to have at last wound up one piece of business, and I could now move on to something else. As to what that something else was, I no longer remember, but it was probably still something of a similar nature.

In actuality, the "grand finale" was not conferred on Ah Q as casually as all that; as to whether I had anticipated it when I began the writing really is something about which I am doubtful. I do seem to remember that I did not anticipate it. But that's the way things go—at the beginning, who can anticipate anyone's "grand finale"? This is not merely in regard to Ah Q; but even in regard to my own "grand finale" to come, I cannot anticipate what it might turn out to be. Will I be regarded as a "scholar" or a "professor"? Or an "academic renegade" or a "hatchet man"? As a "bureaucrat" or as a "pettifogger"? As an "authoritative thinker" or an "intellectual forerunner" or simply a "versatile old hack"? "Artist"? "Warrior"? Or someone who entertains people without fear of fuss like Aledjev in *Worker Shevyrev*? Or? Or? Or?

Ah Q, naturally, could have had any number of other outcomes, but I know nothing about them.

I originally thought that at several points my writing had gone "over the top," but I no longer believe this to be the case. If things that take place in China now are written up as they really are, they will seem *grotesk* [German in the original] in the eyes of people in other countries or to the people in a better China of the future. I often imagine things that seem just too strange, but when I actually encounter things similar to what I imagined in real life, they are invariably even stranger. But prior to these things taking place in real life, based on my shallow knowledge, I could never have imagined them.

About a month ago a robber was executed here by two men in short jackets, each with a revolver, shooting him seven times altogether. I don't know if so many shots were fired because they weren't able to kill him at first, or if they just continued shooting after he was dead. At the time I expressed my feelings to a group of young students, saying: This is something that would have happened in the early years of the Republic, when the firing squad was being used for the first time; over a decade has passed since then, and we should have made some progress and not have made the dead man suffer so much. Beijing, on the other hand, is different: before even reaching the execution ground the criminal's life is taken with a shot to the back of the head by the executioner, so the condemned man does not even know that he is being killed. Beijing is, after all, "the best place in China"; even when it comes to capital punishment, it is far better at it than the provinces.

A few days ago, however, I saw the November 23 edition of the Beijing *World Daily* and realized once again that what I said was inaccurate; on page 6 there was a news item headlined "Du Xiaoshuanzi Dies by Chopping," divided into five paragraphs, one of which is excerpted below:

> Du chopped, others shot. Because the Garrison Command acceded to requests emanating from the members of the Resolute Corps, it decided to employ "decapitation," so prior to Du and the others arriving at the execution ground, a large hay-chopper had been prepared. The chopper

was long and rested on a wooden bed, with a blade both thick and sharp at its center. There was an opening set in the wooden bed beneath the blade such that the blade could be lifted up and down; when Du and the three others entered the execution ground and were bundled off the prison-wagon by the guards, they were told to face north, and to stand facing the execution table that had been made ready. . . . Du did not kneel down, so a police officer from an outer borough asked him if he wanted someone to help him. Du simply smiled without responding, then ran over to the front of the chopper and lay down under it face up. The executioner had already raised the blade, so when Du laid his head down at the proper place, the executioner closed his eyes and chopped with great force, and Du's head and body were severed. As the blood gushed out, Song Zhenshan and the other two kneeling by the side awaiting the firing squad furtively looked on; one of them, one Zhao Zhen, even started to shake. After that a lieutenant took a revolver and positioned himself behind Song and the other two, first killing Song Zhenshan, then Li Yousan and Zhao Zhen, each with one shot. . . . Prior to that, the two sons of the murdered man Cheng Buxi, Zhongzhi and Zhongxin, were spectators at the scene; they let out great sobs, going over to the condemned after the executions had been carried out and shouting at the top of their voices: "Father! Mother! You have been avenged, but what are we to do now?" All those who heard this were grief-stricken, and afterward the two sons were taken home by their relatives.

Had there been a writer of talent in actual touch with the pulse of the times who had on November 22 published a story narrating such an event, I think that many readers would have thought it was talking about events from the time of Judge Bao, in the eleventh century of the Western calendar, some nine hundred years before our time.

But, really, what is to be done?

As for the translations of "The True Story of Ah Q," I have only seen two. The French version was published in the August 1926 edition of *L'Europe*, but it contained only a third of the original, having been abridged. The English version seems to have been translated with greater care, but since I don't understand English, I can't comment on it. I did, however, happen to come across two things that can be discussed further: one is that "three hundred cash, ninety-two to the string" should be translated as "three hundred cash, with ninety-two counting as a hundred"; the second is that "the Persimmon Oil party *(shiyou dang)*" would be better transliterated, because it was originally "the Liberty Party *(ziyou dang),*" but the country folk didn't understand and thus mistook it for *shiyou dang,* something that they were familiar with.

December 3, 1926, written in Xiamen

TRANSLATED BY THEODORE HUTERS

# In Reply to Mr. Youheng

答有恆先生

Mr. Youheng:[18]

I read your many comments published in *Beixin* today. I am grateful for the high hopes you have for me and for your good intentions, which are plainly evident. Now I would like to briefly respond to you and take the opportunity to address those who share similar views.

I have plenty of free time, so I'm not, by any means, too busy to write. But it has, indeed, been a long time since I've published my opinions, a decision I made as of last summer, when I had planned to maintain silence for a period of two years. I don't place much significance on time, though, and have often treated it as a trifling matter.

But the reason for my present silence is not the same reason that led me to my earlier decision; by the time I left Xiamen, my thoughts had already begun to change a bit. The path that led to these transformations is too tedious to bring up here, so I'll just leave the issue aside for the time being and hope to perhaps publish about it in the future. Speaking only of recent times, one of the main reasons is that I'm terrified. This is a kind of terror I have never experienced before.

---

First published in a combined issue, numbers 49 and 50, of *Beixin* on October 1, 1927, and later anthologized in *And That's All* (Eryi ji, 1928). Lu Xun, *Lu Xun quanji* (Complete works of Lu Xun) (Beijing: Renmin wenxue, 2005), 3: 473–480.

I have yet to carefully analyze the reasons behind this "terror." For the time being, I will just mention a thing or two that I have come to understand through careful consideration.

First, one of my wishful illusions has been shattered. Until now, I often felt a sense of optimism. I was under the impression that it was mostly the old who oppress and slaughter the young. As these old people gradually die off, China could then be somewhat revitalized. Now I know this isn't the case. It seems it is mostly the young who are slaughtering the young. They have even less regard for other peoples' lives and youth, which once gone can never be recreated. If this were how they treated animals, it would be considered a case of "destroying and exterminating all living things under heaven."[19] I especially dread reading the smug words of the victors: "struck to death with an axe" . . . "stabbed to death with a spear" . . . I'm by no means a proponent of radical reforms, and I've never opposed capital punishment. But with regard to punishments such as death by a thousand cuts and extermination of the clan, I have in the past expressed extreme revulsion and sorrow. I believe that neither should exist in human societies in the twentieth century. Of course, striking a blow with an axe or stabbing someone with a spear is not the same as death by a thousand cuts, but can't we just put a bullet to the back of the head? The results are the same—the death of one's opponent. But facts are facts—the bloody game has already begun, and the players are the young who appear to revel in the prospect. Now I can no longer see how this drama will end.

Second, I have discovered that I am a . . . what shall I call it? I can't, at the moment, pin down a name for it. I have said before: China has a long history of laying out man-eating feasts; some eat and others are eaten.[20] Those eaten have previously eaten others, and those now eating will later be eaten. But I have now discovered that I myself have helped lay out these feasts. Sir, you have read my works, and now I have a question for you. After reading them, did you feel numb or awakened? Did you feel lethargic or alive? If what you felt is the latter, then my self-indictment has, in large measure, been proven true. In Chinese banquets, there is a dish called "drunken shrimp."[21] The more animated the shrimp, the more elation and thrill experienced by the eater. I am one of those who assist in the preparation of the drunken shrimp. I clarify the minds of the honest yet unfortunate youths and heighten the sensitivity of their emotions, which only doubles their suffering when disaster strikes. At the same time, this allows those who loathe them to derive all the more pleasure from witnessing this more acute suffering. It is my supposition that when it comes to waging a war, be it against the Red Army or the revolutionary forces, the punishment inflicted will be more severe if the enemy captive is educated—a student, for example—rather than a worker or others who are uneducated. Why? Because people derive a special thrill from gazing at the heightened and more subtle expressions of suffering on their faces. If my conjecture is accurate, then my self-indictment has been proven to be entirely true.

So now I finally feel that there is really nothing more to say.

To keep on making fun of the likes of Professor Chen Yuan is something easily done;[22] just yesterday I wrote something along those lines. But it's a pointless exercise; people of their kind are not the problem. At most they have eaten half a shrimp or sipped a few mouthfuls of the vinegar served with it. Moreover, I heard that they've had a falling out with their most esteemed "Mr. Gutong"[23] and have now joined the revolution under the flag of the blue sky and white sun.[24] If the flag of the blue sky and white sun is planted at a far enough distance, perhaps even "Mr. Gutong" may end up joining the revolution. There wouldn't be a problem anymore, everyone joins the revolution, how grand and majestic.

The problem lies with my own backwardness. There's another small matter as well. That is, the punishment for wielding my pen as a dagger, it seems, has now been meted out. Those who plant peonies get flowers, and those who plant devil's weed get thorns, as it should be, so I bear no resentment whatsoever. But what makes me indignant is that the punishment seems a bit too severe, and what makes me sad is that it has implicated a few of my colleagues and students.

What sins have they committed, other than often associating with and not speaking ill of me? Those like them are now declared to be part of "the Lu Xun party" or "*Threads of Talk* clique." This is a great accomplishment of the propaganda put out by the "Research Party" and "Contemporary Review group." So in the past year, Lu Xun has been regarded as an outcast exiled to far-off places. I need to point out that when I was in Xiamen, I was moved into a Western-style building with no neighbors around me; my constant companions were books, and deep into the night I would hear the howling of beasts from below. But I'm not afraid of solitude, and students still came by to chat. But then came the second blow: two of my three chairs were to be removed, they said, because bigshot so-and-so's son had arrived and needed to use them. I was enraged by this and asked: "What if his grandson comes, am I supposed to just sit on the bare floor? I won't allow it!" The chairs weren't removed, but then came the third blow. A smirking professor said: "Celebrity scholar's temper flaring up again." It seems that under the laws of Xiamen, only celebrity scholars are entitled to have extra chairs. In using the word "again" to describe how often I threw these scholarly fits, sir, as you probably know, they were taking a cue from the writing style of the *Spring and Autumn Annals*.[25] Then there was the fourth blow, which came just as I was about to depart. Someone said that the reason I was leaving was that, first, there was no wine to drink and, second, that I was upset when I saw other people's spouses arriving. This, too, was presumably a result of my "celebrity scholar's temper."

This is just a minor incident that came to mind, but from this alone you may be able to forgive me and sympathize with my reasons for being afraid to speak out. I know you wouldn't want me to play the role of the drunken shrimp. If I keep on fighting, I might become "sick in body and mind,"[26] and if I am "sick in body and mind," then I would become the target of mockery. Of course these things are all inconsequential. But why suffer playing the role of the drunken shrimp?

But what was most fortunate this time around was that I was not, in the end, made out to be a communist. A young man once wanted to use as evidence my having published some essays in *New Youth*, edited by Duxiu,[27] to prove that I belonged to the Communist Party. But the accusation was refuted by another youth who knew that, at the time, even Duxiu had not begun preaching communism yet. Even the lighter sentence of "communist sympathizer," in the end, failed to take hold. If I had departed Guangzhou as soon as I left Sun Yat-sen University, I would surely have been so branded.[28] But I didn't leave, and after newspapers clamored "he escaped," "went to Hankou," and the like, nothing came of the matter. There is some promise in this world after all; at least no one claimed that I had the ability to split myself in two and be in different places at one time. For the moment, I don't seem to have any titles pegged on me, though according to the "*Contemporary Review* group," I am the "leader of the *Threads of Talk* clique." This is rather inconsequential and doesn't endanger my life in any way, so long as they don't have other tricks up their sleeves. It would be a bad turn of events for me, however, if the "lead character" Tang Youren[29] were to say that I had received an "edict from Moscow."

With a slip of my pen, I've gone off on a tangent; I'd better return to the issue of my "backwardness." I believe, sir, that you have probably read my lament over the absence of anyone daring to "mourn the death of a rebel" in China. And what about now? You've seen for yourself—have I spoken a word this past half year? I have nonetheless expressed my views in public lectures, though I have had no venues in which to publish my writings and have long since ceased to speak out. None of this counts in my defense, though. In sum, if I were now to again express platitudes such as "save the children," they would sound hollow even to my own ears.

Furthermore, the attacks I directed at society in the past were also futile. No one in the society knew that I was attacking it; had anyone understood, I would have died long ago with no burial plot for my corpse. Attack one member of society such as Chen Yuan and see what happens. Not to mention attacking all four hundred million at once. I have been able to drag out my ignoble existence because the majority of the people are illiterate and unaware of my criticisms, not to mention that my words are without effect, like shooting arrows into the sea. Otherwise, a few random thoughts might have cost me my life. Ordinary people's desire to see the punishment of evil exceeds even that of scholars and warlords. It recently dawned on me that so long as a suggestion remotely associated with reform has no effect on society, it will be tolerated as "rubbish." If the suggestion were to have effect, the one promoting it will likely suffer or be killed. Past or present, in China or abroad, it's the same principle. Take an example before us now. Doesn't Mr. Wu Zhihui[30] also have his own "ism"? Not only has he escaped the public's wrath, he was even able to shout out "Down with so and so . . . and punish with the utmost severity!" and that is because his words are like rubbish. The Red Party wants to implement communism in twenty years, whereas Wu's "ism" would take several centuries to carry out. Who has the leisure to think about what the world of our posterity countless generations down the line might be like?

I have said quite a bit so far and would like to bring things to a close. I'm grateful to you, sir, for your good intentions toward me, from which I detect not even the slightest hint of mockery or malicious intent. So I send my reply in earnest. Of course, I've also taken advantage of the opportunity to vent some complaints. But I want to make it clear that all the things I've mentioned above have nothing to do with false modesty. I know myself and I dissect myself even more mercilessly than I dissect others. Several critics whose bellies are full of malice have tried their utmost to diagnose my illness, all in vain. So this time I have chosen to divulge a little, but it is, of course, just a small part of the whole, and there is still much that I have kept hidden.

I feel that I may not have anything more to say from now on. Once this terror subsides, what will take its place? I still have no way of knowing, but I am afraid it won't be anything good. But I am still trying to save myself with the old remedies—that is, first, by numbing myself and, second, by forgetting. Even as I struggle, I still want to recover some meaning from "amid the pale blood stains,"[31] which will only grow paler with time, and record them on scraps of paper.

September 4

TRANSLATED BY EILEEN J. CHENG

# Preface to *Self-Selected Works*

《自選集》自序

My writing of fiction began in 1918 when a "literary revolution" was being advocated in the pages of the magazine *New Youth*.[32] This type of movement has long since turned into a relic of literary history, but at that time it was, without a doubt, a revolutionary movement.

The works I published in *New Youth* were generally in step with those of other contributors, so I think it's fair to consider them part of the "revolutionary literature" of that era. Yet at the time I was not all that enthusiastic

---

First published in *Lu Xun's Self-Selected Works* (Lu Xun zi xuan ji) (Shanghai: Tianma Shudian, 1933) and later anthologized in *Southern Tunes in Northern Tones* (Nan qiang bei diao ji, 1934). This translation is of the original preface. Subsequent published versions of this essay have slight deviations from the original. Lu Xun, *Lu Xun quanji* (Complete works of Lu Xun) (Beijing: Renmin wenxue, 2005), 4: 468–471.

about "revolutionary literature." Having seen the 1911 Revolution, the Second Revolution,[33] Yuan Shikai's attempt to make himself emperor, and Zhang Xun's restoration,[34] the more I saw the more skeptical I became, and that made me feel disappointed and dejected. A nationalist writer's claim in a tabloid this year that "Lu Xun is full of suspicion" is not inaccurate. I was just then in the process of questioning whether that group of people were really nationalists, or just adept at changing colors. But I was also suspicious of my own disillusionment, because I know that the people and events I have seen are extremely limited; this gave me the strength to take up my pen again.

"Despair, like hope, is an illusion."[35]

Since it wasn't out of any direct enthusiasm for the "literary revolution," what was it that kept me writing? Thinking back on it, it was mostly identification with the feelings of the enthusiasts. Those fighters, I thought, though lonely and in difficult circumstances, were able to come up with a good idea, and so I also called out with a few shouts of my own to encourage them. At first it was for this reason alone. Of course, it was inevitable that my stories were interspersed with scenes that exposed the roots of sickness in the old society, with the hope that this might spur people on to find a cure. But in order to actualize these hopes, I needed to bring myself into step with the vanguard of the movement and thereupon followed my commander's orders to cut out some of the darkness and intersperse my stories with some positive notes, making them display some degree of light. Those were what later formed the volume *Outcry*—a total of fourteen pieces. So these examples of "revolutionary literature" could also be called "literature to order." But what I followed faithfully were orders from the revolutionary vanguard who also happened to be victims of oppression at the time; these were also orders that I myself had wanted to follow from the start, by no means the "sagely instructions" of an emperor, or orders backed by the gold yuan or some military commander's sabre.

Afterward, the *New Youth* group dispersed. Some were promoted to high position, others went into seclusion, some advanced. Having experienced how rapidly members of my own camp could change, the label "author" had fallen on me, and I continued, as before, wandering back and forth in the desert. However, I found myself unable to get out of writing a few words for various and sundry periodicals that might be called "random chats." From that point on, whenever the mood struck me, I would write some short pieces that, immodestly speaking, were "prose poems." After I stopped writing and washed my hands of them, I had them printed as a book and titled it *Weeds*. When I had more complete materials to work with, I resumed writing short stories. It was only because I had become a scattered partisan unable to form a band of my own that, though I had improved my technique a bit and seemed to have unfettered my thinking, my will to do battle had cooled considerably. Where were my new comrades in arms? I felt that to continue in this way would have been awful, so I collected the eleven works I had produced in this period into a volume titled *Hesitation* and bade them farewell, hoping that in future I would no longer continue thus.

> The road is long and the journey far,
> I shall search up and down, through heaven and earth.[36]

I did not expect that this lofty boast would fizzle without a trace. Fleeing Beijing, I took refuge in Xiamen, but in that forlorn tower I wrote only several pieces for *Old Tales Retold* and the ten pieces that make up *Morning Blossoms Plucked at Dusk*. The former are tales from myths, legends, and history; the latter are reminiscences and nothing more.

After that I wrote nothing, "as if all had become a void."

All of what could plausibly be called my "creative work" up to now are in these five volumes, which can actually be read through in a short time. Yet the publishers have requested that I make a selection of them for publication in one single volume. I would speculate that their motivation in doing so might stem, first, from a desire to save money for the readers or, second, from the belief that an author is able to make the best selection of his own works, because he knows them far and above others. I have no reservations about the first proposition but am doubtful about the second. Because there are no pieces that I have expended a particularly great effort on, nor are there ones with which I cut corners on, I don't feel there are any that are exceptionally brilliant or worthy of promotion. So I could find no other course of action than to throw together a volume of twenty-two pieces written on different subjects in different styles. But I have made an effort to eliminate pieces that might place an unnecessary burden on the reader. This is because I still have the idea that I "did not want to infect the young people who were dreaming beautiful dreams, just as I had at the time of my own youth, with the loneliness I have found so bitter."[37] But here I need not make the type of intentional concealment I did back in the days when I was writing *Outcry*, because I now believe that the youth of today and of the future will no longer live in such a dream world.

December 14, 1932—written by Lu Xun at his residence in Shanghai

TRANSLATED BY JON EUGENE VON KOWALLIS

# Preface to the English Edition of *Selected Short Stories of Lu Xun*

英譯本《短篇小說選集》自序

Chinese poetry sometimes spoke to the suffering of the underclass. This is not at all the case for painting or fiction, where the underclass is described as being perfectly cheerful, "in harmony with nature, not worrying about the past or the future,"[38] as if they were birds or flowers, happy and content. Indeed, from the perspective of the intellectual class, the laboring masses of China might as well be of the same category as flora and fauna.

I grew up in a big family in the city, taught from a young age by the ancient texts and my instructors to regard the laboring masses as flora and fauna. At times when I was disgusted by the hypocrisy and corruption of the so-called upper class, I had even envied working men for their peace and harmony. But my maternal grandmother happened to come from the countryside, and visiting her allowed me to become acquainted now and then with a number of peasants. I learned in time that they were oppressed and suffered much pain all their lives, hardly the picture of happy birds and flowers. But I had no means for getting this message across to the public.

---

This preface was written at Edgar Snow's invitation in 1933, when Snow was planning to publish a collection of Lu Xun's short stories in English. The plan never came to fruition. In 1937, Snow grouped seven of Lu Xun's stories with seventeen pieces by other modern Chinese writers and published them under the title of *Living China* (New York: Reynal and Hitchcock). The preface was not included in *Living China*, but it was anthologized in *Supplement to the Collection of the Uncollected* (Ji wai ji shiyi, 1938). Lu Xun, *Lu Xun quanji* (Complete works of Lu Xun) (Beijing: Renmin wenxue, 2005), 7: 411–412.

Later on, I came across novels from abroad, especially those from Russia, Poland, and the smaller countries of the Balkans. I realized then that there are a vast number of laboring people in this world who share the same fate with our suffering masses, and there are also writers who cry out and fight on their behalf. The scenes I had earlier witnessed in the countryside came back to me with added vividness. By chance, I was asked to write something, so I wrote about the depravity of the "upper class" and the misfortunes of the "lower class." They were published one after another in the form of short stories. My original intent was simply to lay it out in front of the readers so as to raise a few questions. They were not meant to be "art" as understood by the literary types of the time.

And yet these pieces caught the attention of a few readers, and though denounced by some literary critics, the stories did not die out. That they would be translated into English and become available to readers of the new continent was not something I could have dreamt of.

Still, I have not written short stories for a long while. These days, the masses bear worse hardship than ever before. My own thinking has also changed somewhat, and I have in addition witnessed the rising tide of new literature. Under the circumstances, I cannot write in the new mode, nor do I want to write in the old mode. This situation calls to mind a fable from an old Chinese book. The inhabitants of Handan were widely admired for their elegant gait. Someone went there to study it but wasn't able to learn it properly. Meanwhile, he had forgotten his own way of walking. So he ended up having to crawl back home.[39] Crawling is what I'm doing right now. But I will keep on learning until I can stand up.

March 22, 1933, Shanghai

TRANSLATED BY HU YING

# How I Came to Write Fiction

## 我怎麼做起小說來

How was it that I came to write fiction? I have already given a brief answer to this question in my preface to *Outcry*. I should add here that when I first became interested in literature, the situation was very different from how it is now. In China at that time, fiction was not considered "literature," and a writer of fiction could in no way merit the title of "littérateur." So no one considered it an estimable career path. Nor did I have the intention of elevating fiction into the "literary garden" of high culture; I merely sought to utilize its power to reform society.

Nor did I wish to be a creative writer. What I thought important was to translate and introduce works—particularly short stories, especially those by authors from among the oppressed peoples of the world. Because anti-Manchu views were prevalent at that time, some young people quoted those authors who cried out against and resisted oppression in order to give voice to their own positions. For that reason, I never read books like *How to Write Fiction*, but I did read quite a few stories, partly because I enjoyed reading them, but mostly because I was looking for material to introduce. I also read literary histories and literary criticism because I wanted to familiarize myself with the character and thought of the authors in order to decide whether to introduce them to China. This had absolutely nothing to do with scholarship or the like.

Because the works I sought out were about outcries and resistance, my inclinations turned toward Eastern Europe; for that reason, I read an especially large number of works by authors from Russia, Poland, and various small countries in the Balkans. I also enthusiastically sought after works from India and Egypt, but could not get ahold of any. I remember my favorite authors at the time were Gogol from Russia and Sienkiewicz from Poland. Among the Japanese were Natsume Sōseki and Mori Ogai.

First published in *Experiences in Creative Writing* (Chuangzuo de jingyan) (Shanghai: Tianma Shudian, 1933) and later anthologized in *Southern Tunes in Northern Tones* (Nan qiang bei diao ji, 1934). Lu Xun, *Lu Xun quanji* (Complete works of Lu Xun) (Beijing: Renmin wenxue, 2005), 4: 525–530.

After returning to China, I got involved in the world of education and for some five or six years had no time to read fiction. But why did I start writing again? Since I've already discussed this in my preface to *Outcry*, there is no need to repeat it here. But the reason I started to write fiction was not that I thought I had the talent to write creatively, but rather that I was staying in a hostel in Beijing and lacked reference materials required to write scholarly articles and had no access to original texts worth translating. So I could only produce something bearing some resemblance to a short story in order to fulfill an obligation—this was "Diary of a Madman." I must have relied on over a hundred of the foreign works I had read previously and a bit of medical knowledge. Other than that, I had no preparation.

But the editors of *New Youth* kept coming back to urge me to write more; each time, after several of their attempts to press me, I would produce another piece. Here I should acknowledge Mr. Chen Duxiu[40] for having been the most persistent among those who urged me to write short stories.

Of course, in taking up the writing of fiction, it is expected that one would have one's own views. For instance, if I were to address the question of "why" I began to write short stories, it was because I still cherished the ideas of "enlightenment" I had held over a decade ago; writing, I believed, was "for life," to change life in the world for the better. I detested the way fiction had in the past been considered "writings to while away the hours in leisure," and I thought that the slogan "art for art's sake" was simply an updated version of the same idea. Therefore, I drew my material mostly from among the unfortunate people of a sick society, hoping that revealing their sickness and suffering might draw attention to their plight so that a cure might be found. I made an effort to avoid being long-winded, being satisfied if I could communicate my meaning without adding any contrasts or embellishments. Traditional Chinese operas did not use backdrops, and the colorful woodblock prints for children sold at New Year's[41] had only a few main figures (although today most have added backgrounds). Believing these methods would also be commensurate with my goals, I refrained from indulging in descriptions of the wind and the moon and avoided lengthy dialogues.

After finishing a story, I would always read it through twice. When I felt something didn't sound right, I would add or delete a few words, so that it would read more smoothly. If there was no appropriate expression in the vernacular, I would resort to using classical phrases and hope that there would be some readers who could understand them. I seldom used expressions that would be intelligible only to myself and refrained from creating new words that would be unintelligible even to myself. Only one critic among many spotted this feature, but he ended up calling me a "stylist." The events I wrote about mostly came from something I had seen or heard, but they were certainly not entirely factual—I would draw on one thing but change or expand upon it until it completely expressed what I intended. The models for characters were also like this—I would not rely on one specific individual but, more often than not, use a mouth from someone in Zhejiang, a face from Beijing, and clothes from Shanxi to create a composite character. When people say this or that story of mine was an attack on such and such a person, it's utter nonsense.

Nevertheless, there is a problem in this method of writing—that is, it makes it hard for one to put down one's pen. Writing in one fell swoop makes one feel that the characters come alive and fulfill their own missions. But if one gets distracted and has to resume writing after having set the story aside, the temperament of the characters may change, and the backdrop may become different from what was originally imagined. For instance, in my story "Broken Mountain," I had originally intended to describe the blooming of sexuality, its creativity and decline; but in the middle of writing, I read an article in a newspaper by a Neo-Confucian critic attacking love poems, which got my ire up so much that I added a little personage into the story and had him run up between Nüwa's legs.[42] This was not only unnecessary but ended up ruining the overall structure of the story. But these things probably went unnoticed by everyone else but me; our eminent literary critic Cheng Fangwu[43] even acclaimed this as an exceptionally brilliant piece.

I imagine if you take just one person as your model in creating a character, you can avoid this sort of problem, but I, myself, have never tried my hand at it. I forget who said that in painting, the best way to capture a person's unique attributes with a minimum number of strokes is to draw the person's eyes. I think that observation is extremely accurate. If you were to draw someone's whole head of hair, however realistic it is down to every minute detail, it would be pointless. I have often attempted to learn this method but unfortunately failed to master it.

I have never insisted on putting in any details that could be left out, nor have I forced myself to write when I could not; but that was because I had another source of income at the time and did not depend on my writing for my livelihood, so it cannot be taken as a general rule for writers.

Additionally, when I wrote I never took any sort of criticism seriously; as immature as the realm of creative output in China was in those days, the field of literary criticism was even more immature. If critics did not elevate someone to the skies, they put him down into the earth. If you took what they said to heart, you either felt yourself over and above ordinary mortals, or thought that nothing short of killing yourself could serve as a fitting apology to the world. In order to benefit writers, criticism should simply say what is good is good and what is bad is bad.

I frequently read essays by foreign literary critics because they owe me no gratitude and bear me no grudges. Although the works under criticism are by others, there are many points from which I can learn. But naturally I am careful to find out which school or faction these critics belong to.

These are all things that transpired a decade ago, after which I discontinued creative writing and made little progress. So when the editor asked me to write an essay on the subject, how could I possibly produce anything? All I can come up with are the above rambling remarks.

By lamplight on March 5

TRANSLATED BY JON EUGENE VON KOWALLIS

# More Random Thoughts after Illness (excerpt)

## On *"Releasing one's frustrations"*

病後雜談之余——關於 "舒憤懣"

## III

Renewed hostility to the Qing dynasty probably started around the reign of Emperor Guangxu, but I never looked into who the "ringleaders" from the literary world were. Mr. Taiyan gained renown as a valiant general who wrote essays opposing the Manchus, but in the unrevised edition of his *Compelled Writings* (Qiu shu), he nonetheless acknowledged the Manchus' ability to govern China, calling them "guest emperors," comparable to the "guest ministers" of the Qin empire.[44] In any case, by the final year of the reign of Guangxu, old books unfavorable to the Qing empire were reprinted in quick succession. Mr. Taiyan revised his notion of the "guest emperor" accordingly; while some essays were omitted, he specified that that particular essay be preserved in the second print edition of *Compelled Writings*. Later, the title of the book was changed to *Investigative Essays* (Jian lun), but I don't know if things were handled in the same manner. Quite a number of the Chinese students in Japan searched the library for written documents from the late Ming to the early Qing that could be used to incite revolution. At that time, printed in one big volume was *Voice of the Han*, a supplementary issue of *World of Hubei Students*. Four phrases from the *Selections of Refined Literature* (Wen xuan) were inscribed on the cover: "express accumulated sentiments of nostalgia, articulate exquisite feelings arising from contemplating ancient times." I no longer recall the third phrase, but the fourth was: "invigorate the glorious reputation of the Han." Without the past there would be no present, yet documents such as these can often be copied only from libraries in foreign countries.

I was born in a remote locale and didn't have the slightest inkling of the distinction between "Manchu" and "Han." Only on restaurant signs did I see

First published in volume 4, issue 3, of the journal *Literature* (Wenxue) in March 1935 and later anthologized in *Essays from the Semi-Concessions* (Qiejie ting zawen, 1937). Lu Xun, *Lu Xun quanji* (Complete works of Lu Xun) (Beijing: Renmin wenxue, 2005), 6: 191–195.

such words as "Manchu and Han Wine Banquet," yet it never aroused my suspicions. Hearing people relaying stories about "this dynasty" was a common occurrence, but the literary inquisition was a matter I had never heard of; Emperor Qianlong's grand affair of journeying south was also seldom recounted anymore. What we heard about most was "fighting the Long Hairs."[45] My family had an elderly female servant who said she was over ten years old at the time of the Long Hairs. She recounted the most stories about the Long Hairs to me but didn't make any distinctions between good and evil. She simply said that there were three terrifying things: naturally, one of them was the "Long Hairs," one was the "Short Hairs," and then there was the "Patterned Green Heads."[46] Only later did I come to understand that the latter two were actually government troops, but based on the experience of the ignorant masses, they were no different from the Long Hairs. It was, rather, some scholars who pointed out to me how despicable the Long Hairs were. We had a few provincial gazettes at home, and flipping through them by chance once, I saw that the names of martyred men and women alone filled up one or two volumes, and among my fellow clansmen, several had been killed off and later knighted as "Hereditary Commandants of the Fleet-as-Clouds Cavalry." And so I came to discern very clearly how despicable the Long Hairs were. Yet it really is a case of "one's worries being like billowing waves"; as time went by and I acquired more experience to substantiate the maidservant's accounts, I was still unable to verify whether the martyred men and women had been killed by the Long Hairs, the Short Hairs, or the Patterned Green Heads. I was really envious of the fortune of the sages who were "not confused when they reached the age of forty."[47]

What first prompted me to the distinction between Manchu and Han was not books, but the queue. On account of this queue, many of our ancients had their heads cut off, and it was only then that the custom took root. By the time I had acquired some knowledge, everyone had long forgotten the bloody history. Instead, they considered those with fully grown hair Long Hairs, and those completely shaven, monks. Only those who shaved a bit here and let their hair grow a bit there were considered respectable people.[48] And then they started playing some fancy tricks with the queue: clowns would tie their queues into a knot and stick a paper flower in it as they pulled their pranks; jesters in traditional dramas would hang their queues on metal rods as they smoked leisurely and showed off their skills; magicians, without using their hands, would simply shake their head and *"shazam"* their queues would fly up and coil around on top of their heads, at which point they'd take up their Guan Yu swords. Moreover, there were practical uses as well: in a fight, one can grab it in order to flee from a dangerous situation; when trying to capture someone, you can pull on it—no need for a rope. If many are captured, one person could string a whole bunch of captives together by grasping the tips of their queues. In Wu Youru's print "Magnificent Scenes from Shanghai," there's an image of a guard tugging at a criminal's queue in a courtroom—but this was considered a "marvelous scene."

Things were fine when I lived in a remote locale, but once in Shanghai, I would unavoidably hear an English term come up now and then: "Pigtail." This term is no longer heard now, and its meaning seemed to be simply that a pig's tail was growing out of a person's head. It's much more polite than the term "swine" used by the Chinese in Shanghai to curse each other nowadays. But the young people back then, it seems, were not as cultivated as the young people today, and they didn't yet understand the concept of "humor," so it actually sounded quite jarring to their ears. People also gradually came to feel that the queue, with its over two-hundred-year history, had become an eyesore: the hair was neither left to grow out fully, nor was it completely shaved off; instead, it was partially shaved into a ring, with some remaining tufts braided into a queue left to trail down one's back, as if designed to be a handle for others to tug at or hold on to. It seems entirely natural that people would, in the end, come to find it revolting, even if the queue isn't a practice appropriated from somewhere else nor the result of having been seduced by the theories of someone whose surname ends with "-sky."[49] (In compliance with government orders, the last two phrases of the sentence above can be changed to "there's nothing surprising about it.")

My queue stayed behind in Japan—half of which I gave to a servant girl at an inn to make a wig, the other half to a barber—and I returned to my native home without it in the early years of the reign of Xuantong. As soon as I arrived in Shanghai, I had to wear a fake queue. At that time, there was an expert in Shanghai who exclusively fitted fake queues. The price was set at four silver yuan per braid, no discounts given. Students who had studied abroad were presumably all familiar with his name. And he really did an exquisite job; so long as people weren't paying close attention, it was quite possible not to run into any trouble. But if people knew that you had studied abroad and examined you carefully, there was a good chance of being exposed. The fake queues didn't quite work in the summer since you couldn't wear a hat, nor in crowds because you had to make sure it didn't get twisted or pulled off. After wearing it for over a month, I thought: If it fell off or was yanked off by someone on the street, wouldn't that be worse than not having a queue to begin with? Might as well not wear it. As the sages said: One must conduct oneself with honesty.

But the price of this honesty was not cheap in the least: the treatment I received when I went out on the streets was completely different from before. In the past, I expected special treatment only when visiting my friends' home as a guest; but now I found that you could garner special treatment on the streets on the way there as well. In a good case scenario, people would just stare at me blankly, but mostly I received cold sneers and bitter cursing. If accused of a "minor" crime, it would be that I had committed adultery, because at the time the punishment meted out to a male adulterer was to first cut off his queue, which I still don't understand the reason for; if accused of a "serious" crime, it would be that I had "consorted with the foreign," or that I was what we now call a "traitor of the Han." A person without a nose walking down the street wouldn't necessarily suffer so, though someone without a shadow *would*, I'm afraid, be subjected to such social abuse.

In my first year after returning to China, I worked as a teacher in Hangzhou, where I could still pass for a foreign devil when I donned a Western suit. In the second year, when I returned to my native Shaoxing to work as a school superintendent, the Western suit didn't cut it anymore; because many people knew me, no matter what I wore, I was always identified as a "traitor." The worst suffering I was subjected to as a result of being queueless was thus in my hometown. I had to be most prudent under the watchful eyes of the Manchu official in the Shaoxing government. Whenever he visited the school, he would carefully scrutinize my short hair and go out of his way to talk to me.

There was a sudden fashion for queue-cutting among the students, and many wanted to cut theirs off. I quickly forbade it. They then sent a representative to interrogate me: just what, exactly, is better, to have a queue or not? Without a second thought, I replied: no queue is better, but I advise you not to cut it off. The students had never accused me of "consorting with the foreign," but from this time on, they deemed me someone whose "words and actions were inconsistent" and looked down on me. Having one's "action consistent with one's words" is of course a worthy enterprise; even today there are so-called "littérateurs" who still pride themselves on this quality. But the students were unaware that as soon as they cut off their queues, all their worth would be placed on their heads. Xuanting Alley, not far from the Shao-xing Middle School, is the place where Miss Qiu Jin[50] was martyred; they often pass by it but have forgotten already.

"How fast indeed!" By October 10 of the year 1911, Shaoxing also hung up white flags as a sign of having joined the revolution. The greatest and most unforgettable benefit I received from the revolution was that I could hold my bare head high as I sauntered on the street leisurely without hearing any kind of mocking or cursing. When a few old friends who didn't have queues came to visit from the countryside, we would touch our bare heads as soon as we saw each other and laugh heartily, saying: Ha ha, this day has finally arrived.

If someone were to ask me to praise the achievements of the revolution as a way of "releasing my frustrations," the first thing I would mention is cutting off the queue.

December 17

TRANSLATED BY EILEEN J. CHENG

# Death

死

While compiling a selected volume of Kaethe Kollwitz's[51] woodcuts for publication, I asked Ms. Agnes Smedley to write a preface. I felt that this was a most appropriate request since the two were very well acquainted. Not long after receiving it, I pressed Mr. Mao Dun to do a translation, now published in the selected volume. A passage in it reads:

---

Written a month before Lu Xun's death at the age of fifty-six. First published in volume 1, issue 2, of *Midstream* (Zhongliu) on September 20, 1936, and later anthologized in the last volume of *Essays from the Semi-Concessions, Final Volume* (Qiejie ting zawen mo bian, 1937). Lu Xun, *Lu Xun quanji* (Complete works of Lu Xun) (Beijing: Renmin wenxue, 2005), 6: 631–636.

Over many years, Kaethe Kollwitz—who never once took advantage of the honors bestowed upon her—produced a large quantity of paintings, ink and pencil sketches, woodcuts, and etchings. An examination of these works shows that they are driven by two dominant themes: the theme of her early works is resistance, and the themes of her later years include maternal love, the security provided by the maternal, salvation, and death. Suffering and tragedy enshroud her works, along with a passionate desire to protect the oppressed.

Once I asked her: "In the past, the main theme of your works was resistance but now it appears that you're quite unable to cast aside the notion of death. Why is this?" In an anguished tone of voice, she replied: "Maybe it's because I'm getting older by the day!"

When I read up to this point, I paused to reflect. I started calculating: She began using "death" as a subject of her artworks around 1910; at the time, she was only forty-three or forty-four years old. My own reflections on the subject this year had, of course, something to do with my age. But when I think back to over a decade or so ago, death had yet to resonate with me so deeply. Perhaps it is because people have long dealt with life and death so casually, considering it to be of little significance, that we, too, have come to regard it lightly, quite unlike the seriousness with which the Europeans view it. Some foreigners say that the Chinese are most afraid of death. This is, in fact, incorrect—though, naturally, there are bound to be those who sort of just die off without even realizing it.

Beliefs regarding the afterlife may have further contributed to people's casual attitude toward death. Everyone knows we Chinese believe in ghosts (in more recent times also referred to as "spirits"). Though no longer human after death, one can nevertheless exist as a ghost, which is better than nothing. But the imagined duration of one's existence as a ghost varies according to one's wealth when alive. Poor people's belief in transmigration after death stems mainly from Buddhism. What is referred to as transmigration in Buddhism is, of course, an onerous process that is by no means simple, but the poor are often unlearned and don't understand this. Which explains why criminals, bound and tied on their way to the execution grounds, shout "a hero will rise up again in another twenty years" with no hint of fear on their faces. Moreover, it's been said that ghosts wear the same clothes they had on at the time of death. Since the poor don't own good clothing, as ghosts, they certainly won't appear any more dignified; far better to reincarnate immediately as a naked baby. Has there ever been the case of a family with a newborn that arrived dressed in beggar's rags or in swimwear? Never. It's a relief, then, to have a completely fresh start. Perhaps someone might ask: if one believes in transmigration, then there's no knowing if in your next life you might sink into yet more destitute circumstances or literally come back as a beast, which would be even more horrifying. But my feeling is that the poor don't think this way. They firmly believe that they have not committed sins vile enough, nor attained the status, power, and wealth, that would warrant their return in the form of a beast.

Yet those with status, power, and wealth don't feel that they deserve to return as beasts either; some of them worship Buddha in their homes while simultaneously promoting reading the classics and reviving ancient ways, preparing to attain Buddhahood and Sagehood at once. They believe that at death they will transcend the laws of transmigration, just as they were able to transcend ethical standards of behavior in their lifetime. The modestly wealthy, they don't feel they should transmigrate either; but they don't have any grand ambitions and are simply content with their lot as ghosts. So as soon as they approach the age of fifty, they search for a burial plot and have coffins made; they burn paper money to make an advance deposit into their accounts in the netherworld, bear progeny who will ensure that they have sacrificial food to eat. This really is a life far more blessed than that of a living person's. Suppose that I had transformed into a ghost and left behind good descendants in the human realm. Why would I bother hawking my writings piece by piece or going to Beixin Press to collect my debts? All I have to do is lie comfortably in repose in my coffin made from the precious *nan* tree or petrified wood; come New Year or some other holiday, I would have a sumptuous feast and a pile of money laid out before me. What bliss!

Unlike those of wealth and rank, who are exempt from the laws of the netherworld, it is generally speaking to the advantage of the poor to be reborn immediately after death and for the modestly well-off to exist as ghosts for as long as possible. Those in this latter category are willing to exist as ghosts because their lives (this is improper word usage, but I can't think of an appropriate term at the moment) as ghosts are essentially extensions of their human lives, which they have yet to grow weary of. In the netherworld, there are, of course, also rulers who are extremely strict and unbiased, but they believe that these rulers will make special accommodations for them alone and also accept some small gifts, just as good officials are wont to do in the human realm.

There is another group of people who are rather cavalier and probably wouldn't think much about death even as it comes knocking. I have always belonged to this "cavalier clique." Thirty years ago when I studied medicine, I had contemplated the question of whether the soul existed; the conclusion was that I didn't know. Then I contemplated whether death itself was an agonizing experience; the conclusions varied. Afterward, I stopped further contemplation and forgot about it all. In the past decade, I sometimes wrote essays to commemorate the death of friends, but it seems that I never really thought about my own death. In the past two years I have been ill often, and once stricken, the illness dragged on for a relatively long time, which would invariably remind me of my age. I was, of course, also prompted by the continual reminders that came from the pens of writers, well intended and malicious.

Starting last year, whenever I was recuperating from an illness, I would recline in my wicker chair and inevitably think about all the things I had to work on after recovering: what essays to write, what books to translate or publish. After arriving at a definitive plan, I would conclude by saying: that's settled, then—but I'm going to have to get to work at once. This line of thought, of having to "get to work at once" never occurred to me before and came from the subliminal reminders prompting me about my age. But I never directly thought about death.

Not until my major bout of illness this year did I start contemplating the prospect of death. At first, when I fell ill, I did the same thing I had in the past: I went to the Japanese Dr. S[52] for a diagnosis. Though not a specialist in tuberculosis, he was elderly, had a lot of experience, and was senior to me when it came to medical training. I was also very well acquainted with him, and he was forthcoming in his opinions. Naturally, a doctor would still be circumspect when it comes to what he relays to his patient, regardless of how well acquainted they are with each other. But Dr. S had already given me at least two or three warnings, which I didn't take to heart or tell anyone about. Probably because my illness had dragged on for so long and my health seemed so precarious, a few friends secretly came up with a plan to ask Dr. D, an American citizen, to examine me. He is the only European[53] tuberculosis specialist in Shanghai. After tapping my body and listening to my heart and lungs, he praised me as a typical specimen of the Chinese, with a most remarkable resistance to disease. Yet he also pronounced that my death was near at hand, adding that had I been European, I would have died five or six years ago. This verdict made my more sensitive friends shed tears. I didn't ask the doctor for a prescription because I thought that since his medical training had been done in Europe, he would surely not have learned to write a prescription for a patient who had already been dead for five years. But Dr. D's diagnosis was, in fact, extremely accurate; the image of my chest shown on an x-ray taken later more or less matched his diagnosis.

I didn't really take his pronouncement to heart, but it still affected me as I lay in bed day and night with no energy to talk or read books. I couldn't even hold a newspaper in my hands, and I had yet to cultivate my mind to become as "still as water from an ancient well." But from this point on, I sometimes actually thought about "death." My thoughts, however, weren't tuned to things like "a hero will rise up again in another twenty years" or how long I would reside in the coffin made of *nan* wood, but rather to some of the trivial matters that needed to be taken care of before death. It wasn't until this moment that I knew for certain I didn't believe in ghosts after death. The only thing that occurred to me was to write a will. Had I been royalty with extraordinary wealth, my sons and sons-in-law would have pressed me to write a will long ago, but no one brought up the matter then. Still I thought I might as well leave one anyway. At the time I seem to have thought about quite a few matters, all related to what I would write in my will for my next of kin. They included the following:

1. Do not, on account of the funeral, accept a penny from anyone—old friends exempted.
2. Just quickly put the body in the coffin and bury it at once.
3. Do not hold any commemorative activities.
4. Forget me and mind your own lives. If you don't, you're just fools.
5. When the child grows up, if he's lacking in talent, then let him get by in life doing something ordinary. Under no circumstances should he become a phony writer or artist.
6. Promises made by others, do not take them seriously.

7. Under no circumstances associate with people who harm others yet profess to oppose retaliation and to advocate tolerance.

There were of course other things besides these but I have now forgotten. I just recall once, when I was ill with a fever, thinking about a deathbed ritual that Europeans often conduct, in which one seeks pardon from others and pardons others as well. It's safe to say that I have many enemies who resent me. If a person influenced by modern trends were to ask me about this ritual, how would I respond? I gave it some thought and decided: "Let them go on hating me, I shan't forgive a single one of them either."

But no such ritual was conducted, and I didn't write a will either. I just lay there in silence, and sometimes a pressing thought would surface: so this is what dying feels like, it's not so miserable after all. But perhaps the moment right before death might not be like this; even so, death only happens once in a lifetime and no matter what I should be able to endure it. . . . Afterward, things took a turn and I recovered. Up until now, I suspect these experiences probably aren't accurate reflections of what it is like before death. If one were really about to die, one might not even have any of these thoughts. But just exactly what it will be like, I don't know either.

September 5

TRANSLATED BY EILEEN J. CHENG

# Preface to *Essays from the Semi-Concessions*
## 《且介亭雜文》序言

In recent years, more "miscellaneous essays" have been produced than in the past, and they have been attacked even more than before. For example, the likes of the self-proclaimed poet Shao Xunmei, the former "third type of person"[54] Shi Zhecun and Du Heng (also known as Su Wen), and the half-baked college student Lin Xijuan all have a deep hatred of the miscellaneous

---

First published in *Essays from the Semi-Concessions*, vol. 1 (Qiejie ting zawen, 1937). Lu Xun, *Lu Xun quanji* (Complete works of Lu Xun) (Beijing: Renmin wenxue, 2005), 6: 3–5.

essay and have indicted it on various counts. Yet all in vain: as the number of writers have started growing, so too have their readers.

The "miscellaneous essay" is not some novel product of recent times; it has, in fact, existed "since ancient times." Essays can be categorized by different subjects or chronologically by date of completion (annals). Different kinds of essays, all collected in one volume regardless of their form, are called a "miscellany." Categorization by subject enables readers to reflect on the content, while annals help readers understand the trends of the times. If one wants to assess the important personages and affairs of an age, then one has to read annals. The prevalence of newly written biographical chronicles of the ancients is proof that many people are already aware of this. All the more so in pressing times like the present, when the mission of the writer is to immediately refute or challenge things that are harmful, to serve as a reactive nerve and tool for attack and defense. Dedication to a great masterpiece and planning for the culture of the future are certainly good things. But writers who struggle for the present are fighting for the present *and* the future, for if we lose the present, there is no future to speak of.

In any struggle, there must be direction. This is the great enemy of the likes of Shao, Shi, Du, and Lin. In truth, what they despise is substance, and though they have donned the cloaks of "litérateurs," beneath those cloaks hide "preachers of death,"[55] whose existence is inimical to our survival.

This collection, along with *Fringed Literature*, is the accumulation of all the essays I have written in the past year when the "miscellaneous essay" was under attack, whether overtly or covertly, directly or indirectly. Of course I dare not call them "poetic testaments of an age"; in their midst are signs of the times, but they are by no means a hero's treasure chest that, when opened, will shine with brilliance. I'm just hawking my wares by the roadside deep in the night. What I have to offer are no more than a few nails and a few small dishes made of clay, but I hope and also believe that some people will find in them things of use.

December 30, 1935, recorded in the semi-concessions of Shanghai

TRANSLATED BY EILEEN J. CHENG

# SECTION II

*In Memoriam*

# Warriors and Flies

# 戰士和蒼蠅

Schopenhauer said something along these lines: in assessing a man's greatness, the size of his spirit stands in inverse proportion to that of his physical body. For the latter, the further the distance, the smaller it appears; for the former, the further the distance, the greater it appears.

Precisely because the closer someone is to us, the more ordinary he seems and the more visible his flaws and wounds, he appears to be one of us, not a god, a demon, or a strange beast. He is human and nothing more. But this is also precisely why he is a great man.

When a warrior dies in battle, the first things flies detect are his flaws and wounds. Biting and buzzing merrily, they take pride in this discovery, presuming to be even more of a hero than the dead warrior. But the warrior is dead and no longer swats them away. So the flies buzz on even more merrily, presuming that the sounds they make are everlasting because in their completeness, they are far superior to the warriors.

And indeed no one has detected the flaws and wounds of flies.

Yet warriors with flaws are still warriors after all, and perfect flies are nothing more than flies.

Away with you, flies! Even though you have wings and can still buzz about, you will never surpass warriors, you vermin!

March 21, 1925

TRANSLATED BY EILEEN J. CHENG

---

In "Must-Read Books for Young People" (in this volume), Lu Xun notes that this essay was written to commemorate Sun Yat-sen (1866–1925), a revolutionary and the first president of the Republic of China, who died on March 12, 1925. The flies here refer to the critics attacking Sun posthumously. First published in issue 14 of *Mass Literary Arts Weekly* (Minzhong wenyi zhou kan), a supplement to *Capital News* (Jing bao), on March 24, 1925, and later anthologized in *Inauspicious Star* (Huagai ji, 1926). Lu Xun, *Lu Xun quanji* (Complete works of Lu Xun) (Beijing: Renmin wenxue, 2005), 3: 40–41.

# Roses without Blooms, Part II (excerpt)

## 無花的薔薇之二

### IV

This is no longer the time to write things like "Roses without Blooms."

Although my writings consist mostly of thorns, they still require some degree of peace of mind to write.

Now I hear that a massacre has just occurred in Beijing.[1] Just as I was penning the pointless words above, many young people were being shot at or cut down. Alas, people's souls are unable to communicate with each other!

### V

On March 18 in the fifteenth year of the Republic of China, Duan Qirui's government ordered guards with guns and bayonets to surround and slaughter the unarmed protesters in front of the gates of the State Council, the hundreds of young men and women whose intent was to lend their support in China's diplomatic dealings with foreign powers. An order was even issued, slandering them as "mobsters"!

Such brutal and vicious acts are not to be seen among beasts and are rare even among humans. The only case bearing some resemblance is when Tsar Nicholas II of Russia ordered the Cossacks to open fire on the masses.[2]

### VI

China is being devoured by tigers and wolves, but no one cares. The only ones who do are a few young students who should have been studying in peace but who were so disturbed by the volatile state of affairs that they were unable to do so. If the authorities had just an ounce of decency in them,

---

In "Roses without Blooms, Part I," published on March 8, Lu Xun explains that the title was a modified translation of Arthur Schopenhauer's line, "No roses without thorns, but many a thorn without a rose." Part II was first published in issue 72 of *Threads of Talk* (*Yusi*) on March 29, 1926, and later anthologized in *Sequel to Inauspicious Star* (*Huagai ji xubian*, 1927). In Lu Xun, *Lu Xun quanji* (Complete works of Lu Xun) (Beijing: Renmin wenxue, 2005), 3: 277–281.

shouldn't they have admitted their faults and been stricken with just a bit of conscience?

And yet they had them slaughtered!

## VII

Even if these sorts of young people were killed off all at once, the murderers would by no means be victors.

China itself would perish along with its patriots. Having accumulated some wealth, the murderers might be able to go on raising their progeny for quite a while, but they will get their due in the end. What joy could there be in spawning "a long string of progeny"?[3] Though their extinction may be postponed, they would have to live in a barren land most unsuited to human habitation; they would have to burrow in the deepest of mines; they would have to toil in the most defiled of occupations. . . .

## VIII

If China is not to perish, then as past history teaches us, the future will prove to be a great surprise to the murderers—

This is not the end of an incident, but just the beginning.

Lies written in ink cannot cover up facts written in blood.

Blood debts must be repaid in kind. The longer the delay in payment, the higher the interest!

## IX

All the above is empty talk. These words written with pen, what relevance do they have?

Rather, it is actual bullets that shed the blood of young people. This blood cannot be covered up by lies written in ink, nor can it be lulled by eulogies written in ink; no power can suppress it, for it can no longer be deceived nor killed.

Written on March 18, the darkest day since the founding of the Republic

TRANSLATED BY HU YING

# In Memory of Liu Hezhen

## 紀念劉和珍君

## I

On March 25 of the fifteenth year of the Republic of China, the Beijing Women's Normal College held a memorial service for Liu Hezhen and Yang Dequn, both of whom were killed on the 18th in front of Duan Qirui's government offices.[4] On that day, as I was pacing alone outside the auditorium, I encountered Miss Cheng, who came up to me and asked: "Sir, have you written something for Liu Hezhen?" I said: "I haven't." She then solemnly urged me: "Sir, why don't you write something? Liu Hezhen was very fond of reading your essays when she was alive."

This I knew. The circulation of the journals I edited, probably because they often ceased publication without notice, was consistently dismal. Yet in spite of financial hardship, she was among those who steadfastly subscribed to a whole year of *Wilderness* (Mangyuan). I, too, had felt the need to write something early on, for though it may have no relevance for the dead whatsoever, it seems that this is the only thing the living can do. If I believed in "one's soul living on in the heavens," then naturally I would derive a greater sense of comfort—but at this moment, it seems this is the only thing I can do.

Yet I really have nothing to say. I just feel that the world we live in is inhuman. The blood of over forty youths has saturated my surroundings, making it difficult for me to see, hear, or breathe; what could I possibly have to say? Releasing one's sorrow in song can only come after the pain has settled. The insidious remarks made by a few so-called scholars and literary men that ensued made me feel especially dejected. I am already beyond indignation. I will savor the dark desolation of this inhuman world and display my

First published in issue 74 of *Threads of Talk* (Yusi) on April 12, 1926, and later anthologized in *Sequel to Inauspicious Star* (Huagai ji xubian, 1927). Lu Xun appends the term of respect 君 (*jun*, sometimes translated as "sir"), commonly used between men, to the name of his female student Liu Hezhen in the title. This same term is appended to the names of the women who were injured or killed (including Liu Hezhen) mentioned in the essay. They have been left untranslated. Lu Xun, *Lu Xun quanji* (Complete works of Lu Xun) (Beijing: Renmin wenxue, 2005), 3: 289–295.

utmost despair before this inhuman world, letting it delight in my pain. Let this be the humble offering of one still living, presented at the altar of the dead.

## II

True warriors have the courage to confront the misery of life and look at bloodshed without fear. What sorrow and bliss they must feel! Yet the Creator often has the mediocre person in mind in his designs, so he lets the swift flow of time wash away traces of the past, leaving behind only pale red bloodstains and a faint trace of sorrow; this allows people, for the time being, to drag out their ignoble existences amid the pale red bloodstains with a faint trace of sorrow, so that this seemingly human yet inhuman world of ours can go on. When will such a world come to an end?

We still live in such a world. I, too, had felt the need to write something early on. Two weeks have elapsed since March 18 and the savior called forgetting is about to descend, and so I must write something now.

## III

Among the over forty youths killed was Liu Hezhen, a student of mine. "Student," this is how I had thought of her and referred to her, but now I am a bit hesitant to do so. Rather, I should offer her my sorrow and pay my respects. She is not a student of "one who continues to drag out his ignoble existence," but a Chinese youth who died for China.

The first time I came across her name was early last summer, when the principal of the Women's Normal College, Yang Yinyu, expelled six members of the student union from the school. She was one of them, but I didn't know her then. It was only later, likely when Liu Baizhao dispatched male and female military officers to forcibly drag them off the campus that someone pointed out a student to me and said: That's Liu Hezhen. Only then was I able to attach the name to an actual body, but I was inwardly astonished. I had imagined that the students who had been so unwavering in the face of the authorities and had resisted a principal with strong backing would, of course, be bold and fierce. Yet she often smiled and her manner was gentle. After we rented temporary accommodations in Zongmao Alley to use as classrooms, she started attending my lectures, and so our encounters became more frequent, and she was, as before, always smiling with a gentle manner about her. It was only after the college was restored to its old ways and some of the staff, believing they had already fulfilled their duties, prepared to resign, that I saw her fretting over the future of the college, distraught to the point of tears. After this, it seems we never saw each other again. At least in my recollection, that was our final parting.

## IV

It wasn't until the morning of the 18th that I heard a crowd had presented a petition to the acting government; that afternoon, I received the sad news that the forces had open fired and that the injured and dead numbered in the hundreds and that Liu Hezhen was among those killed. I was quite skeptical about these reports, however. I've never had qualms about ascribing the worst of intentions to my fellow Chinese, but at the time, I could neither imagine nor believe that they would stoop to such despicable brutality and that the blood of the smiling and amiable Liu Hezhen would be splattered so senselessly—and before the gates of the government building, at that.

But on that day it was proven true, and the evidence is her corpse; another piece of evidence is the corpse of Yang Dequn. And it further proves that this was not a mere killing, but a brutal slaughter, because her body still had bruises left from the blows of a baton.

But the Duan government issued a decree declaring them to be "violent rabble-rousers"!

Then came the rumors saying that they had been manipulated by others.

Cruel images, I can no longer bear looking at them, and the rumors are especially hard for me to bear. What more is there left for me to say? I now understand the reason why a dying race remains silent. Silence, oh silence! If we do not explode from the silence, then we shall perish in silence.

## V

But I still have more to say.

I didn't witness this myself, but I heard that at the time she, Liu Hezhen, marched ahead cheerfully. Of course, she was just going to file a petition; no one with an ounce of compassion in them could have ever guessed that there would be such a trap. But she was shot in front of the government offices and the bullet went in through her back and pierced sideways through her heart and lungs. It was a fatal wound, but she didn't die immediately. Zhang Jingshu, who went along with her, took four bullets when she tried to prop her up. One shot was from a handgun, and she fell over immediately. Yang Dequn, who also went along, wanted to prop *her* up, and she, too, was shot. The bullet went through her left shoulder and exited her right chest area and she, too, immediately fell over. Yet she was still able to sit up, but she died when a soldier struck two brutal blows to her head and chest.

The ever-smiling and amiable Liu Hezhen has indeed died—this is the truth, and her corpse is the evidence. The silently courageous and friendly Yang Dequn is also dead, and her corpse is the evidence. Only Zhang Jingshu, who was just as courageous and compassionate as the others, remains alive, moaning in the hospital. When the three women were calmly shot one after the other by the bullets of guns invented by civilized men, what astounding greatness they displayed! The great feats achieved by Chinese generals in slaughtering women and children and the military prowess displayed by the Allied Forces[5] to teach students a lesson have, unfortunately, been completely blotted out by these few streaks of blood.

But those Chinese and foreign murderers still hold their heads high, unaware that each of their faces is stained with blood. . . .

## VI

Time flows on swiftly as always, and the streets and cities are peaceful once more. The loss of a few lives doesn't matter much in China; at most they supply fodder for the after-meal chatter of idlers who have no ill will, or they give those idlers with malicious intentions seeds for rumormongering. As for any other deeper significance, I feel that there is little, because this is really nothing more than a case of some innocent people filing a petition. The ongoing history of human bloodbaths is similar to the process of coal formation—large quantities of wood are used up to produce just a small piece of coal. But the petition no longer exists, nor the lives of the innocent.

Yet since there are bloodstains, naturally the incident will take on a deeper significance. At least they will soak into the hearts of family, teachers, friends, and lovers; though the color of the blood will fade to pink with the passage of time, the familiar smiles and amiable natures will be preserved eternally in the faint traces of sorrow. Tao Qian once said:

> Relatives may still feel sorrow,
> but others are already singing.
> Dead and gone, what can I say?
> I entrust my body to the mountains.[6]

If things could truly be like this, then that would be quite enough.

# VII

As I said earlier, I have never had qualms about ascribing the worst of intentions to my fellow Chinese. But this time, there were a few things that I found to be beyond my imagination: one is the extent of the brutality of those in power; another, the despicableness of the rumormongers; and yet another is that Chinese women would exhibit such calmness before death.

It was last year that I started seeing for myself how Chinese women took matters in hand. Few as these instances were, I nonetheless found myself frequently marveling at their capability, their persistence, and their resolute attitude. In this instance, their attempts to save one another in the rain of bullets, with little regard for their own lives, are tributes to the steely courage of Chinese women. Though they fell victim to a malicious plot and their memory will be suppressed for several thousand years, there is no evidence that that memory will, in the end, die in vain. If one were to search for some kind of meaning that the deaths and injuries from this incident hold for the future, perhaps it can be found in this.

Those who drag on their ignoble existence amid pale bloodstains will vaguely make out faint glimmers of hope; true warriors will tread onward with even greater resolve.

Alas, I am unable to speak, but with this I commemorate Liu Hezhen.

April 1, 1926

TRANSLATED BY EILEEN J. CHENG

# Remembrance for the Sake of Forgetting

為了忘卻的紀念

## I

For a long time now I have been meaning to write a few words to commemorate several young writers. This is for no other reason than that I have, in the past two years, often found myself assailed by pangs of grief and rage that have yet to cease. I was hoping that doing so would allow me to shake off my sorrow, giving me some measure of relief. To put it plainly, it is so that I can forget them.

Two years ago today, that is, on the night of the 7th or the morning of the 8th of July 1931, five of our young writers were murdered.[7] The Shanghai papers at the time didn't dare report on the matter; or perhaps they were unwilling to or thought it unworthy of printing. Only in *Literary News* were there some essays with veiled references. In the 11th issue (May 25), there was a piece by Mr. Lin Mang titled "Notes of My Impression of Bai Mang," which read:

> He wrote a good number of poems and also translated a few by the Hungarian poet Petöfi. When Lu Xun, editor of the journal *Torrent* at the time, received his manuscript submission, he wrote a letter requesting a meeting. But Bai Mang was one of those people who didn't care to meet with celebrities. In the end, it was Lu Xun who came to call on him and did his utmost to encourage him to engage in literary work. But in the end, Bai Mang wasn't able to just sit and write in his dingy room, so he once again resumed his own path. Not long after, he was arrested once again. . . .

The account of our dealings relayed here is, in fact, inaccurate. Bai Mang was not that arrogant. He did come to my residence, but it wasn't because I had asked to meet him. I myself am not so arrogant as to offhandedly write a letter to summon a contributor I didn't even know. The reason for our

First published in volume 2, issue 6, of *Les contemporaines* (Xiandai) on April 1, 1933, and later anthologized in *Southern Tunes in Northern Tones* (Nan qiang bei diao ji, 1934). Lu Xun, *Lu Xun quanji* (Complete works of Lu Xun) (Beijing: Renmin wenxue, 2005), 4: 493–504.

meeting was rather ordinary. At the time, he had submitted a translation of "Biography of Petöfi" from German, so I wrote a letter asking for the original text, which was included in the beginning of an anthology of Petöfi's poems. Since mailing it wasn't convenient, he brought the book over personally. He looked to be a youth of about twenty, his appearance quite respectable, his complexion dark. I have forgotten what we talked about at the time; I only remember that he said his surname was Xu and that he was from Xiang-shan. I asked him why the lady who collected his letters for him had such a strange name (strange in just what sense I have now forgotten). He said she just liked the strange name and thought it romantic, and that he didn't get on so well with her anymore. This is all that remains with me now.

That night, I hastily compared his translation with the original. I knew that apart from the errors in a few spots, there was also a deliberate mistranslation. He didn't seem to like the phrase "national poet," all instances of which were changed to "poet of the masses." The next day I received a letter from him, saying that he regretted meeting with me. He had talked a lot, whereas I had said very little, and the few words I spoke were cold, making him feel somewhat intimidated. I then wrote a letter in reply, explaining that it was entirely normal not to say very much on a first meeting and also telling him that he shouldn't have changed the original text to suit his own taste. Since his book was in my possession, I sent him two volumes of Petöfi's works from my collection, asking if it were possible for him to translate a few additional poems for readers' reference. He did, in fact, translate a few more poems and brought them over in person, and we talked more than in the first encounter. The biography and poems were later published in volume 2, number 5, of *Torrent*, which was the final issue of the journal.

The third time we met, I recall, was on a hot day. Someone knocked on the door, and I went to open it. It was Bai Mang. He was wearing a thick padded robe, his face streaming with sweat, and both of us couldn't help bursting out in laughter. Only then did he tell me he was a revolutionary and that he had just been released after being arrested; his clothes and books had all been confiscated, including the two books I had given him. The robe he was wearing was borrowed from a friend who didn't have a thin-lined one, and since he had to wear a robe that was long, he was left with no choice but to sweat profusely. I believe this instance was probably what Mr. Lin Mang was referring to when he said "he was arrested once again."

I was delighted that he had been released and immediately paid him the fees for his essays so that he could buy a thin-lined robe. At the same time, I also lamented the fate of those two books of mine: having fallen into the hands of the police, they were like fine pearls cast into darkness. There was nothing special about the two books to begin with, one a volume of essays, the other an anthology of poems; according to the German translator, it was his own compilation and no such complete volume of Petőfi's works existed even in Hungary. And since they were published by Reclam's Universal-Bibliothek, they could be found everywhere in Germany and cost less than one *yuan*. But to me, they were treasures, because these books were special-ordered from Germany through the Maruzen Bookstore thirty years ago, at a time when I loved Petőfi with a passion. At the time I was even afraid that the store clerks wouldn't take the order since the books were so cheap, and so I made the request rather timidly. Afterward, I generally kept the books with me, but as my sentiments changed with circumstance, I no longer felt like translating them. So I made up my mind to give them to this young man who had a passionate love for the poems of Petőfi as I once did, thinking that I had found them a good home. And so I took this matter rather seriously, requesting Rou Shi to deliver them personally. Who would have ever guessed that they would wind up in the hands of the "three stripes."[8] What a grave injustice indeed!

## II

That I don't ask to meet prospective contributors is not entirely out of modesty; a large factor is that it saves me a good deal of trouble. From my longtime experience, I know that the majority of young people, in particular young people engaged in literature, are very sensitive and have a strong sense of pride. A slight misstep can easily lead to a misunderstanding, so most of the time I deliberately avoid them. I'm afraid just to meet them, let alone ask them for favors. But when I was in Shanghai, there was one person with whom I dared to joke around casually, and even ask for help handling some private matters—that was Rou Shi, who had delivered the books to Bai Mang.

I don't recall when or where Rou Shi and I first met. I seem to recall he once said that he had heard my lectures in Beijing, so it may have been eight or nine years ago. I also forget how we started seeing each other regularly in Shanghai. Anyhow, at the time he lived in Jingyun Alley, which was about four or five houses down from my residence and somehow we just started seeing each other regularly. It was probably during our first meeting that he told me his surname was Zhao and his given name Pingfu [the characters for "peace" and "return"]. But he also spoke of the strong airs put on by the wealthy gentry in his hometown and said there was one in particular who thought the name Pingfu was a good one and wanted to give it to his son; so he was told not to use the name anymore. So I suspect his original name was "Pingfu," the characters for "peace" and "good fortune," which is why the gentleman took a fancy to it. I doubt he would have been so taken with the character "fu" if it was the character for "return." His hometown was in Ninghai in Taizhou, and you could tell right away from his tough character, which was typical of Taizhou. He could also be quite set in his outdated ways, sometimes suddenly making me think of Fang Xiaoru,[9] who, it seems, had a similar bearing.

He secluded himself in his own quarters engaging in literary endeavors, producing creative works as well as translations. After spending many days together, we found ourselves quite compatible, so we arranged to meet a few other youths of the same persuasion to establish the Morning Blossoms Society. Our goal was to introduce literature from Eastern and Northern Europe and import foreign woodcuts, because we all felt that we should support and cultivate art and literature that was robust and unpretentious. Then we published *Morning Blossoms Tri-Monthly*, *Collected Short Stories of the Contemporary World*, and *Literary Garden of Morning Blossoms*, all of which were guided by this principle. There was only one publication, *Selected Paintings of Fukiya Koji*, that we printed as a way of wiping out the so-called "artists" of the Shanghai bund, that is, to expose the paper tiger Ye Lingfeng.[10]

But Rou Shi himself didn't have money. He borrowed over 200 yuan for printing books. Apart from buying paper, he handled the majority of the manuscript-related work and errands, such as going to the press, producing illustrations, proofreading, etc. But often things were not to his liking, and when he talked about them, his brow would furrow. When you read his old works, they all seemed to have a pessimistic air about them, but in fact, he wasn't like that in nature; he believed people were good. When I would sometimes mention how people could be deceitful, sell out their friends, and suck on the blood of others, his forehead would glisten with sweat and he would widen his nearsighted eyes in surprise and say in protest: "Is this really the case? Surely things have not come to this?"

But not long after, the Morning Blossoms Society went bankrupt. I don't want to go into the reasons, but at any rate, that idealistic noggin of Rou Shi's was the first to hit a brick wall. Our efforts were wasted, and we still had to borrow 100 yuan to pay for the paper. Afterward, he expressed less skepticism toward my theory that human nature was evil and at times even sighed, saying, "Have things really come to this?" But he still believed that people were good.

He then sent the books that remained at the Morning Blossoms Society—all rightfully his—to the Tomorrow Bookstore and Bright China Bookstore in hopes of recouping some money while translating as much as he could to repay the debts; *Collected Short Stories from Denmark* and Gorky's novel *The Artamanovs' Business* were sold to the Commercial Press. I believe the manuscripts of these translations may have been burned in the battles over Shanghai last year, though.

He gradually changed his outdated ways and finally even mustered the courage to go for walks together with women from his hometown or female friends, though they were often separated by at least three to four feet. This was a bad practice, because sometimes when I ran into him on the street, if there was some pretty girl within three or four feet of him, I would start suspecting that she was a friend of his. But when *we* walked together, we always walked very close to each other; he would practically prop me up because he was afraid I would be hit by a car or a tram. For my part, I was concerned about his need to take care of others despite his nearsightedness, so we would both be at a loss and uneasy the whole way. If I could help it, I didn't go out with him. I saw that it was tiresome for him, and so it was for me as well.

If something benefited others at his own personal cost, be it from the perspective of old morality or new morality, he would willingly take it on and assume the burden himself.

In the end, he finally decided to change. There was one instance when he told me very clearly that from then on we had to transform the content and form of our writing. I said: "I'm afraid this might be difficult, it's like telling someone accustomed to using a sword that he can now only swing a stick. How is this possible?" He responded simply and concisely, saying: "You just need to learn!"

It wasn't just empty talk either, he really did start learning things anew. At this time, he brought a friend to visit me, a Miss Feng Keng. We chatted for a while, and in the end, I felt that there was a big barrier between us. I suspected that she had a bit of a romantic streak and an eagerness for quick results. I also suspected that Rou Shi's recent ambition to produce a novel was her idea. But then I started questioning myself: perhaps Rou Shi's determined response earlier may have struck a sore spot, exposing my own laziness, and so I may have unconsciously transferred my frustrations onto her. In truth, I'm no better than the overly sensitive and prideful literary youths I had been afraid of encountering.

Her constitution was frail, and she wasn't beautiful either.

## III

Not until after the founding of the League of Left-Wing Writers did I realize that the Bai Mang I knew was the Yin Fu who published poems in *The Pioneer*. Once at a general meeting, I brought along a German translation of a travelogue written by an American journalist to give to him; there was no deep significance to it other than the fact that I thought it might help him practice his German. But he didn't show up. So I had to again ask Rou Shi to deliver it to him.

But not long after, it turned out that they were both arrested at the same time, and that book of mine was confiscated and wound up in the hands of the "three stripes."

## IV

Tomorrow Bookstore was coming out with a journal, and Rou Shi was invited to be the editor; he accepted. The bookstore also wanted to publish my translations and asked him to inquire with me about how to handle royalties. So I copied out the contract I had signed with the Beixin Bookstore and gave it to him. He stuffed it into his pocket and rushed off. It was the evening of January 16, 1931. Little did I know that this would be the last I would ever see of him and that it would turn out to be our final farewell.

The next day he was arrested at a meeting, my publisher's contract still in his pocket. I heard that the authorities were searching for me because of it. The book contract was legitimate, but I had no desire to go to those shady places to explain and defend myself. I recall that in the *Complete Biography of Yue Fei*, there is a story about a high-ranking Buddhist monk who, seated in a lotus position, transcended to the other world just before the deputy He Li arrived at the temple gates to arrest him. He even left a verse that went along the lines of "He Li comes from the East, I am going toward the West." This is the only good method that slaves can conjure up to escape the sea of suffering. Since there was no righteous swordsman in sight, this was the most convenient way out. I'm no eminent monk, I'm not entitled to the release that comes with nirvana and I'm also still very attached to worldly life. And so I fled.

That night, I burned all the old letters from my friends. Then—with my woman and our child in tow—I went to a guesthouse. Within a few days, I heard that rumors about me—of my arrest or murder—had circulated rampantly, but there was little news of Rou Shi. Some said the police had taken him to the Tomorrow Bookstore to check whether or not he was an editor there. Others said the police had taken him to Beixin Bookstore to check whether or not he was Rou Shi. His hands were in cuffs—indicating the severity of his case. But just exactly what the details of the case were, nobody knew.

During his imprisonment, I saw two letters he had written to someone from his hometown. The first one went like this:

I, along with 35 other fellow offenders (seven women), arrived at Longhua yesterday. Last night we were put in handcuffs, an exception to the rule that political offenders were never shackled. Since so many people are implicated in the case, it seems unlikely that I will be released anytime soon, so I hope you can handle matters at the bookstore on my behalf. I'm doing well right now, learning German from brother Yin Fu, please tell Mr. Zhou about this. Ask Mr. Zhou not to worry, none of us have been tortured. The police and people at the Public Security Bureau asked for Mr. Zhou's address a few times, but how would I know it? Please don't worry. Best wishes!

Zhao Shaoxiong, January 24

The above was written on the front side.

> I'd like two or three Western-style tin rice bowls. If you aren't allowed to see me, you can have them passed on to Zhao Shaoxiong.

The above was written on the back side.

His state of mind hadn't changed. He still wanted to learn German and put even more effort into it. He was still concerned about me, just as when we had been out walking in the street together. But some things he said in the letter were incorrect. The shackling of political prisoners did not start with him. He had always held the world of officialdom in too high esteem and believed that from the beginning of civilization until now, it was only in their time that the cruelty began, when in fact this wasn't the case. As expected, his second letter was quite different. The phrases he used were quite forlorn and bitter. He also said Ms. Feng's whole face had swollen up. Unfortunately, I didn't copy this letter down. By that time, even more rumors had proliferated: some said that he could be bailed out, others said that he was already on his way to being released in Nanjing, but none could be verified. More people telegraphed to inquire after me and even my mother in Beijing became so agitated that she fell ill. I had no choice but to send letters one after another to explain the situation. Things continued on like this for twenty days or so.

The weather grew colder, and I wondered, did Rou Shi have blankets where he was? We did. Had he received the Western-style tin bowls yet? . . . But then suddenly I received a reliable account saying that Rou Shi and the other twenty-three people had already been executed by gunfire at the Longhua Police Headquarters on either the night of February 7 or the morning of the 8th. His body took ten bullets.

So this is how things turned out! . . .

One evening, deep into the night, I stood in the courtyard of the guesthouse, surrounded by piles of who knows what kind of rubbish. Everyone was fast asleep, including my woman and child. The feeling that I had lost a good friend and that China had lost a fine youth weighed heavily on me. In the midst of my sorrow and anger, I fell into a calm silence. Yet as was my habit of old, I raised my head from this calm silence and strung together the following lines of verse:

Accustomed to the long nights of spring,
I flee with my wife and child in tow, my hair white.
In my dreams, I dimly make out the tears of my loving mother;
The warlord flags raised in the city, ever changing.
Stoically, I watch as friends become new ghosts;
In outrage, I write a short poem in the face of a thicket of swords.
Reciting it, I furrow my brows, there's no place to publish it.
The moonlight glimmers upon my black robe, like ripples of water.

Afterward, I wasn't sure about the last two lines, but this is what I wrote down and sent to a Japanese musician in the end.

But in China, government bans were tighter than the seals on canned goods, and there was no place to publish such things. I recall that Rou Shi had gone back to his hometown at the end of the year and stayed for a long while, and was reprimanded for it by his friends when he returned to Shanghai. He was furious and told me that his mother had lost sight in both eyes and wanted him to stay a few more days, so how could he leave? I understood Rou Shi's and his blind mother's deep devotion to one another. When *Big Dipper* first came out, I wanted to write an essay about Rou Shi, but I couldn't, so I selected a woodblock of Madame Kaethe Kollwitz's titled "The Sacrifice." In it, a mother solemnly offers her son as a sacrifice. This was, known to me alone, a way to commemorate Rou Shi.

Of the four literary youths who met their deaths at the same time, there was Li Weisen, whom I had never encountered, and Hu Yepin, whom I saw once in Shanghai and chatted with briefly. The one I was most familiar with was Bai Mang, also known as Yin Fu. He had corresponded with me and submitted his manuscripts for publication, none of which I can find now. I must have burned them all on the night of the 17th without knowing then that Bai Mang was among the arrested. That volume of *Petőfi's Collected Poems* still remains with me, though. I flipped through it once, and there wasn't much there, except four lines of translation written in ink next to the poem *Wahlspruch* (Maxim), which read:

Life is precious,
the value of love even more so;

*The Sacrifice*, by Kaethe Kollwitz (1923)

But in the name of freedom,
both can be abandoned

On the second page was written the three characters "Xu Peigen," which I suspect is his real name.

## V

On this day two years ago, I was taking refuge in a guesthouse while they were on their way to the execution ground. On this day a year ago, when I was fleeing to the British concessions under a hail of artillery fire, they had by then long been buried in the ground, who knows where. Only on this day this year am I sitting in my old residence, everyone fast asleep, including my woman and child. Again, the feeling that I had lost a good friend and that China had lost a fine youth weighed heavily on me. In the midst of sorrow and anger, I fell into a calm silence. Yet as was my habit of old, I raised my head from this calm silence and wrote down the words above.

If I kept on writing, there would be no place for me to publish in the China of today. When I was young, I read Xiang Ziqi's "Rhapsody on Reflecting on the Past" and faulted him for writing a mere few lines: it is as if the poem ends before it even begins. But now I understand.

It isn't the young people who are writing in memory of the elderly. In the past thirty years, I have personally witnessed the shedding of many young people's blood, congealing layer upon layer, burying me until I cannot breathe. All I can do is use the ink of my brush to write a few essays as a way of burrowing a hole through the mud from which I can forcibly draw a few more wretched breaths. What kind of world is it we live in? The night is so long and the road so far, it might be better just to forget and not speak of them. But I know that even if I'm not the one to do so, in the future, there will still come a time when they will be remembered and spoken of again.

February 7–8

TRANSLATED BY EILEEN J. CHENG

# In Memory of Wei Suyuan

## 憶韋素園君

I still have a few memories, fragmented though they are. I feel that my memories are like fish scales scraped off with a knife: a few still cling to the fish, while others have fallen into the water. Stir up the water and a few of these scales may churn up to the surface, glittering, though flecked with blood, which I'm afraid may sully the eyes of connoisseurs.

There are several friends now wishing to commemorate Mr. Wei Suyuan, so I must also say a few words. Yes, I have this obligation. So there is nothing for me to do other than stir up the waters around me and see what rises to the surface.

It was one day perhaps over ten years ago, when I was a lecturer at Peking University, that I encountered a young man with incredibly long hair and beard in the teacher's common room; it was Li Jiye. I probably became acquainted with Suyuan through Li Jiye's introduction, although I forget the exact circumstances. What remains in my memory now is that Suyuan was already occupying a small hotel room, planning his publications.

That small room was none other than the Weiming Press.

At the time I was in the midst of editing and publishing two small series: one was the Wuhe Series, which only accepted creative work, and the other was the Weiming Series, which only accepted translations; both were published by the Beixin Press. Neither publishers nor readers like translations, something as true now as it was then, so the Weiming Series was decidedly less than popular. It just so happened that Suyuan and his friends wanted to introduce foreign literature to China, and they discussed with Li Xiaofeng the idea of transferring the Weiming Series over to their management, to which Li readily agreed, after which the series left Beixin. All the manuscript submissions were our own, and after raising another sum to cover publication costs, we were ready to begin. Because of the series name, we also

First published in volume 3, issue 4, of *Literature* (Wenxue) in October 1934 and later anthologized in *Essays from the Semi-Concessions* (Qiejie ting zawen, 1937). Lu Xun, *Lu Xun quanji* (Complete works of Lu Xun) (Beijing: Renmin wenxue, 2005), 6: 65–72.

called our press Weiming [no name]—which did not mean "having no name," but rather "having no name as yet," as with a child "not yet of age."

The members of the Weiming Press had no lofty ambitions or high ideals, but rather a will shared by one and all to proceed earnestly and steadily. The backbone of the operation was Suyuan.

So he sat in the small and decrepit room that constituted the press's office, although much of the reason for this was because of his illness, which prevented him from going to school to study, so it naturally fell to him to hold the fort.

My earliest recollection is seeing Suyuan in this broken-down fortress, a thin, clever, and quite serious young man. Several rows of old and worn foreign books sat beneath the window, testifying to the fact that he was at once poor and dedicated to literature. At the same time, however, he left a negative impression: I thought that because he seldom smiled, he would be very hard to get along with. "Seldom smiling" was actually a trait of all the colleagues at the Weiming Press, but Suyuan manifested it most clearly, and one could sense it immediately. But I later realized that my judgment had been erroneous, and that it was not at all difficult to get along with him. That he didn't smile much was most likely a result of the difference in our ages and a particular attitude he had toward me; a pity I couldn't change into a young person and prove irrefutably that the differences between us could be overcome. I believe that this was something that Jiye and the others understood.

But by the time I realized my error, I also discovered his fatal flaw: he was too conscientious, so that although he appeared to be calm, he was in fact extremely intense. Can conscientiousness be considered a fatal flaw? At the very least one must say that it was so then and is so now, since as soon as one becomes conscientious, it is easy to become too intense: when this is given expression, it may lead one to sacrifice one's life, and when endured silently, it will gnaw away at one's heart. I have a small example here—actually, all we have are small examples.

At the time I had already fled to Xiamen because of the repression of Premier Duan Qirui and his lackeys, but their animalistic fury was still omnipresent in Beijing. Lin Suyuan, installed as head of the Women's Normal College by the Duan clique, had led a detachment of troops to take over the school; after a demonstration of military force, he had denominated a number of the teachers who had stayed on as "communists." The label has long been a convenient tool used by certain people for "getting the job done"; this method is a long-standing one, and there is hardly anything remarkable about it. But Suyuan allowed his intensity to get the better of him, and from that time on, he detested the two characters "Suyuan" and stopped using them in the letters he wrote me for a period of time, addressing himself as "Shuyuan" instead. At the same time there was a dispute within the press: Gao Changhong had sent a letter from Shanghai saying that Suyuan had suppressed Xiang Peiliang's manuscript and asking me to intercede. I said not a word. So Gao then began his chiding in *The Tempest*, first at Suyuan, then at me. I thought it beyond hilarious for Suyuan to suppress Peiliang's manuscript in Beijing, for Gao Changhong to complain on Peiliang's behalf from Shanghai, and for him to want me to adjudicate the matter from Xiamen. Moreover, in any organization, even a small literary one, when times get tough, some insider is sure to cause trouble, and there is nothing extraordinary about it. Suyuan, however, took things very seriously; he not only wrote me a letter narrating the whole affair, but also wrote a piece in a magazine vindicating himself. But is there any way to clear oneself in the court of "geniuses"? I couldn't help but utter a long sigh, thinking he was only a man of letters, and also quite ill; if he had to throw himself so completely into dealing with problems within and without, he wouldn't be able to endure it for long. This was, of course, but a minor concern, yet when such a burden is placed on someone of such conscientious intensity, it can have major implications.

Not long thereafter, the Weiming Press was shut down by the authorities, and several people were detained. Perhaps Suyuan had already begun to cough up blood and had gone to the hospital, so he was not among them. Later, however, the detainees were released, and the Weiming Press was allowed to open again; this now shutting down, now opening, now arresting, and now releasing is a game I don't understand even to this day.

I arrived in Guangzhou the next year—early fall of 1927—and continued to receive letters from him regularly. He was in a hospital in the Western Hills, writing while lying down propped up by a pillow, since his doctor would not allow him to sit up. His wording was more distinct than ever, and his thinking even clearer and more expansive, which made me worry even more about his health. One day I received a book out of the blue; it was a cloth edition of Gogol's "The Overcoat," translated by Suyuan. With a shiver, I understood at once: he was obviously sending me a memento. Had he already realized that his life was near its end?

I couldn't bear to leaf through the book again, but I had no choice.

Because of this I remembered that a friend of Suyuan's had also coughed up blood one day in front of Suyuan, which threw Suyuan into a panic. In an affectionate but anxious voice, he gave the following command: "You are not allowed to spit up blood again!" At that moment I thought of Ibsen's *Brand*. Didn't the protagonist order the dead to rise again, but since he didn't have any supernatural powers, wound up just burying himself under an avalanche?

I saw both Brand and Suyuan up in the sky, but there was nothing I could say.

At the end of May 1929, it was by good fortune that I was able to go to the hospital in the Western Hills to chat with Suyuan. Due to sunbathing, his skin had become quite dark, but his spirits had not flagged. The two of us, along with several friends, were quite happy, but my happiness was from time to time intermixed with sadness. I would suddenly think of his lover, who, after securing his permission, had already become engaged to someone else. It would suddenly occur to me that even his quite modest ambition to introduce foreign literature to China would be difficult to achieve. I would suddenly wonder as well that lying here peacefully, was he waiting to recover or waiting to perish? I would also suddenly wonder why he had sent me a hardcover copy of "The Overcoat." . . .

A large portrait of Dostoevsky was hanging on the wall. I respect and admire this gentleman, yet also resent the calm ruthlessness of his writing. He lays out mental tortures and reels in unfortunates one by one, and makes a show of interrogating them before us. And now his gloomy gaze is fixed on Suyuan and his sickbed, as if to tell me: this unfortunate can also be incorporated into my work.

This was, of course, a small misfortune, but for Suyuan, it was a very serious one.

On August 1, 1932, at 5:30 A.M., Suyuan died of his illness in the Tongren Hospital in Beiping, and all his plans and hopes followed him into oblivion. What I regret is that since I had to seek sanctuary from the authorities, I have burned all his letters, so all I have to remember him by is a copy of "The Overcoat," which I always keep by my side.

In the blink of an eye, two years have passed since Suyuan died of his illness. In the interim, no one on the literary stage has spoken of it. This can't really be considered strange—he was neither a genius nor a hero; he simply led a quiet existence, and after he died, it was natural that he would but vanish quietly as well. But as far as we are concerned, he was a young man worth commemorating, as he quietly kept the Weiming Press going.

The Weiming Press is by now all but defunct, and its existence was short-lived. Yet from the time Suyuan started managing it, it introduced Gogol, Dostoevsky, Andreev, van Eeden, Ehrenburg's "The Tobacco Pouch," and Lavrenev's "The Forty-First." It also issued the New Weiming Collection, which included Wei Congwu's "Junshan," Tai Jingnong's *Sons of the Soil* and *The Pagoda Builders*, as well as my *Morning Blossoms Plucked at Dusk*, all of which were considered worth reading at the time. Reality hasn't been merciful to either the frivolous or treacherous youngsters; they have all disappeared, but the translations of the Weiming Press have yet to wither in the garden of literature.

Yes, but Suyuan was neither genius nor hero, much less the pinnacle of a great edifice or a beautiful blossom in a renowned garden. He was, however, a building stone at the base of the edifice and a lump of earth in the garden, the kind of person that China is most in need of. He is not in the line of sight of connoisseurs, but those who build and cultivate would never cast him aside.

The real misfortune suffered by men of letters lies not in being ignored and attacked in their lifetime, but comes after death when their words and conduct cease to exist; idlers pass themselves off as their confidantes spreading gossip and rumor every which way for the sake of self-promotion. For the sake of making a little money, even a corpse becomes a tool by which they seek to secure fame and fortune, and it is this that is truly lamentable. I am now using these several thousand words to memorialize the Suyuan whom I knew so well, but I hope that no part of this has been tainted by self-advancement. Other than this, I will say no more.

I don't know if there will still be a chance to commemorate him in the future, but if this is the only time, then, Suyuan, farewell!

The night of July 16, 1934

TRANSLATED BY THEODORE HUTERS

# On "Gossip Is a Fearful Thing"

## 論 "人言可畏"

"Gossip is a fearful thing"—this phrase was found in the note left by the film star Ruan Lingyu after she took her own life.[11] This incident created a sensation at the time, but after some idle chatter, it gradually cooled down. Once *The Film Star Breathed Her Last* finishes its stage run, it will completely fizzle out into thin air, just like the suicide of Ai Xia last year.[12] Their deaths serve only to add a few grains of salt to the vast human ocean, offering a bit of flavor to the mouths that engage in nonsensical chatter, but before too long, everything will still taste bland, bland, bland.

The phrase created a bit of a stir at first. Some commentators claimed that the newspapers' excessive exposure of her lawsuit was to blame for her death. Soon afterward, a journalist came out with a public rebuttal, saying that the power of the press and the clout of the media nowadays are much too pathetic to have any effect on anyone's fate. Moreover, the reports were mostly based on official sources rather than fabricated hearsay, as can be verified by checking the back issues. Thus Ruan Lingyu's death had nothing whatsoever to do with newspaper reporters.

These words seem to be true enough, but—not quite.

It is indeed true that newspapers today are not what they should be. It is also true that commentators cannot speak freely and have lost prestige. Perceptive people will not lay excessive blame on the journalists. And yet the power of the press has not completely plummeted: it might not harm some but can still hurt others. It may be weak before the powerful, but it still remains quite strong to those weaker than itself. Thus, though sometimes the press has to bite its tongue and swallow its bile, other times it can still strut its stuff. And the likes of Ruan Lingyu provide the perfect fodder for the press to brandish what little power it has left. For though quite the celebrity, she had no power at all. And petty urbanites always love to hear of some

First published in volume 2, issue 5, of *Taibai* on May 20, 1935, under the pseudonym Zhao Lingyi and later anthologized in *Essays from the Semi-Concessions, Volume 2* (Qietie ting zawen er ji, 1937). Lu Xun, *Lu Xun quanji* (Complete works of Lu Xun) (Beijing: Renmin wenxue, 2005), 6: 343–346.

scandal, especially when it involves someone they are quite familiar with. Once those old women hanging out in the alleyways of Shanghai catch whiff of some strange man entering and leaving the house of their neighbor Second Sister, they chew over it with relish. But they wouldn't be interested in listening if you were to tell them that some woman in Gansu was having an affair or that a woman in Xinjiang was remarrying.

Because Ruan Lingyu appeared on the silver screen and is known to everyone, she is perfect fodder for some lively discussions in the newspapers or at the very least good for sales. Reading stories about her, some readers would think: "I might not be as pretty as Ruan Lingyu, but I'm more respectable." Or "I might not be as capable as Ruan Lingyu, but I was born of better stock." Even after her suicide, she enables people to indulge in such thoughts: "I don't have Ruan Lingyu's talents, but I'm more courageous, because I didn't kill myself." It is quite a bargain to dispense with a few coins and discover your superiority. But for a professional actress, once the audience starts to entertain ideas like these, it is enough to drive her to the end of her path. So, instead of freely engaging in clichéd discussions about social systems or one's strength of character, of which we ourselves may not know much about anyway, we should first put ourselves in her place and consider the situation. Then we are likely to see that Ruan Lingyu's belief that "gossip is a fearful thing" is true enough, and the idea that her death has something to do with newspaper reporting is also true enough. But the journalist's retort that the reports are mostly based on official facts is also true. There are those newspapers in Shanghai, neither too large nor too small, in which much of the social news comes from legal cases that have gone through the Public Security Bureau or the Municipal Council in the International Settlement. Reporters have this bad habit whereby they like to add in some colorful descriptions, especially if the case involves women. Since these sorts of cases do not involve powerful public figures, more color can be added with impunity. The age and appearance of men are typically written about in a straightforward manner, but when it comes to women, journalists need to display their literary talent: either she is "past her prime but still enchanting," or she is "just budding, exquisite and lovely." When a young girl runs away and it has yet to be determined whether she has eloped or been seduced, the man of talent claims: "Alone in her bed, she is not used to his absence." How in the world would you know? A peasant woman marrying for the second time is a common occurrence in the poor countryside. But under the pen of a man of talent, he bestows it a grand topic: "Such extraordinary lasciviousness, comparable to that of Empress Wu Zetian."[13] How in the world would you know the extent of her lasciviousness? These offensive words probably may not affect the country woman much, since she is not literate and those who know her may not read the papers anyway.

But to an educated person, especially a woman in the public eye, such words are enough to injure, not to mention the effect of words that are intentionally lurid or especially sensational. And yet such words, ingrained in the Chinese, flow from the pen with ease, with nary a thought from the writer. At the moment, it doesn't occur to him that he is turning women into playthings, nor that he is supposed to be the voice of the people. The words, no matter how colorful, will not hurt the powerful; all it takes is a letter to the editor and before long an erratum or apology would be printed. But someone without power or courage like Ruan Lingyu is forced to suffer a bitter fate—her face smeared with mud that cannot be washed away. Some may ask, why couldn't she have fought back? Without a newspaper of her own, what could she have done? She suffered injustice, but there was no culprit nor principal offender. Whom was she supposed to fight against? If we put ourselves in her place and consider the situation, we are likely to see that her belief that "gossip is a fearful thing" is true enough, and the idea that her death has something to do with newspaper reporting is also true enough.

Still, as mentioned before, it is also true that the press has lost its power. But I don't think it has gotten to the point, as the journalist demurred, where it has become worthless and therefore bears no more responsibility whatsoever. For it can still determine the fate of those weaker beings such as Ruan Lingyu. That is to say, the newspaper can still do harm and, naturally, it can also do good. Words like "we print what we hear" or "we have no power" should not be the routine excuses that an engaged and responsible journalist should mouth, because they are, in fact, not true—newspapers do make choices and do exert influence.

As for Ruan Lingyu's suicide, I don't intend to launch a defense on her behalf. I don't approve of suicide, and I don't have any plans to take my own life. But the reason that I don't plan on taking my own life isn't because I think such an act beneath me, but because I am unable to. These days if a person commits suicide, stern critics inevitably condemn him loudly, and

Ruan Lingyu is of course no exception. And yet I think taking one's own life is not that easy, not nearly as effortless and easily accomplished as those of us who are not planning on killing ourselves and look down upon it might imagine. If there is anyone out there who thinks it's easy, just try it out and see for yourself!

Naturally, there are likely many brave enough to make the attempt, except they would be loath to do it because they bear a great responsibility to society, which is, needless to say, an excellent thing. But I hope they would keep a notebook and write down the great deeds they have accomplished. When their great grandchildren come along, they can pull it out and count the items and see how it all tallies up.

May 5th

TRANSLATED BY HU YING

# A Few Matters regarding Mr. Zhang Taiyan
## 關於太炎先生二三事

Some time ago, Shanghai officials and gentrymen held a memorial service for Mr. Taiyan. Fewer than a hundred people attended, and the ceremony ended on a desolate note. Someone then lamented that the young people now are less passionate about scholars of our own country than they are about the foreign Gorky.[14] Such a lament is actually misplaced. Ordinary folk have never dared to show up to gatherings for officials and gentry. And besides, Gorky was a militant writer, whereas Mr. Taiyan, though first known as a revolutionary, later retired to live the quiet life of a scholar, erecting a wall, built with his own hands and with the help of others, to cut himself off from his times. There are, of course, those who commemorate him, but he will probably be forgotten by most.

---

First published in *A Few Matters* (Er san shi) in *Gongzuo yu xuexi congkan* series on March 10, 1937, and later anthologized in *Essays from the Semi-Concessions, Final Volume* (Qiejie ting zawen mo bian, 1937). The original title refers to Zhang Taiyan as "Mr. Taiyan." Leaving out the surname conveys a sense of intimacy; "Zhang" is included in the translation for clarification. Lu Xun, *Lu Xun quanji* (Complete works of Lu Xun) (Beijing: Renmin wenxue, 2005), 6: 565–571.

## A Few Matters regarding Mr. Zhang Taiyan

I believe his contributions to the history of the revolution are actually even greater than his contributions to the history of scholarship. I remember over thirty years ago, when the woodblock edition of *Compelled Writings* (Qiu shu) had just been published, I couldn't figure out how to punctuate the sentences let alone understand them; this was likely the case for many of the youths then as well. I knew of the existence of a Mr. Taiyan in China not because of his works on the Confucian classics and ancient philology, but because he had refuted Kang Youwei, had written a preface for Zou Rong's *Revolutionary Army*, and had been incarcerated in a prison in the Shanghai concessions. At the time, some students from Zhejiang province studying in Japan were in the process of putting out the journal *Zhejiang Tide*. In it, they published poems Mr. Taiyan had written in prison, but the poems, it turned out, were not hard to understand. They moved me and to this day I haven't forgotten them; two are copied below:

| | |
|---|---|
| **To Zou Rong from Prison** | 狱中赠邹容 |
| Zou Rong, my younger brother, hair flowing, ventured off to Japan. | 邹容吾小弟，被发下瀛洲。 |
| A swift snip of the scissors, he was rid of his queue; on dried beef he sustained himself. | 快剪刀除辫，干牛肉作糇。 |
| When a hero is put in prison, heaven and earth too become despondent. | 英雄一入狱，天地亦悲秋。 |
| Facing execution, let us join hands, two heads like heaven and earth. | 临命须掺手，乾坤只两头。 |
| **On Learning of Shen Yuxi's Death in Prison** | 狱中闻沈禹希见杀 |
| Long had I not seen Master Shen, I knew him hidden among the rivers and lakes. | 不见沈生久，江湖知隐沦， |
| The wailing wind grieves for this gallant fighter; his head now hangs from a Hebei Gate. | 萧萧悲壮士，今在易京门。 |
| With goblins he deigned not compete for the flame;[15] his writings shatter my soul. | 螭魅羞争焰，文章总断魂。 |
| Wait for me in the Nether world; the north and the south shall have a few new graves | 中阴当待我，南北几新坟。 |

Released from prison in June 1906, he sailed to Japan that same day. Not long after arriving in Tokyo, he began editing *People's Paper* (Min bao). I was fond of reading *People's Paper*, not on account of Mr. Taiyan's archaic and ab-struse writing style, which was difficult to understand, or his lectures on Buddhist doctrines and discussions on "parallel evolution of opposing forces," but because of his quarrels with Liang Qichao, who wanted to preserve the monarchy, and his quarrels with "xx" over xxx and with xxx[16] who claimed that reading the *Dream of the Red Chamber* was a way to attain Buddhahood. He was an unstoppable, awe-inspiring force. I also went to listen to his lectures at the time, not because he was a scholar, but because he was an erudite revolutionary. To this day, his voice and expressions still appear vividly before me, but I remember not a word of his lectures on the *Analysis of Graphs and Explications of Characters* (Shuo wen jie zi).

After the 1911 revolution and the founding of the Republic, his ideal had been realized, and so he should have been able to accomplish great things, but his ambitions were still thwarted. This is completely different from the case of Gorky, who was respected in his lifetime and honored after death. I believe the reason they had such different fates was because Gorky's early ideals were all realized in the end; he was one with the masses, and he shared their same joys and frustrations. Even though his goal to overthrow the Man-chus had been accomplished, what was most important to Mr. Taiyan— "First, to use religion to inspire people's confidence and strengthen their morality; second, to use the national essence to arouse racial awareness and patriotic sentiments" (see *People's Paper*, volume 6)—remained nothing more than sublime fantasies. Not long after, Yuan Shikai usurped the reins of power to suit his own purposes, which made him further lose his bearings, and all that remained to him were his empty writings. Now, our term "Republic of China," which originated from his "Explicating the People's Republic" (first seen in *People's Paper*), remains the only great tribute to him. Yet I'm afraid that there aren't many people left who are aware of this. Later, he distanced himself from the people and gradually became more dispirited, participating in the *touhu* ceremony[17] and accepting gifts, for which critics often reproached him. But these are merely minor flaws on a piece of pure jade, not a reflection of a later decline in his character. In as-sessing his life, we find no one else had the gall to dangle his big medal[18] as an ornament on a fan or appear in front of the gates of the presidential palace loudly cursing Yuan Shikai's malicious intentions; no one else had his un-flagging revolutionary ardor, which he maintained even after seven arrests and three imprisonments. This is the spirit of a sage and a model for future ages. Recently some "literary philistines," colluding with the tabloids, have written essays smugly deriding Mr. Taiyan. This really is a case of "petty people not wanting others to succeed" and "an ant shaking a giant tree, ridiculously ignorant of its own limitations!"

But after the revolution, in hopes of leaving a legacy for later generations, Mr. Taiyan gradually concealed his cutting edge. He personally edited *The Collected Works of Zhang*, published in Zhejiang. Likely because he felt that attacks and cursing were contrary to the style of the ancient Confucian tradition and would incur the censure of scholars, his earlier essays, which are filled with a fighting spirit and had appeared previously in journals, were mostly omitted. The two poems cited above are not to be found in his *Records of Poetry* either. Few works were collected in the 1933 edition of the second volume of *The Collected Works of Zhang*, published in Beijing, which was even more restrained in nature and didn't include old works, so naturally there were no essays with a fighting spirit in it. Mr. Taiyan then wrapped himself in the resplendent robes of scholarship and appeared as a great Confucian master. Many people sought him out, wanting to be his disciple, such that a volume of his *Records of Disciples* was hastily compiled. In the newspapers recently, I saw an announcement about copyrights of his works and a note about a third volume of his works. It appears that some of his works will be published posthumously, but I don't know if they will include his earlier essays that had a fighting spirit. These essays with a fighting spirit are Mr. Taiyan's greatest and most lasting accomplishments. If they are not included, I feel that they should be collected together and published so that he will be known to posterity and live in the hearts of fighters. But at this moment in time, I'm afraid that things may not turn out as I hope. Alas!

October 9, 1936

TRANSLATED BY EILEEN J. CHENG

# A Few Matters Recalled in Connection with Mr. Zhang Taiyan

## 因太炎先生而想起的二三事

Having written out this title, I started feeling slightly hesitant, fearing the empty verbiage might exceed actual content, or, as the saying goes, "loud thunderclaps but tiny raindrops." After I completed "A Few Matters regarding Mr. Zhang Taiyan," it occurred to me that there were still a few more minor anecdotes I could relate, but because I had no energy left, I had no choice but to stop. When I woke up the next day, the newspaper had already arrived, and as soon as I opened it I inadvertently rubbed the top of my head and exclaimed in surprise: "Why it's the twenty-fifth anniversary of Double Ten Day—that means the Republic of China has been around for a quarter of a century already. What a thrill!" By "thrill" I was reflecting on how quickly time flies. Later, as I was flipping through the pages of the literary supplement and happened to see some essays by new writers talking about how much they detested the old fogeys, it was like having my head doused with a bucket of cold water. I thought to myself: young people must indeed find it hard to tolerate oldsters. In my case, for instance, my temperament seems to be growing more and more eccentric by the day; a mere twenty-five years have passed, and yet I insist on calling it a "quarter of a century" to describe how long a period of time it has been. What do I think I'm accomplishing with such a fuss? And this gesture of rubbing my head also really marks me off as someone who has fallen behind the times.

I have been using this gesture now for a quarter of a century whenever I feel delighted or moved, as if to say: "I've finally cut off my queue." It originated as a sign of triumph, a state of mind that cannot be shared by the youth of today. If a man appeared today wearing a queue, adults in the prime of

First published in *Wilderness* (Mangyuan) in the *Gongzuo yu xuexi congkan* series on March 25, 1937, and later anthologized in *Essays from the Semi-Concessions, Final Volume* (Qiejie ting zawen mo bian, 1937). Written two days before his death and unfinished, it is Lu Xun's last essay. The original title refers to Zhang Taiyan as "Mr. Taiyan." Leaving out the surname conveys a sense of intimacy; "Zhang" is included in the translation for clarification. Lu Xun, *Lu Xun quanji* (Complete works of Lu Xun) (Beijing: Renmin wenxue, 2005), 6: 576–582.

their thirties as well as youngsters in their twenties would probably look on it as an eccentricity or even find it amusing, whereas I would still feel pangs of resentment and outrage because I had been one of those who suffered on account of the queue and viewed the decision to cut it off as a benchmark. The main reason I love the Republic of China with such fervor and fear its decline is largely due to the fact that it gave us the freedom to cut off our queues. If at the outset they had insisted that to preserve a relic of our ancient heritage we would not be allowed to cut off our queues, I would likely not have loved the Republic so much. But when it comes to the likes of Zhang Xun[19] or Duan Qirui,[20] I'm really ashamed to admit I do not possess the same degree of magnanimity as certain gentlemanly commentators.

When I was still a child, the old people would point out to me that the flagpole outside a barber's stand would, three hundred years ago, have had heads dangling from it. When the Manchus first "came through the pass" and conquered China, they gave the order that queues should be worn. So barbers would grab men on the streets and shave off the hair above their foreheads. If anyone refused, his head would be cut off and hung on the pole, and then the barbers would go on to grab others. The method of shaving the head back then was simply to wet down the hair and begin scraping with a razor—rather distressing, but the tales of hanging heads did not frighten me, for if I was unwilling to have my forehead shaven, the barber not only did not try to behead me, he would pull some candy out from behind the pole and tell me I could eat it as soon as he was finished; by then our barbers had adopted a "soft sell" approach. When one gets used to seeing something, it no longer seems strange, so with regard to the queue, we didn't see it as anything ugly back then. Not to mention that there were many ways the queue could be worn: in terms of form, it could be loosely or tightly bound, tied with three interwoven threads or adorned with loose threads. The short unbound hair that dangles down (in what we refer to today as the Liu Hai style)[21] could vary in length, and the longer loose hair could be tied into two thin queues and twisted around the top of the head, so that on looking at one's reflection one might feel one's own masculine beauty enhanced. Speaking of its uses, in a fight the queue could be yanked; when adultery committed it could be cut off; in an opera it could be used to suspend an actor from an iron pole; a father could use it to whip his children; an acrobat could, with a shake of his head, make it take flight and dance in the air like a dragon or a snake. Yesterday, on the street, I saw a policeman grab two suspects, one with each hand, and thus one man was capable of arresting two. But if this had been before the 1911 revolution, one policeman could have held onto at least ten queues with one hand, so in terms of quelling public disorder, it was also quite convenient. Unfortunately, after what was called the "ban on maritime trade" had been lifted, our scholars gradually began to read foreign books, and we compared ourselves with others; even if we had not been described by foreigners as wearing "pigtails," we would have inevitably found no logical reason or necessity for having to shave off not all, but only part of our hair, leaving a tuft to be braided into a pointy queue that stuck out from our heads like the sprout of an arrowhead plant.

I think even young people born in the Republic must know all this. During the Guangxu reign era (1875–1908), there was one Kang Youwei who tried to bring about reforms but was unsuccessful, and as a reaction, the Boxer Uprising came about and then the Armies of the Eight Allied Nations occupied our capital, the date of which (1900) is easy to remember because it marked the end of the nineteenth century. Thereupon the officials and people of the Manchu Qing dynasty demanded reforms again, and just as had been done before, officials were sent overseas on inspection tours and students were sent overseas to study. I was one of the students sent to Japan by the viceroy of Jiangsu, Anhui, and Jiangxi provinces. Of course, by then I had long known something of anti-Manchu views, the heinousness of the queue, the book burnings, and the persecution of scholars, but really what struck me first was the inconvenience of the queue.

All the students who went to Japan were in a hurry to acquire what they understood as "new knowledge." Aside from studying the Japanese language in preparation for entry into schools offering subjects in their intended area of specialization, they would go to associations organized by fellow provincials, run around to bookstores, attend meetings, and listen to speeches. I forget the name of the place where I had my initial experience of that sort, but I do remember how impressive it all was at first: a dashing young man with a white bandana wrapped around his head was up on stage making an anti-Manchu speech, which he intoned in his Wuxi accent. But as I continued listening, he came to a point at which he said: "As sure as I stand before you now a-cussin' that old hag, she must be back there a-cussin' Wu Zhihui too. . . ." The whole audience broke into hysterical laughter, and I could bear it no longer. It seemed to me that Chinese students overseas were no more than a frivolous lot. Of course, by "that old hag," he was referring to the Empress Dowager. Now there was no doubt in my mind that Wu Zhihui had stood before us at a meeting in Tokyo "a-cussin'" the Empress Dowager, but I found it highly unlikely that a similar meeting was being convened in Beijing by an elderly empress bent on hurling invective at Wu Zhihui. I'm not against perking up a dry speech with a bit of humor and diatribe, but that type of pointless inanity can serve no purpose at all and may, in fact, prove deleterious. Nevertheless, Mr. Wu at that time was famous in student circles for the scuffle he had gotten in with the Qing ambassador to Japan, Cai Jun,[22] from which he earned a scar of honor now concealed by his white bandanna. Shortly afterward he was arrested for deportation, and as they were leading him on the road that runs along the moat next to the Imperial Palace in Tokyo, he suddenly broke free and jumped into the water, only to be fished out and packed on his way back to China. This is what Zhang Taiyan was referring to when, in his battle of pens with Wu, he wrote: "'Twas a leap, not into the depths, but into a ditch so shallow that his face was exposed."[23] Actually the moat outside the Imperial Palace in Tokyo is not all that small nor all that narrow, but since he was under police escort at the time, even if his face had not been exposed, he still would have been pulled out in time. Their pen-war grew more and more rancorous, with each eventually hurling virulent invective at the other. This year when Mr. Wu sneered at Mr. Zhang for accepting certain privileges from the Nationalist government, this incident came up again, showing that he had not forgotten this grievance from over thirty years ago, indicating the depth of his animosity. But *The Collected Works of Zhang* he personally compiled did not include any of these combative essays. Although he had fought unrelentingly against the Manchus, he was deeply influenced by several Qing Confucian scholars and probably intended to emulate their worthy example by not sullying his works with such remarks. But as I see it, this sort of magnanimity will only work against him in the long term, as it will allow these issues to be revived by others, tarnishing his reputation in the eyes of posterity.

Cutting off one's queue was a big deal in those days. When he got rid of his queue, Zhang Taiyan wrote "Ridding Myself of the Queue" (Jie bian fa), in which he says:

In this, the autumnal seventh moon of the 2741st year after the establishment of the Republic,[24] I have turned thirty-three. The Manchu government is immoral; it has persecuted and slaughtered the greatest scholars of our country and has provoked powerful neighbors, murdering their envoys and plundering the cargos of their merchants, until we now find ourselves besieged on every side. Filled with righteous anger at the outrages of these eastern barbarian tribesmen, and the compromised position into which our Han race has been forced, I weep ceaselessly out of anger and declare: "Having passed my thirtieth year, I have reached the age to stand firm, yet still find myself forced to wear barbarian costume and obey their rules. Unless I can cut off and be rid of this humiliation, I shall have disgraced our ancestors. I shall bind my hair in order to restore the appearance of the ancients, but insufficient time prevents me from obtaining clothing in the ancient styles." Thereupon I further declare: "In the past, Ming loyalists Qi Bansun and the monk Yinxuan cut off their hair before their deaths.[25] The Guliang Commentary to the *Spring and Autumn Annals* states: "In the state of Wu, men cut their hair short." And in the *History of the Han Dynasty*, the "Biography of Yan Zhu"[26] tells us: "In Yue they sever their hair." I am a native of the Wu-Yue region and hence to cut it off is in keeping with our ancient ways.

This essay appears in the first woodblock edition and the second edition of his book *Compelled Writings* (Qiu shu), but after it was re-edited, the book title was changed to *Investigative Essays* (Jian lun), and this piece was removed. My cutting off the queue had nothing to do with the fact that I am a man of Yue. In ancient times in Yue they "cropped the hair and tattooed the body,"[27] but I didn't do this to follow in the ways of my forefathers, nor was my motivation in the least bit revolutionary. It was simply that I found the queue inconvenient: first, it was inconvenient when I took off my cap, second, it was inconvenient when I did calisthenics, and third, it was irritating to have to roll it up on top of my head. In actuality, there were quite a few instances of queue-cutters stealthily re-growing their queues after returning to China, so as to become loyal subjects of the Qing dynasty again. By contrast, Huang Keqiang[28] never cut off his queue when he was a student at a normal college in Tokyo, nor did he ever start yelling about revolution; he simply showed a hint of his rebellious Chu temperament: when the Japanese dean of students issued a new dress code that forbade students from exposing their bare arms, Huang deliberately stripped to the waist and, enamel wash-basin in hand, sauntered conspicuously across the main courtyard from the bathroom to his study.

1936

TRANSLATED BY JON EUGENE VON KOWALLIS

# PART 2

Reflections on Culture

# SECTION III

*On Tradition*

# My Views on Chastity

## 我之節烈觀

"Social mores are going from bad to worse! The soul of our people is becoming more degenerate by the day! The country is going to the dogs!" These sorts of complaints have long been heard in China. But in different eras, what is meant by "degeneracy" has changed somewhat: it used to be that "A" was bad, and now it is "B." Except for documents "intended for the eyes of the emperor" in which one dares not make such wild statements, pretty much all other writings have this plaintive tone. The advantage of such a complaint is that you get to point out the errors of others while exempting yourself from all that is "degenerate." That's why it's not only gentlemen who sigh to each other; even murderers, arsonists, adulterers, swindlers, and all other scoundrels, in the intervals between carrying out their misdeeds, also shake their heads and moan: "They are becoming more depraved by the day!"

Inciting evil can indeed corrupt one's morals; but even those who don't actively encourage it but merely stand by, enjoy the show, or deplore it, can also have a corrupting effect. Thus in the past year there have been a few who were not content with empty words and, after lamenting the situation, came up with plans to remedy it. First, there was Kang Youwei who, gesticulating excitedly, claimed that "constitutional monarchy" was the way to go, which Chen Duxiu called nonsense.[1] And then there were the spiritualists, who somehow came up with the antiquated and abstruse idea of summoning the ghost of "Mencius the sage" to help them devise a plan, which was then derided by Chen Bainian, Qian Xuantong, and Liu Bannong as baloney.[2]

These articles refuting them appeared in *New Youth*, and reading them makes me gravely disappointed. For we are already in the twentieth century, and the light of dawn has been glimmering before the eyes of humanity for some time now. If an article appeared in *New Youth* debating whether the earth was round or square, readers would most certainly be dumbfounded.

First published in volume 5, issue 2, of *New Youth* (Xin qingnian) in August 1918 under the pseudonym Tang Si and later anthologized in *Graves* (Fen, 1927). Lu Xun, *Lu Xun quanji* (Complete works of Lu Xun) (Beijing: Renmin wenxue, 2005), 1: 121–133.

And yet the arguments made nowadays are not much different from things like the earth is not square. How can this disparity between our times and the level of debate not make us gravely disappointed and even afraid?

These days, constitutional monarchy is not talked about much anymore, though the spiritualists still seem to be communing with their ghosts. Yet at this time there is another group of people who are unsatisfied, shaking their heads and lamenting that "people are becoming more degenerate." And so they came up with yet another remedy, which they call "extolling chastity."

Such brilliant approaches have been touted on all levels since the call for the "Revival of the Monarchy in accordance with Antiquity."[3] Now is just the time to formally raise the banner. In article after article, writers have been loudly "extolling chastity"! If one doesn't speak of chastity, one would not be able to rise above all those who are "becoming more degenerate by the day."

The two characters for chastity, constancy (*jie*) and martyrdom (*lie*), used to apply to the virtues of men as well. Thus we had terms such as "man of constancy" (*jieshi*) and "male martyr" (*lieshi*). But chastity as extolled today applies exclusively to women, not men. According to today's moralists, *jie* means that a woman does not remarry or run off with a lover after her husband dies. The younger she is when her husband dies, and the poorer her family, then the more chaste she is regarded. There are two kinds of chastity martyrs: a woman who commits suicide when her husband or fiancé dies; and a woman who, when confronted with a rapist, kills herself or is killed in the act of resistance. The more cruel and horrendous her death, the more exemplary she is as a chastity martyr. If she is unable to defend herself and then kills herself after being violated, there will be talk. If she is lucky and her case falls in the hands of a charitable moralist, then perhaps he would consider the circumstances and still grant her the title "chaste." But the learned scholars would not be so willing to write her eulogies. If forced to write one, they would inevitably close their piece with a few sighs of "pity, what a pity."

In summary, if a woman's husband dies, she should stay a widow or die. If she encounters a rapist, she should die. If these women are extolled properly, then social mores and the condition of people's souls will improve, and China as a country will be saved. That's the gist of it.

Kang Youwei had to rely on the name of the emperor, and the spiritualists depended on the words of ghosts; "extolling chastity," however, is entirely in the hands of the people, which seems to imply that we are becoming more self-reliant. Still, there are several questions that I feel compelled to raise, and I will pursue their answers to the best of my ability. I am also convinced that this idea of saving the world through "extolling chastity" is widely held by our fellow citizens, while the most vocal proponents are but the spokesmen. Although the mouthpiece makes the sound, the entire body, from the limbs to the facial features to the nervous system to the internal organs, every part is involved. Thus I present my queries and responses to the majority of my fellow citizens.

My first question is: How do unchaste and unmartyred women harm the country? (The Chinese see those who do not keep their chastity as having "lost chastity," but there is no special term for those who do not commit suicide. For lack of a better term, I call them collectively "unchaste and unmartyred.") Looking at the current situation, that "the country is about to be lost" is clear enough: there is no shortage of reprehensible crimes; likewise, war, banditry, flood, drought, and famine follow closely on the heels of one another. But these phenomena result from the absence of new morality and new knowledge, as actions and thought merely repeat the past. This is why the many kinds of benightedness now resemble the chaotic times of antiquity. In any case, the realms of politics, the military, learning, and commerce are all occupied by men, not by "unchaste and unmartyred" women. It is rather unlikely that powerful men fell under the evil influence of unchaste and unmartyred women, lost their moral sense, and thus committed those wicked deeds. As for the flood, drought, and famine, they result from the absence of new knowledge, as people worship the dragon spirit, cut down forests, while neglecting the management of waterways. They have even less to do with women. True, war and banditry tend to produce many unchaste and unmartyred women. But even here, the soldiers and bandits come first, unchaste and unmartyred women follow. It isn't as if the women were first unchaste, which then invited the coming of soldiers and bandits. My second question is: Why is it that the job of saving the world falls on women alone? If we were to follow the old school of thought, women belong to the *yin* element, and their place is the inner sphere of the home, as chattel of men. Thus the task of governing the state and saving the nation belongs to men, who are of the *yang* element and whose place is in the outer sphere of the world. Surely, such a major task should not fall on the shoulders of those of the *yin* element. On the other hand, if we were to abide by the new ways of thinking, then men and women are equal and their obligations are comparable. Though they have their duties, they should only have their share. Men, the other half of the population, should fulfill their responsibility, not just in eliminating violence, but in developing their own virtues. Men's natural responsibility does not reside in punishing and lecturing women alone.

My third question is: What is the effect of extolling chastity? Using chastity as a yardstick, we can divide women alive today into three categories: those who are chaste and should be extolled (martyrs by definition are dead, so they are excluded from this category); those who are unchaste; and those who have yet to be married, or whose husbands are still alive and who haven't encountered a rapist, so their chastity is yet to be determined. The first kind is very good and should be extolled. No more need be said. The second kind is bad, and since Chinese tradition does not allow repentance, once a woman has done wrong, she can only die of shame. So, there is nothing more to be said for these women either. The most important is the third category. Now that they have been properly taught, they must all have resolve in their minds: "If my husband dies, I will never marry again. If I encounter a rapist, I will immediately kill myself!" Let us ask: Do these decisions have anything to do with public morality in China, which, as I pointed out earlier, is determined by men? Which brings up more related questions: The chaste and martyred, once extolled, are naturally the moral exemplars. But though everyone may aspire to learn from a sage, not everyone can become an exemplar of chastity. A young woman in the third category may very well have high aspirations, but if her husband enjoys longevity and the world is peaceful, she would have to hold her grudges and be satisfied to live out her life as a lesser being. So far, we have only used familiar common sense to consider the matter, and already we have found many contradictions. If we allow for a whiff of the twentieth century, then there are two more problems.

First: Is chastity moral? Morality should be something required of everyone and be within the reach of everyone. It should be beneficial to oneself and to others. Only then can such a morality have existing value. What is called "chastity and martyrdom" now does not apply to men; nor is this honor attainable by all women. Thus it cannot be considered a virtue and held as a model of behavior. The reasons have been discussed in an article "On Chastity" recently published in New Youth.[4] Although the article mainly discusses the issue of women's sexual constancy while their husbands are alive, the same reasoning is applicable after the death of their husbands. The remaining issue of martyrdom, which is especially peculiar, is still worth some further examination. From the perspective of the categorization above, the first type of martyrdom is actually the same as chastity; the difference is that the woman dies in maintaining it. Because moralists like to use death to categorize people, these women have been categorized as martyrs. The second type is a different kind of martyrdom altogether: when a weak being (women are still weaker in current society) suddenly encounters a violent man, if her father, brothers, and husband are unable to save her and her neighbors do not come to her aid, and she dies; she may die after being raped, or else it may be the case that she does not die at all. In time, her father, brothers, husband, and neighbors come together with a few learned scholars and moralists. They do not speak of how ashamed they are of their own cowardice and impotence; nor do they discuss how to punish the criminal. Instead, they wag their tongues and speculate: Did she die or not? Was she raped or not? How good it is that she died, or how bad it is that she lived? Thus they produce many glorious women martyrs, as well as many much-maligned nonmartyrs. If we think it over sensibly, we would have to say this sort of thing shouldn't occur in the human realm, let alone be considered moral.

Second: Are polygamous men qualified to extol chastity? The old moralists would say, of course they are: for as men, they are quite unique and they own the world. Pointing to the classics that espouse *yin-yang* elements and the doctrine of inner and outer spheres, they show off their abilities in front of women. And yet times have changed and people have gotten a glimpse of the light of dawn. They know the talk of *yin-yang* and the inner and outer sphere is utter nonsense. Even if dual elements exist, there is no way of proving that *yang* is greater than *yin* and that the outer sphere is superior to the inner. In any case, society and nation are not made of men alone. So we have to accept the truth that the sexes are equal. If men and women are equal, then there must be contracts that govern both. Men cannot request women be bound by rules they themselves do not abide by. If a marriage is arranged through a sale, a swindle, or some kind of tribute, the man has no grounds on which to demand his wife's faithfulness during his life. What right does a polygamous man have to praise a woman for her chastity?

I am done for now presenting my queries and responses. For a system that makes so little sense, how did it survive for so many years? To answer this question, we need to first look at how chastity originated, how it was put into practice, and why it has not been reformed.

In ancient society, women were usually the chattel of men. Killing or eating her was acceptable. When he died, she could be buried as a sacrificial object, along with other objects he had treasured and weapons he had used while alive. No objection there either. Later on, the practice of burying women alive was gradually changed while the custom of preserving one's chastity came into being. But that was mostly because a widow was considered the wife of a ghost, and as she was followed by her ghost husband, nobody would dare marry her. It wasn't because she wasn't allowed to remarry. Customs such as these may still exist in primitive societies today. While we cannot be sure of what happened in the high antiquity in China, by the end of the Zhou dynasty [c. 1046 BCE–256 BCE], human sacrifice included both men and women, and widows were free to remarry without being subjected to restrictions; from this we can see that such practices had died out some time ago. From the Han dynasty [206 BCE–220 AD] to the Tang dynasty [618–907], no one advocated chastity. It was only in the Song dynasty [960–1279] that a bunch of professional Confucians began talking about how "it is a small matter to starve to death and a great matter to lose one's chastity."[5] They seemed shocked to see the term "twice wed" in historical records. Whether their reaction was genuine or feigned is hard to ascertain now. Theirs was also a time when "people were becoming more degenerate by the day" and "the country was going to the dogs!" Perhaps the professional Confucians meant to use the talk of women's chastity to castigate men? But beating around the bush like this is rather contemptible, and it's hard to tell what they were really driving at. Whether this contributed to the addition of a few more chaste women, we cannot know for sure. But officials, civilians or soldiers, they appeared unmoved by it all. In the end, China with "the oldest civilization in the world and the highest moral standards," was taken by "Yeke Mongghol Ulus" Kublai Khan, Temür Khan, and Külüg Khan.[6] Still later, the emperors changed surnames a few times, and yet the idea of chastity flourished. The more emperors expected loyalty from their ministers, the more men demanded chastity from women. By the Qing dynasty [1644–1911], the Confucians became sterner still. When they read about a princess's remarriage in the history of the Tang dynasty, they'd become enraged at the writer and exclaim: "What! How could you not conceal this sort of thing for royalty! What insanity!" If the Tang dynasty writer were alive today, he would surely be stripped of his office, to "rectify men's hearts and correct their morals."

So when people are about to be conquered, chastity tends to flourish and chastity martyrs are especially esteemed. Since women belong to men, if their men die, they shouldn't remarry; if their men live, then of course they shouldn't be taken by others. And yet if men themselves are conquered and don't have the power to protect nor the courage to resist, they devise this innovative little scheme of advocating female suicide. There are also those rich men who in the chaos of wartime perhaps cannot look after all of their wives, concubines, and daughters. If they run into rebels or government soldiers, then nothing can be done. They would have to save themselves and bid their women to become martyrs, because dead women are of no interest to rebel soldiers. Once order is restored, they can make their way back at their own leisure and write a few eulogies. Fortunately, remarrying is considered entirely natural for men, so they can acquire new wives and that would be the end of it. This is why we have essays like "Combined Biographies of Two Martyred Women" and "Epitaph for Seven Concubines."[7] Even the collected works of Qian Qianyi are filled with eulogies for "chaste woman Zhao" and "martyr Qian."[8]

Only a society that tolerates utter selfishness, where women must be ruled by chastity and men may have multiple wives, can produce such a warped morality. That this moral regime becomes increasingly more severe and exacting is not surprising. But since men are its proponents and women its victims, why have women not uttered a word of dissent? Because "the female is born to submit,"[9] so it is natural for women to submit to the wishes of others. Education is said to be pointless for women; even speaking can be a crime. Thus her spirit, like her body, becomes warped. This is why she has no objection to the warped moral strictures. Even if a woman has her own views, there is no opportunity for her to voice them. If she writes a few poems on "gazing upon the moon from the boudoir" or "admiring the flowers in the garden," she worries that men would accuse her of lascivious thoughts. How would she dare to disrupt "the righteous order of heaven and earth"? Only in fiction do we encounter women who somehow do not maintain their chastity. But according to the storytellers, once she remarries, the ghost of her former husband seizes her and carries her off to hell. Or else, despised by everyone, she becomes a beggar and is turned away at every door. In the end, she dies in utter misery.

We thus see how women cannot but "submit." What about men, then? Why is it that none of them champion the truth and just let it slide? After the Han dynasty, public discourse was monopolized by "professional Confucians." By the Song and Yuan dynasties, it got so bad that we can barely find a single volume not penned by a professional Confucian or a word not uttered by the elites. Except for Buddhists or Daoists who could speak with imperial dispensation, other "heterodox" voices could not go beyond the private chamber. In any case, most men were influenced by the idea that "a learned man is yielding"[10] and thought that to break any new ground is a major taboo.[11] Even if someone saw the truth, he would not want to defend it with his life. Take the preservation of chastity, for example. Everyone knows it takes both sexes, men and women, to make it happen. And yet only the woman is blamed, and little attention is paid to the man who sullied her chastity or the criminal who committed rape. In any case, it's trickier to pick on men than women, and bringing someone to justice is more difficult than uttering a few words of praise. Although a few men felt uneasy and mildly suggested that it is unnecessary for girls to remain unmarried or commit suicide after the death of their betrothed, nobody paid them any mind.[12] If they kept at it, society would not have tolerated it, and pretty soon they would find themselves treated just like the unchaste women. Thus they, too, learned to be "yielding" and stopped speaking on the subject. This is why to this day the issue of chastity has not seen any reform.

(I should make it clear at this point that I personally know quite a few people who are proponents of extolling chastity. I dare say there are among them good people with perfectly good intentions. But their idea for saving the world just isn't right. It is as if they meant to go west but headed north instead. But just because they are good people doesn't mean they can somehow end up in the west when they have headed north. Thus I'm hoping they will turn themselves around.)

There is still one more question: Is it hard to be chaste? The answer is: very hard. Even men know it is very hard, and that's why they praise it. Public opinion is that chastity depends entirely on women. Though a man seduces a woman, he is not answerable for it. If a man propositions a woman and she rejects him, then she is chaste. If she dies in the process, then she is a chastity martyr. The man's name is not tarnished, and society is said to be decent, resembling ancient times. If the woman accepts him, then she is unchaste. Again, the man's name is not tarnished, but social mores have been injured by the woman! Similar logic applies elsewhere as well. This is why, throughout history, women have been scapegoats for the fall of the empire and the breakdown of the family.

For more than three thousand years, women have been shouldering the crimes of humanity for no good reason. Since men do not have to bear any responsibility nor are they capable of self-reflection, they can go on seducing women as they please, and literati writers even make romantic stories out of it. A woman is thus beset by danger. With the exceptions of her father, brothers, and husband, every man carries a whiff of the potential seducer. That is why I say it is very hard to be chaste.

Is it painful to be chaste? The answer is: very painful. All men know it is very painful, and that's why they praise it. Everybody wants to live; it goes without saying that to be a martyr means death. But the chaste widow needs to live on. Let's set aside for now the psychological pain she must face. Mere physical subsistence itself is already a major difficulty. If women were economically independent and people had the spirit of mutual assistance, then a widow might be able to survive on her own. Unfortunately in China, the opposite is true. So, if she is well-to-do, she may still survive, but if she is poor, she will surely starve to death. Only after starving to death would she perhaps be given an imperial honor and her name recorded in the local gazetteer. At the back of tomes of county or prefectural records, there are invariably a few volumes for "chastity martyrs." Under their surnames Zhao, Qian, Sun, or Li, each gets a line or half a line of mention, but nobody ever reads these pages. Even for those moralists who extolled chastity their whole lives, if you were to ask them to name the top ten chastity martyrs of his own county, I'm afraid he wouldn't be able to. Alive or dead, chastity martyrs in fact have little to do with society in general. That is why I say it is very painful to be chaste.

Following the same logic, is it any less difficult to be unchaste? The answer: also very difficult. The social consensus is such that women who lose their chastity are the lowest of the low and are to be ostracized by society.

Many ideas like this have been passed down unthinkingly from ancient times and are completely irrational, and yet the sheer weight of tradition and numbers can crush to death those who do not conform. Who knows how many in the past, including the chastity martyrs, have been murdered by these types of killing squads, which have neither ringleaders nor consciousness. The only difference is that these chastity martyrs are occasionally rewarded posthumously by being written into gazetteers, whereas those who lost their chastity are despised by all and sundry and must suffer meaningless abuse. That is why I say it is also very difficult to be unchaste. Do women themselves want to become chastity exemplars and chastity martyrs? The answer is: no, they do not. All human beings have hopes or objectives for their lives. Although a hope may aim high or low, it must be meaningful. An objective is good if it benefits both oneself and others, but at the very least it should benefit oneself. Preserving one's chastity is very hard and painful and benefits neither oneself nor others. It's quite unreasonable to say that women do it willingly.

This is why if you were to say to a young woman, sincerely and with all your heart, that you wish her to become a chastity martyr, she would surely become angry. You might even receive a blow from her father, brothers, or husband. Still, the practice of chastity remains indestructible, supported by the crushing weight of its history and numbers. Yet everyone is afraid of this "chastity," afraid that such a label would be nailed onto oneself or those closest to oneself. That is why I say it is not something anyone wants. Based on the above facts and reasoning, I conclude that chastity is extremely hard, extremely painful; nobody wants it for themselves; it benefits neither oneself nor others, nor does it benefit society or the country; it is something that holds no meaning for posterity and has long lost its value to exist in modern times.

Before we finish, there is still one more question: If chastity has lost its meaning and value, does it mean that chaste women have been suffering for nothing? Here's my answer: there is value in grieving over their suffering. These women deserve our compassion. They had the misfortune of being trapped by history and numbers and they have sacrificed themselves for nothing. We should hold a great memorial service for them.

After mourning those of the past, we will make a pledge: may we be pure in intent, more intelligent and braver, and aspire for better things. May we discard hypocritical masks. May we eliminate delusion and tyranny that harm ourselves and others.

After mourning those of the past, we will make a pledge: may we eliminate the meaningless pain and suffering in our lives. May we eliminate the delusion and tyranny that cause pain and suffering and make us delight in the pain and suffering of others.

We will also make a pledge: may all people enjoy true happiness.

July 1918

TRANSLATED BY HU YING

# Impromptu Reflections No. 38: On Arrogance and Inheritance

隨感錄三十五

The Chinese have always been a little arrogant. What a shame it's not the "arrogance of the individual" but only the "arrogance of mass patriotism." This is why they are unable to rise up and move forward after they fail in cultural competition.

The "arrogance of the individual" lies in eccentricity; it's a declaration of war against the common masses. Except for those who suffer clinically from delusions of grandeur, most afflicted with this sort of arrogance possess an element of genius or, as Max Nordau and others claim, of madness. They are bound to feel they are superior to the masses in thought and knowledge and that they are misunderstood by the masses, so they rail at the vulgarity and mundaneness of the world and gradually become cynics or "enemies of the people." And yet all new thought must come from them; political, religious, and moral reform originates with them. A country that has more citizens

First published in volume 5, issue 5, of *New Youth* (Xin qingnian) on November 15, 1918, and later anthologized in *Hot Wind* (Re feng, 1925). Lu Xun, *Lu Xun quanji* (Complete works of Lu Xun) (Beijing: Renmin wenxue, 2005), 1: 327–332. Yu-sheng Lin points out that Zhou Zuoren actually claimed to have written this essay, though it was originally published under the name "Xun," one of Lu Xun's pen names and was selected by Lu Xun to be included in *Hot Wind*. See Yu-sheng Lin, *The Crisis of Chinese Consciousness: Radical Anti-traditionalism in the May Fourth Era* (Madison: University of Wisconsin Press, 1979), 116n27.

afflicted with this sort of "arrogance of the individual" is truly blessed, truly fortunate!

"Collective arrogance" and "patriotic arrogance" represent an alliance of the like-minded against those who are different, a declaration of war against a minority of geniuses. (Declaring war against the civilizations of other countries is of secondary importance.) These people themselves have no particular talent to boast of, so they use the country as their shadow; they raise high the country's customs and institutions and praise them to no end; and since their "national essence" is so glorious, naturally they too are glorious. They themselves don't need to join in battle if there's an attack, for there are a huge number of people, their eyes wide and tongues wagging, crouching under the shadow; they need only make use of the expertise of "the mob" to cause a commotion and secure victory.[13] As part of the collective, the "I" naturally shares in any victory; and with so many others in the group, the "I" won't necessarily suffer losses in defeat. In general, this kind of mentality is most evident when the group unites to stir things up; it is the psychology of the crowd. Their actions seem to be fierce, when in reality they are base and cowardly. What results, then, are restoration of ancient ways, monarchism, xenophobic appeals in support of the Qing and the elimination of foreigners, and the like, for which we have long had a deep appreciation. A people who manifest this "collective, patriotic arrogance" are indeed a tragic and sorry lot.

Unfortunately, it is just this sort of arrogance that is most apparent in China: "Nothing the ancients ever said or did was wrong; so how dare we talk of reform when we cannot even emulate them?" Although there may be slight variations in the ideas of the different schools of patriotic arrogance, they are fundamentally alike. We can divide them into the following five types:

A says: "China is a vast land of great material abundance; it has the oldest civilization and the world's highest morality." This is just plain swagger.

B says: "Although foreign material civilization is advanced, Chinese spiritual civilization is far superior."

C says: "All things foreign existed first in China: this particular science or that philosophical precept, for example." (These last two schools of thought are branches of the larger Ancient-Modern / Chinese-Foreign School that follow Zhang Zhidong's maxim, "Chinese learning for the essence. Western learning for practical application.")

D says: "Foreign countries have beggars too." Or alternatively: "They, too, have mud huts, prostitutes, and bedbugs." (This being a negative form of resistance.)

E says: "China is better off with barbarism." Or: "So you say Chinese thought is muddled,[14] fine, but it is the crystallization of the enduring efforts of our race. It has been muddled from the time of our ancestors and will continue to be muddled down through our descendants, muddled from the past to the future. . . . We are four hundred million strong. Do you think you can really annihilate us?" (This takes D's argument one step further; instead of dragging others down in the water, it revels in our own ugliness and uses it as a means to look down on others. As for the uncompromising tone, it smacks of Niu Er's loud-mouthed bullying in *The Water Margin*.

Of the five, the language of the first four, though preposterous, is more excusable than that of the last, because it still shows a bit of nerve. For example, when the sons of a declining family look on another that is in ascendance, they spout great words and put on airs, or they seek out a flaw in the other to somehow relieve their own embarrassment. Though utterly laughable, it can still be considered a slight step above someone whose nose has fallen off and who shows his face to everyone because it came from a venerable disease inherited from his ancestors.

The patriotism of faction E is the last to make an appearance and most disappoints me when I hear it, not only because its intentions are fearful, but because it comes closest to the truth. Muddle-headed ancestors raise muddle-headed descendants—this is a principle of heredity. Once the racial essence has been created, be it good or bad, it is difficult to change. In his *Les lois psychologiques de l'évolution des peuples*, the Frenchman Gustave Le Bon says (I present the gist of the original wording, which I have forgotten): "Our every movement and action, though it may appear to be self-motivated, is in fact restrained by the ghosts of the dead. In sheer numbers, people in our current generation are no match for the hundreds of generations of ghosts that have preceded us." Among the several hundreds of generations of our ancestors, we find no shortage of muddle-headed people: Neo-Confucians who discourse on the Way and Daoists who speak of *yin* and *yang* and the Five Elements; "immortals" who meditate and practice alchemy; and actors who paint their faces and do acrobatics. Though at present we all mean to live respectably as "humans," it is difficult to prevent the muddled elements in our veins from doing their mischief. We are not our own masters; suddenly we find ourselves studying Daoist physiognomy or the art of theater faces. This is most disconcerting. But I keep hoping that the harm inherited from this muddled thought will be less severe than that of syphilis and ultimately present no real risk. We have discovered a 606 medicine to cure syphilis of the body. I hope that there is also a 707 to cure the disease of the mind. Indeed, that medicine has already been discovered, and it is science. I only hope that those friends who have spiritually "lost their noses" will not again raise the banner of "venerable disease inherited from the ancestors" to oppose the use of this medicine. Then the day will come when the disease of being muddled will be completely cured. Though the influence of our ancestors is great, if from now on we set our sights on changing, if we sweep away all muddled thought and the things that foster it (the texts of both the Confucians and Daoists) and take the appropriate medicine, we might still be able to reduce the virus ever so slightly, if not immediately. That way, several generations from now, when we have become ancestors, we will have thrown off the influences of our own muddled ancestry and reached a turning point at which we will no longer have to fear Le Bon's words.

This is my cure for "a people in arrested development." As for the part about "annihilation," that's a load of nonsense not worth mentioning. Why should mankind even speak that fearful word *annihilation*? Only those like the brutal Zhang Xianzhong had such intentions, and today they are cursed by mankind; moreover, how effective were they in the end? But I do have a few words of advice for the good sirs who espouse the views of category E mentioned above. The word *annihilation* can frighten people, but it cannot frighten nature. Nature has no mercy; when it sees a people heading toward its own annihilation, it invites them to proceed without the least courtesy. We all want to live and hope that others live. We cannot bear to speak of others' annihilation, because we fear that if they tread that path, they will drag us to annihilation with them. So we feel anxious. I would not object even to being "barbarians," if it were possible to prosper and live truly free and happy lives with things the way they are now. But is there anyone who dares say that this is possible?

November 15, 1918

TRANSLATED BY KIRK A. DENTON

# On Conducting Ourselves as Fathers Today

我們現在怎樣做父親

My idea in writing this essay is actually to think about how to reform the family. Since kinship authority in China is powerful, and paternal authority even more powerful, I particularly want to express an opinion on fathers and sons, a relationship previously considered sacrosanct and inviolable. In short, it is just that revolution is about to revolutionize the old man himself. But why such a grandiose, long-winded title? There are two reasons.

In the first place, China's "disciple of the sage" particularly detests it when other people meddle with two matters. We can pass over the first, which is of no concern to our present generation; the other is his concept of traditional morality, a matter that people of my generation inevitably have occasion to touch on. In consequence, we inevitably become involved, earning such imprecations as "uprooting morality" and "acting like beasts in the field." He and his colleagues believe that fathers have absolute authority and power over sons: whatever the elder generation says must of course be correct, whereas their juniors are in error before they have opened their mouths. Yet grandfathers, fathers, sons, and grandsons are each of them rungs on life's ladder, not positions that are fixed and immutable. Today's sons become tomorrow's fathers and in turn grandfathers. I know that those of my contemporaries and readers who are not already fathers, are fathers-to-be, and all of us expect to become ancestors in due course. To save trouble, therefore, we should cast aside all ceremony and seize the high ground at the earliest opportunity to claim the dignity due to fathers and pronounce on matters concerning ourselves and our children. This would not only minimize future difficulties as these matters are put into practice, but it is also an accepted logical progression in China, so that "the disciple of the sage"

First published in volume 6, issue 6, of *New Youth* (Xin qingnian) in November 1919 under the pen name Tang Si and later anthologized in *Graves* (Fen, 1927). The target is the famous translator and writer Lin Shu (1854–1924), a defender of conservative Confucian values derided by Lu Xun as a "disciple of the sage." Lu Xun repeatedly quotes extracts from a variety of Confucian texts upholding traditional morality. The result is an odd mixture of casual speech, classical phrases, and absurd pomposity. Lu Xun, *Lu Xun quanji* (Complete works of Lu Xun) (Beijing: Renmin wenxue, 2005), 1: 134–149.

need not be alarmed: in short, we score two goals with one shot. To that end, my topic is "On Conducting Ourselves as Fathers Today."

Second, I have already touched on the question of families in "Impromptu Reflections" (nos. 25, 40, and 49) in *New Youth*, to the effect that it is up to us to start by emancipating our own descendants. The emancipation of our sons and daughters is actually a very ordinary matter and of course doesn't need discussion. But the poison of old customs and old thinking has affected China's elderly so deeply that they inevitably fail to realize this. Young people pay no attention if they hear a crow cawing in the morning, but elderly people, who are superstitious about crows, will remain flustered the rest of the day. It's pathetic, but it can't be helped. The only solution is to start with enlightened people emancipating their own children. Although they themselves bear a tremendous burden, they can prop open the gates of darkness, releasing the children into a bright, open space where they can spend their lives happily as rational human beings.

Again, when I happened to mention that I was not in any way an original writer, it ended up with me being abused in the article "New Lessons" in a Shanghai newspaper. But when my generation writes commentaries on current matters, we need to review our own selves first and avoid passing ourselves off as experts; this is the only way in which we can do justice to ourselves and others in a responsible manner. I'm aware that it's not just that I'm not an original writer, I'm not even the kind of person who discovers truths. Everything I say or write comes from the lessons learned from what I've heard or seen in everyday life; I make no claim to know about ultimate truths. It's even more the case that I can't predict what change and progress in theories will take place a few years from now; I simply believe there will surely be more change and progress compared with today. That's why I'm talking about "On Conducting Ourselves as Fathers Today."

What seems to me reasonable today is extremely simple. To judge by the phenomena in the natural world, we must first maintain life, then extend it, and finally develop it (that is, evolution). This is what living beings do, and it's what fathers do.

There's no need to discuss here the values in being alive, or the scale of different values. Yet it's only common sense to know that the most important thing for living beings is life. What constitutes living beings is just that—

life; without it they've lost what it means to be a living being. To maintain life, we are all equipped with instincts, the most obvious being the desire for food. It is through this desire that we ingest food, which produces warmth and thus maintains life.

However, each individual being inevitably grows old and dies, so in order to extend life, there is another instinct—sexual desire. Sexual desire leads to sexual intercourse, and sexual intercourse leads to producing offspring and thus extends life. That is, the desire for food is a means to maintain the individual and its current life, while sexual desire is a means to maintain posterity and eternal life. Food and drink are not evil or dirty, nor is sexual intercourse. The result of food and drink is the nourishment of the individual; it isn't doing oneself a favor. The result of sexual intercourse is the production of offspring, but that, of course, can't be seen as doing our sons and daughters a favor either. As we each proceed on the long journey of life, the only distinction between us is that some come first and others follow, and there's no telling who is being favored by whom.

It's unfortunate that traditional views in China happen to be the exact opposite of this principle. Although the bond between husband and wife is formally described as only the third of the five main human relationships, it's held to be the starting point; although sexual intercourse is entirely normal, it's held to be dirty; and although childbearing is normal, it's held to be a huge achievement. Most people secretly harbor dirty thoughts about marriage. Relatives and friends make filthy jokes about it, and the couple themselves feel ashamed; they still behave furtively even when they have children and are fearful of announcing it. It's only in regard to the child that people start to brag. There's not an iota of difference between such conduct and the rich who've made their wealth by theft. It's not my contention—as people who attack me have asserted—that sexual intercourse between human beings should be as promiscuous as it is among animals, or like the vile conduct of scoundrels who openly gloat over their conquests. What I do say is that from now on people whose minds have been emancipated should clean up the foul ideas that characterize the Orient, so that they become a little purer and a little wiser, understanding that husband and wife are companions, colleagues, and creators of new life. The sons and daughters they give birth to are assuredly the people who will take charge of this new life, but they won't be in charge forever; they'll hand over to their sons and daughters, just as their parents did. Whether they lead or follow, all play their part in these transitions.

Why must life be continued? It's in order for it to develop and evolve. Since individuals can't avoid death and there are no limits to evolution, we can only extend it by taking the path of evolution. Taking this path requires an inner energy, just as a unicellular organism has an inner energy that enables it to multiply after a long process of accumulation, or as invertebrate animals develop into vertebrates. It's for this reason that later forms of life are more significant and complete than earlier forms, and in consequence more valuable and precious. The earlier life-forms should be sacrificed for the later ones.

Unfortunately, however, it again so happens that traditional views in China are the exact opposite of this principle. Primacy should be held by the young, but it is the elders who occupy it; emphasis should be on the future, but instead it's on the past. The elder generation, having sacrificed itself to its predecessors, lacks the strength to survive and expects its successors to sacrifice themselves for its sake, destroying all capacity for development.

Nor is it my contention either—as people who attack me have asserted— that grandsons should beat up their grandfathers all day long and daughters abuse their mothers constantly. It's that from now on emancipated people should first cleanse their minds of the false ideas that stem from ancient Oriental tradition; they must strengthen their sense of responsibility toward their sons and daughters and drastically reduce their sense of privilege and authority, in preparation for a reformed ethics in which the younger generation has primacy. When in turn the younger generation achieves a position of authority, they won't occupy it forever but will act responsibly toward their juniors. Whether they come first or follow behind, all play their part in these transitions.

My conclusion that no favors are being exercised between father and son is a large part of the reason for "the disciple of the sage" and his colleagues seeing red. Their mistake is in the elder generation's primacy, where its belief in self-interest and privilege is strong while its sense of obligation and responsibility is weak. In holding that the father-son relationship can be reduced to the phrase "my father gave me life," they mean the son belongs entirely to the father. What's especially disgraceful is the implied expectation of a return favor: since the son belongs to the father, he must be sacrificed for the sake of the father. They are completely unaware that the laws of the natural world are the exact opposite. Since ancient times, our conduct has defied heaven's will, and in consequence human abilities have been significantly reduced and social progress has accordingly come to a halt. We can't say that this stasis will necessarily end in extinction, but we are closer to the path of stasis and extinction than to progress.

The natural world order is inevitably flawed, but there is nothing wrong with the way it joins together young and old. It has no use for favors but endows animals with an instinct that we call love. Apart from species like fish whose offspring are too numerous to be loved individually, animals as a rule show great love for their young; not only are they free of any self-interest, they even sacrifice themselves for their young to secure their future life as they embark on the long path of development.

Humankind is no exception. In the majority of European and American families, primacy is given to the young and the weak in keeping with basic biological principles. Even in China, as long as you keep your heart pure and don't cross the path trampled by the sage's disciple, you can discover this instinct quite naturally. For example, a village woman suckling her infant wouldn't think that she was conferring a favor, and a peasant taking a wife would never consider it a form of usury. It's only when you have children that you instinctively love them and want them to survive; and more than that, you want them to surpass you: this is evolution. Love like this, utterly remote from systems of trade and profit, is the tie or bond that strengthens human relationships. Adopting old-fashioned terminology (that is, eliminating the word *love* and substituting it with *favors* or *expecting a return*) not only wrecks the moral bond between father and son but is the very reverse of a parent's true feelings, one that sows the seeds of monstrous outcomes.

There's a ballad called "In Praise of Filial Piety" that goes something like this:

While you go off to school,
Your mother makes your meal,
She's heating almond broth for you,
Before her you must kneel!

The writer no doubt considered himself a champion of morality. It wouldn't have occurred to him that the almond broth of the rich and the soybean milk of the poor are of equal value in terms of love, their value lying in the affection of the parents at the time being free of any thought of reward; otherwise, it's a commercial transaction in which drinking almond broth amounts to feeding pigs on human breast milk in order to fatten them. In terms of morality, it is utterly without value.

So what I now accept as right and proper is simply love.

Most people across the world acknowledge that self-love is justified. It's essential to maintaining life and basic to the continuation of life. The future is determined by what happens in the present; parental defects may lead to the extinction of their descendants and a crisis in their lives. Ibsen's play *Ghosts* is mainly about male-female problems, but we can also find the horrors of heredity in it. Oswald is an artist who wants to live, but because his father was a libertine, he is born diseased and unable to lead a normal life. He adores his mother and can't bear for her to nurse him during his illness, so he hides some morphine with the intention of asking the maid, Regina, to administer it to him so that he can commit suicide. Regina leaves, however, and he has no choice but to entrust his mother with the task:

> OSWALD: You'll have to help me now, mother.
> MRS ALVING: I?
> OSWALD: Who better than you?
> MRS ALVING: I! Your mother!
> OSWALD: For that very reason.
> MRS ALVING: I, who gave you life!
> OSWALD: I never asked you for life. And what kind of life have you
> given me? I don't want it! You take it back![15]

This passage is one that should make those of us who are fathers tremble in fear and admiration; it is imperative that we not betray our conscience and allow our sons to suffer. There are many such cases in China. People who work in hospitals are constantly witness to tragic cases of children suffering from inborn disease, and the people who proudly bring them in are usually the parents. But syphilis is not the only dreadful hereditary disease. Many other mental and physical defects can be passed on, and in the long run society itself suffers from their aftereffects. We don't have to concern ourselves with the fate of mankind here; for the sake of our own sons and daughters, we can say that people without self-love lack the qualification to be fathers. If they insist on becoming fathers, they are no better than usurpers who fashion their own crowns yet never count as legitimate rulers. In the future, when learning has advanced and society has been reformed, it will be up to the eugenicists to deal with the descendants who have managed to survive.

Supposing the parents haven't passed on any mental or physical defects to their children, and provided that no accidents have occurred, the children will of course be healthy, and it can be expected that the goal of continuing life will be achieved. But the duties of parents haven't yet been completed, because although life continues, it must not be brought to a halt: the new life must develop. The higher forms of animals not only nurture and protect their young but also teach them essential survival skills. For example, birds teach their young how to fly and predators teach theirs how to attack. Humans, who are several stages further advanced, instinctively want their children to advance still further. This is also love (which I've discussed above in regard to the present, but here it's in regard to the future). Anyone whose mind is not ossified would wish their children to be stronger, healthier, cleverer, and morally better than they are themselves, and happier as well; that is, children should transcend their parents and transcend the past as well. To achieve this there must be change, and descendants should change the ways of their ancestors. The old saying that to be called filial a son must observe his father's principles of conduct during the three years of mourning is perverse, the root of infantile disorder. Had the unicellular organisms of the ancient world upheld this doctrine, they would never have dared divide and multiply, and humankind would never have inhabited this world.

Fortunately, although this doctrine has harmed many people, it failed to wipe out human instincts. People who haven't read the works of the old sages could still from time to time display these instincts in the shadow of the Confucian ethical code. It's for this reason that the Chinese, although withered and atrophied, haven't yet been exterminated.

Therefore, people whose minds have been emancipated should from now on expand and deepen this instinctive love, sacrificing themselves for the new generation with unselfish love. The starting point for this is understanding. The mistake that the West used to make about children was to regard them as adults in the making; China's mistake was to regard them as miniature adults. It's only recently that a substantial body of scholarly research has revealed that the world of children is quite different from the adult world. If you don't start with understanding but stumble ahead regardless, it will be a major obstacle to child development. It follows that institutions should take childhood as their primary focus. Awareness of this is now common in Japan, where facilities for children and studies on childhood are both flourishing.

Next is guidance. Life must evolve, since circumstances are in continual flux; given that later generations will certainly differ from their predecessors, we can't unreasonably force them into the same mold. Elders should be guides and advisers, not people who issue orders. It's not just that they shouldn't require their juniors to venerate them; what's more important is that they must devote themselves to cultivating in their children hardy physiques, a pure and lofty morality, and an open, free mentality that can accommodate new ideas, so they'll have the strength to swim in these new world currents and not drown in them.

Third comes emancipation. Our children are both part of us and separate from us, and are also part of humankind. Since they are part of us, it is our duty to educate them so as to endow them with the ability to become self-sufficient; and since they are separate from us, we are also obliged to emancipate them, so they become independent adults wholly in charge of their own destinies.

This is how parents should treat their children: be in good health when they bear children, strive to educate them, and fully emancipate them.

Nevertheless, some people may fear that parents be left with nothing but a hollow, empty existence ahead of them. These fearful, foolish notions derive from mistaken ideas from the past; they will disappear of their own accord once the laws of biology are understood. Parents who wish to emancipate their children, however, also need to prepare themselves to be capable of doing so. That's to say that despite being tainted by the past, they should continue to have wide interests and cultivated pleasures in full possession of their independent skills and mentality. Do you want to be happy? Even your future life will be happy. Do you want to forsake old age and be young again? Enjoy a second youth? Your children are your second youth, they're already independent and better for it. Only when you've completed your responsibilities as an elder will life's consolations be yours. On the other hand, if your ideals and skills remain set in the past, and you pride yourself on your seniority while stirring up family quarrels, it will inevitably lead to the pain of a hollow, empty existence.

Some may fear that emancipation will create distance between father and son. It's long been known that European and American families are not as autocratic as in China; but although we used to compare them to savage beasts, these days even the disciple of the sage defends these families, claiming that they are free of rebellious youth. This shows that it's only with emancipation that families remain close, and that it's the lack of constraints on the younger generation by their elders that explains why there aren't any rebellious youth protesting against constraints. In any case, the use of intimidation and bribery can't guarantee holding onto power indefinitely. In China, for instance, regulations during the Han, the Tang, and the late Qing dynasties allowed that filial piety be sufficient qualification to promote sons to official positions. Despite the encouragement of paternal and even imperial favor, however, there've been few cases of people slicing flesh off their limbs to feed their parents. This is clear evidence that the old doctrines and practices in China since ancient times have had little effect; they only made the wicked more hypocritical while the good gratuitously suffered pain without profit to themselves or others.

Love alone is true. Lu Cui, a Han dynasty official, once attempted to discredit Kong Rong, a direct descendant of Confucius, by attributing to him the following statement: "What kinship does a father have to his son? His original idea is a matter of lust. A son's kinship to his mother is like an object in a jar, which loses any connection with the jar once it is taken out." (Toward the end of the Han dynasty, the Kong family produced some outstanding figures—unlike today's dissolute descendants—and it's possible that Kong Rong actually said this. Nevertheless, it is amusing that Lu Cui and his ruler, Cao Cao, were attacking him.) However, it's still not quite accurate, despite being a direct attack on the old doctrines. When parents produce children, they feel an instinctive love for them, a love that is both deep and enduring and that can't be put aside. The world hasn't yet reached the stage of universal harmony, and love exists in different degrees, but a child's love for its parents is particularly intense and intimate; it can't be put aside either. So the prospect of distance need not concern us. There may be some exceptions, people who are beyond the reach of love. Still, if love is beyond their reach, so also are concepts such as favors and threats, reputation and status, principle and propriety.

Some may fear that following emancipation elder generations will suffer hardship. This fear operates on two levels. First, although China is said to be a place where virtue is prized, we are in fact conspicuously deficient in mutual aid and love. The virtues of filial piety and chastity are simply ways in which to persecute the young and frail while bystanders bear no responsibility. In this kind of society, it is not only the old who find that life is difficult, it's the same for the emancipated younger generation. Second, most Chinese men and women grow old before their time (some teenagers actually look decrepit) and are in even more need of support by the time they approach senility. It's for these reasons I contend that parents who emancipate their children must make preparations, for reform is especially necessary in a society such as this in order for people to be able to lead rational lives. When large numbers of people are prepared and carrying out reforms, our hopes will naturally be realized in the course of time. When it comes to other countries' experience, Herbert Spencer never married, but I've not heard he was frustrated or bored; James Watt lost his children while they were still young and yet lived to an old age and died peacefully in his sleep. Surely life will only get better, especially for people with children!

Some may fear that following emancipation children may suffer hardship. This also operates on two levels and is the same as I've noted above, except that they suffer because of disability in old age in the one case and the inexperience of youth in the other. For this reason, people who are emancipated are even more conscious of their responsibility for reforming society. There are many mistakes in the traditional conventions that have been handed down in China. One is seclusion, in the belief that if children can be separated from society they won't be adversely influenced by it. Another is to teach them a capacity for doing wrong, in the belief that this is the only way to survive in society. Elders who make use of these methods, although with the best intentions of prolonging their lives, are making a serious logical mistake. There's also another method, which is to teach them to conform by passing on to them tricks on how to socialize. The people who were spouting the theories of pragmatism a few years ago were similarly mistaken when they proposed teaching school students to scrutinize foreign money because counterfeit money had appeared in the marketplace. Although we may be obliged on occasion to conform to social conventions, it's by no means always the right way to act. On the contrary, as long as society is immoral and vice is common, it would be wrong to conform on all accounts. Should we do so, we would be turning our backs on rational living and end up going backward on the evolutionary path. So the fundamental solution is simply to reform society.

It's a matter of simple fact that the old Chinese ideal of family relationships (including that between father and son) collapsed long ago. It's not true that it flourished right up to the present, it's been the case for a long time. The very fact that so much energy was exerted in praise of having five generations under one roof is enough to show how troublesome actual cohabitation proved to be. The desperate advocacy of filial piety similarly shows how few sons in fact exhibited such piety. And the reason for this is entirely their insistence on promoting false virtues and scorning true human feelings. When we turn the pages of the great family genealogies, we see that the founder's move to a new home is usually made as a single man, who goes on to establish a family and a livelihood; once an extended family settles there and genealogies are published, the family is already on the way to decay and dissolution.

In the future, when superstition has been smashed, sons will no longer weep in a bamboo grove or lie on ice; and when medicine has advanced, there will be no need for them to eat feces or slice flesh off their limbs.[16] For economic reasons, marriage will be delayed and children will be born later, so that by the time the children can be self-supporting, their parents will have grown old, and it will be too late for the children to depend on them for their upbringing; the parents will have performed their duty. The tide of world affairs forces itself upon us, and this is how we can survive; were it otherwise, it would lead to destruction. With more people being emancipated and making a greater effort, crises, it may be hoped, will be lessened.

Nevertheless, as I've said above, if the Chinese family in fact collapsed long ago (and not as the disciple of the sage has claimed in writing), why is there still no sign of progress even now? That's easy to explain. First, what is due to collapse will of course collapse; troublemakers will of course make trouble; and the people who make the rules will of course go on making rules. Without vigilance or any thought of reform, the old ways linger. Second, family quarrels have always been common, and they've only come to be called "revolutionary" since the new terminology became fashionable. Yet they still amount to the same old cursing about money spent on prostitutes and fights about gambling. This has nothing whatsoever to do with revolution as advocated by emancipated people. The younger generation who call their quarrels "revolution" are stuck in the past, and there is no way they will liberate their own children when they become adults. There are some who can't be bothered with discipline, but others hunt out the classic *Book of Filial Piety* and order their children to read it from front to back in the belief that the children will learn from the ancients how to sacrifice themselves for their parents. The blame for this lies wholly with the old morality, customs, and ways; there's no way it's the fault of biology.

If, as I've said above, living beings should extend life in order for evolution to take place, it may seem entirely rational to have several wives and concubines in order to avoid the worst kind of unfilial behavior, that is, to have no sons. This is also easy to respond to. It's unfortunate for people who have no sons to carry on their line, but it's even more unfilial to use improper methods to extend life that bring harm to others. Monogamy is the most rational system in today's society, and polygamy can actually lead to degeneracy. Degeneration is close to retrogression, the reverse of the goal of extending life. To have no sons may mean the extinction of the individual, but to have sons in a regressive situation may lead to the destruction of others. The spirit of self-sacrifice for others will always be part of humanity; furthermore, since living beings have been interrelated ever since they first came to exist, they are connected to a huge number of others, so that a person's bloodline can never become completely extinct. This being the case, biology by no means justifies polygamy.

To sum up, parents who are emancipated should act without any expectation of return when they sacrifice themselves for the benefit of others. This isn't easy, however, and it's even more difficult in China. To be considerate toward their elders and liberate their juniors requires emancipated people in China to pay old debts while opening new paths. This means, as I said at the outset, "Although they themselves bear a tremendous burden, they can prop open the gates of darkness, releasing the children into a bright, open space where they can spend their lives happily as rational human beings." This is a great, important task and also a difficult, arduous one.

Nevertheless, there are still older people who are not only unwilling to liberate their children but even forbid their children to liberate *their* children; they want their grandchildren and great-grandchildren to make meaningless sacrifices. It is a problem, but as a peace-loving man, I can't tackle it right now.

October 1919

TRANSLATED BY BONNIE S. MCDOUGALL

# Before the Appearance of Geniuses
未有天才之前

A lecture given to the Friends of the Affiliated Middle School of
Beijing Normal University, January 17, 1924

I'm afraid that my lecture will be of no benefit or interest to this esteemed audience since I'm really not a very knowledgeable person. But having stalled for far too long, I have no choice but to come here at last and say a few words.

I have noticed that among the demands people have made upon the world of letters, clamors for geniuses to appear are among the loudest. This call seems to provide evidence of two things: one, China still has yet to produce a single genius; and, two, no one likes the literature we have now. Are there really no geniuses? Perhaps they exist somewhere, but we have yet to see them. If we rely on what we see and hear, we perhaps can safely say there aren't any. We lack not just geniuses, but also the masses that would help nurture such geniuses. Geniuses are not strange creatures that arise of their own in some deep forest; they emerge from the masses that nurture them and allow them to grow. Therefore, if these masses do not exist, then there can be no geniuses. Once Napoleon crossed the Alps and proclaimed, "I am

---

Based on a lecture Lu Xun delivered on January 17, 1924, to the alumni of the Affiliated Middle School of Beijing Normal University and published in the first issue of the school's 1924 alumni newsletter. The essay was later reprinted with minor revisions in the *Supplement to Capital News* (Jingbao fukan) on December 27, 1924, and anthologized in *Graves* (Fen, 1927). Lu Xun, *Lu Xun quanji* (Complete works of Lu Xun) (Beijing: Renmin wenxue, 2005), 1: 174–178.

even taller than the Alps!" A majestic achievement for sure, but let us not forget that right behind him were a number of soldiers; if those soldiers had not been there, Napoleon would have either been captured or repelled by the enemy, and his words and deeds would have crossed the line from being heroic to those of a madman. Thus I believe that before we demand the appearance of geniuses, we should first demand the appearance of masses that can nurture such geniuses. For example, if one desires to see a tall tree or a beautiful flower, there must first be good soil; without such soil, neither flower nor tree can thrive. Therefore, soil is actually more important than flowers and trees. Flowers and trees cannot exist without soil just in the same way that Napoleon could not succeed without his able soldiers.

But the opinions and trends in present-day society doggedly demand genius, on the one hand, and yet wish for its destruction, on the other; some are even prepared to sweep clean the very soil on which such genius can grow. I offer some examples.

One of these arguments may be termed "preserving the national heritage." Since new currents of thoughts first arrived in China, they have never had much influence. Even so, some codgers, and even a few youths, have been scared out of their wits and ranting about national heritage. They say that "China has its own good things; neglecting to preserve them and instead going out to seek the new is just as bad as abandoning our ancestral heritage." Bringing up our ancestors to make this point naturally makes for weighty rhetoric. However, I have never believed that a new mandarin coat can't be made just because the old coat has not yet been properly cleaned and folded. With regard to the present, each person can do as he pleases. If the old gentlemen want to go about preserving the national heritage, they can naturally go bury themselves among their dead books. The young, by contrast, can pursue their own vital scholarship and new art. To each his own, and no harm is done to anyone. It is only when each side hoists its flag and clamors for its cause that China risks tearing itself away from the rest of the world altogether. To insist that everyone must behave in a certain way is the height of absurdity. When we strike up a conversation with an antiques dealer, he naturally will praise the qualities of his wares, but at no point does he rail against painters, peasants, carpenters, and other such craftsmen for having forgotten their ancestors. In fact, the antiques dealer is far cleverer than most national heritage scholars.

Another argument may be dubbed "the worship of originality." On the surface, it appears to be consistent with the demand for geniuses, but it is in fact quite different. This argument in its quintessence excludes ideas and styles from abroad. Therefore, it also risks isolating China from global currents. Many people are already sick of hearing such names as Tolstoy, Turgenev, and Dostoevsky, but which of their works have actually been translated in China? When vision is confined to one's own nation, any mention of a "Peter" or "John" arouses irritation; only works about Zhang So-and-So or Li So-and-So are acceptable. So when Chinese writers do emerge, the good ones among them cannot help but borrow a little technique and expression from foreign works. However fine the writing style, their thoughts often can't match those of translated works. They will even inject traditional ideas into their work to suit Chinese people's outdated tastes. And readers fall into their traps, their horizons receding ever more, as if confined in an old snare. Writers and readers are thus mired in a vicious cycle of cause and effect, rejecting foreign currents and upholding national essence; how, then, can geniuses appear? Even if one were to emerge, he would not survive long.

The masses in this kind of environment are but dust, not fertile soil; neither beautiful flower nor tall tree can grow there!

And then there are the malicious criticisms. The public has also long demanded the appearance of critics, and many critics have emerged at present. Unfortunately, among these critics are quite a few hacks. A work will barely appear in front of them before they are already grinding their inkstones and scribbling high-minded critiques declaring that the piece is "alas, far too naive. China needs geniuses!" Afterward, even noncritics will voice the same criticism, having heard it from elsewhere. The first cries of a newly born genius will be identical to those of an ordinary baby and will certainly not be like a fine poem. Because they are still immature, young geniuses will wither and die if prematurely attacked. I personally have witnessed several writers who were so mercilessly attacked by such hacks that they were left frozen and shaken. Those writers may not naturally have been geniuses; all the same, I lay my hopes with ordinary people just as well.

Malicious critics love to trample over land that bears tender sprouts; it brings them great exhilaration. But it is disastrous for the tender sprouts—both ordinary sprouts and sprouts of genius. Naiveté relates to maturity as a child does to an elder, and there is nothing shameful in this. Works of art are the same; there is nothing shameful if in the beginning they are naive. As long as they are not subject to vicious attack, they will thrive and mature. Only debauchery and corruption are beyond remedy. Those who are childish, some of whom are adults, so long as they possess naive hearts, will say naive things. They say things simply for the sake of saying things. Once the words have been spoken or even go as far as to land in print, then they consider the matter over and done with; they could care less whether it is subjected to criticism, whatever camp it may come from.

I would guess that most of you in this audience would like to see geniuses appear. But this is the situation: not only is it difficult to produce geniuses, the soil to cultivate such genius is hard to come by as well. I think that genius is for the most part innate; as long as there is the soil to cultivate such genius, then nearly everyone can become one. Cultivating soil is more important than simply demanding genius; otherwise, even if there were hundreds and thousands of geniuses, without soil they cannot flourish and will end up like bean sprouts served on a plate.

To cultivate soil, we must broaden our minds. This means we must accept new currents of thought and leave behind the old ways so that we can accommodate and understand the geniuses that will appear in the future. We must also not be afraid to engage in more humble endeavors. Those who can write something original should naturally do so. Otherwise, translating, introducing, appreciating, reading, browsing, and reading for leisure are all acceptable as well. It may seem ridiculous to treat literature as a form of amusement, but this is still better than subjecting it to vicious attack.

Of course, merely discussing the relative merits of soil and genius is a waste of breath. However, unless we persevere in difficult conditions, I'm afraid cultivating soil is not something that can be easily done. But things can only be accomplished with human effort, and action is far more realistic than waiting in vain for a heaven-sent genius to arrive. This is what is noble in cultivating the soil, and where great hope also lies. Moreover, cultivating good soil bears its own rewards. When a lovely flower emerges from the soil, people will naturally appreciate it, and the soil itself can also take pleasure in appreciating it. One need not be the flower itself to feel joyful and carefree—if we take as a premise that the soil itself may also have a spirit of its own.

TRANSLATED BY ROY BING CHAN

# Jottings under Lamplight

## 燈下漫筆

### I

There was a time in 1912 or 1913 when the credit-worthiness of the banknotes of a number of national banks in Beijing was growing by the day; it can truly be said to have been soaring by the day. I've heard that even country folk who had always been obsessed with silver realized that banknotes were not only convenient but reliable and were thus quite happy to accept them and keep them in circulation. Those who were somewhat more discerning—not necessarily those of the "special intellectual class"—had long since stopped carrying around heavy and burdensome silver coins and enduring the unnecessary nuisance it entailed. In retrospect, aside from those who had a particular love of silver or collected it as a hobby, almost everyone used banknotes, and mostly notes issued by Chinese banks at that. A pity, however, that this practice later suddenly suffered a considerable setback.

In the same year that Yuan Shikai decided to become emperor [1916], Cai E fled Beijing for Yunnan to start an insurrection. One of the aftereffects was that both the Bank of Communications and the Bank of China ceased to exchange their banknotes for silver. Although the banks stopped honoring them, the government still had the authority to force merchants to continue using the bills; but the merchants had their own way of circumventing this: they didn't say they wouldn't accept them, but said instead that they couldn't make change. I don't know how it worked if you tried to buy things with notes denominated in the tens or hundreds, but who would actually be willing to pay a whole dollar for a pen or a pack of cigarettes? Not only would you be unwilling, you wouldn't have had that many dollar bills to begin with. If you tried to exchange them for copper coins, even at a reduced rate, the merchants would say they had no copper coins. Then how could you expect friends or relatives to have money when you went to ask them for a loan? At

First published in 1925 in two parts in the journal *Wilderness* (Mangyuan): the first on May 1, issue 2; the second on May 22, issue 5. Later anthologized in *Graves* (Fen, 1927). Lu Xun, *Lu Xun quanji* (Complete works of Lu Xun) (Beijing: Renmin wenxue, 2005), 1: 222–232.

that point, you would be willing to lower your standards, ignore patriotism, and ask for notes issued by foreign banks. But foreign banknotes at the time were equivalent to silver, so if you asked for a loan of such notes, it was the same as lending you actual silver.

I still remember that I had thirty or forty dollars in notes issued by the two banks at the time, but I had suddenly become a pauper, almost to the point of having to forgo food, and I was more than a bit panicked. The frame of mind of the Russian rich who held paper rubles at the time of the revolution was no doubt quite similar, or at most just a bit more intense. So I could only resort to making inquiries—could banknotes be converted to silver at a discount? I was told there was no market. Fortunately, a covert market eventually developed, with bills going for just over 60 percent of their face value. I was delighted and immediately sold half of my paper money right then. Later the rate went up to 70 percent, which made me even more delighted, and I converted all my banknotes to silver, which weighed heavily in my pocket, as if representing the full weight of my existence. Had it been normal times, if a money changer shorted me even a penny, I would have found it absolutely unacceptable.

But just as I stuffed a bag of silver in my pocket and began feeling a weighty comfort and delight, another thought suddenly dawned on me: how easily we become slaves, and once it happens, we are even utterly delighted by it.

There are tyrannical powers that "do not treat people as humans," and not only as less than human, but even as inferior to livestock, as simply worthless things; once people begin to envy livestock and to heave sighs about how "people living in chaos are not as well off as dogs living in peace," the eventual result is that people are valued more or less as livestock. It's like the law in the Yuan dynasty that required the compensation of an ox when one killed someone else's slave; at this point, people quite willingly submit and celebrate this as an age of peace and prosperity. Why so? Because although they are no longer considered human, they are at least considered as equals to livestock.

We don't have to reverently study all the *Twenty-Four Imperial Histories* or go to a research center to find the spiritual superiority of our civilization. All one need do is flip through the *Abbreviated Mirror* that children read— or if you think that too weighty read *The Chronology of Historical Eras*—and you will know that what China, the "ancient nation of over three thousand years of culture,"[17] has been up to this entire time is nothing other than such small tricks. In things like those recently composed works known as "history textbooks," however, it is hard to make it out; it is as if they are saying: "we have always been doing quite well."

The fact of the matter, however, is that the Chinese people have never earned the right to be "humans," gaining at best only the status of "slaves," which is still the case today; actually, being worse off than slaves is so common as to be unremarkable. The Chinese people are typically neutral, and when war comes they don't even know to which side they belong, so they can belong to all sides. When bandits come, the people belong to the government, so of course they must be slaughtered; when official troops arrive, the people should then technically be one of their kind, but they're still slaughtered, as if they were on the side of the bandits. At such times, the people wish only for a fixed master. They wouldn't dare dream that he would treat them as his subjects, but rather merely as his livestock; they would willingly seek their own grass to graze on and ask only that he decide which way they should run to find it.

If someone comes along who can actually make decisions on their behalf and set down a particular code of slavery, then this would be considered a "magnificent imperial benefice." A pity that it is quite often the case that there isn't anyone who can set down such a code. To list only the conspicuous examples: during the barbarian invasions and multiple kingdoms of the fourth and fifth centuries, the Huang Chao rebellion of 875–884, the five dynasties of the century that followed, and the end of the Song and beginning of the Yuan dynasties in the mid-fourteenth century, aside from the usual taxation and corvée labor, people had to suffer unexpected catastrophes. The temperament of the seventeenth-century rebel Zhang Xianzhong was even more peculiar: he killed those who didn't pay taxes or submit to corvée labor, but he also killed those who did; he killed those who resisted but also those who surrendered; he smashed to pieces the conventions of slavery. At the time the common people hoped for another sort of master, one who would take greater consideration of the conventions of slavery, regardless of whether the regulations had always existed or were newly promulgated, so long as there was a set of conventions that enabled them to get back on the path to slavery.

"May the ascendant sun perish, and I shall perish along with you"[18] is merely angry talk, and you seldom encounter those determined to put it into practice. In fact, it may generally be the case that following a time of rampant banditry and extreme chaos, there will be someone stronger, or smarter, or craftier, or from another ethnicity who more or less imposes order on the realm. Regulations are established: how to perform corvée labor, how to pay taxes, how to kowtow, how to worship the sages. Moreover, these rules are not arbitrary like the ones nowadays. Thereupon, there is "general rejoicing," and as the saying has it, "great peace reigns in the realm."

No matter how extravagantly our more ostentatious scholars set things out when they write history—and their fine intentions are palpable indeed—the rhetoric they adopt in such excellent topics as "The Era of the Origins of the Han Race" or "The Era of the Flourishing of the Han Race" or "The Era of the Resurgence of the Han Race" is rather too circuitous. The more forthright way of putting it would be thus:

1. The Era of Longing, but Failing, to Become Slaves
2. The Era of Provisionally Securing Status as Slaves

This cycle is what our "ancestral scholars" referred to as "periods of peace and periods of disorder." From the standpoint of the "loyal subjects" that followed, those who created unrest were simply clearing a path for the "master," hence the saying "eliminating obstacles for the Sagacious Lord of Heaven." I can't be certain just which era we are in now. Seeing classicists' faith in the national essence, writers praising our indigenous culture, and Neo-Confucians so intent upon returning to antiquity, however, it is clear that none of them are content with the present. But in exactly which direction are we headed, after all? When the common people encounter some incomprehensible war, those who are a little better off head for the foreign concessions, while women and children take refuge in churches, because such places are relatively "secure," and they don't, in the meantime, have to be in the position of longing, but failing, to become slaves. In short, those intent upon returning to antiquity or taking refuge, regardless of whether they are wise or foolish, worthy or not, all seem to be pining for a time of peace and prosperity three hundred years ago, that is an "Era of Provisionally Securing Status as Slaves."

But are we all like the ancients, forever content with an era that "has always been thus"? Are we all like the archaists, unsatisfied with the present and pining for a time of peace and prosperity three hundred years ago?

Of course, we may not be content with the present either, but we don't need to look backward, because there is a road that lies ahead. And creating a third type of era that has never existed in Chinese history before is the mission of our Chinese youth today!

## II

But more and more people are praising China's ancient civilization, including foreigners. I often think that if whoever it is that comes to China were able to frown in disgust and abhor China, I would offer my sincere gratitude, because he assuredly would not wish to feast on the flesh of the Chinese people!

In his article "The Charm of Beijing," Yusuke Tsurumi notes that there was a Caucasian who came to China intending to stay temporarily, for only a year, but was still in Beijing five years later and didn't want to leave. One day the two of them were dining together:

> Once seated at the round mahogany table, with rare fish and game offered to us in a constant stream, we began talking of such things as antiques, paintings, and politics. There was a Chinese-style shade on the electric lamp and a soft glow suffused curios displayed in the room. Such matters as the *Proletariat* seemed to be nothing but a passing breeze.
>
> I was on the one hand intoxicated by the atmosphere of Chinese life, while on the other pondering over the things that held such charm for foreigners. The Mongols conquered China, but were in turn conquered by the beauty of Chinese life; the Manchus also conquered China but were conquered by the beauty of Chinese life. Now, Westerners are the same; though *Democracy* and such and such are constantly on their lips, they have also been charmed by the beauty of the life constructed over six thousand years by the Chinese. Once one has lived in Beijing, there is no forgetting the flavor of life there. Neither the acres of dust blown up in the windy season nor the war games played by the warlords every three months can erase the charm of Chinese life.

I have as yet no means of refuting these words of his. Our ancient worthies have not only provided us with maxims with which to preserve our ancient ways, but have also sacrificed our children and treasures to provide sumptuous feasts for our conquerors. The Chinese people's ability to endure hardship and its practice of having many children are the stuff of these feasts, and even today remain sources of pride for our patriots. When Westerners first came to China, they were called barbarians, which of course made them frown in disapproval, but now the opportune moment has arrived: after having feted the Toba, the Jurchen, the Mongols, and the Manchus, the time to put on feasts for the Westerners has come.

When they go out, they ride in automobiles; and when they walk, they receive protection. Even when the road is cleared for officials, foreigners still have freedom of movement. When they are robbed, they receive compensation. When the bandit Sun Meiyao hijacked a train and made them stand in front of his troops as hostages, government troops didn't dare open fire. So why wouldn't they enjoy sumptuous feasts in their lavish mansions? And when they are enjoying their feasts, it is of course also the time for them to praise China's ancient culture; there are, however, certain optimistic patriots who are perhaps actually cheered by this, thinking the foreigners have begun to be assimilated. The ancients used women as a buffer by which to secure a short-term peace, euphemistically fooling themselves by calling it "peace through matrimony," while people now use our children and treasure as slavish tribute, euphemistically referring to it as "assimilation." So the only people of true conscience and worthy of admiration are those foreigners, now deemed qualified to attend the banquet, but who nonetheless still curse the condition of modern China!

But we ourselves have long since paved the way for this, with our gradations of noble and base, major and minor, high and low. If we are bullied and abused, we can still bully and abuse others; we can be eaten, but we can also eat others. There is a hierarchy of strict control that cannot be tampered with, nor does anyone wish to tamper with it. Because if it is tampered with, there may be some advantages, but there will also be some harm. Let's have a glance at the fine laws and good intentions of the ancients—

> As there are ten periods in a day, there are ten grades of men. So the inferiors serve the superiors as the superiors wait upon the gods. Therefore the king rules over the dukes, the dukes over the great officers, the great officers over the ordinary officers, the ordinary officers over the lictors, the lictors over the mass, the mass over the underlings, the underlings

over the servants, the servants over the helpers. (From the *Chronicle of Zuo*, seventh year of Duke Zhao)

But the "helper" has no one to rule over; is this not too much suffering? Not to worry, because they have wives inferior in status to them and sons who are weaker still. And even his sons have much hope: when they grow up and are promoted to the status of "helper," they will also have wives and sons who are inferior to and weaker than them and whom they can order around. In a chain like this, each finds his own station, and anyone who objects will be accused of not being content with his lot!

Although these are ancient matters, and the seventh year of the Duke of Zhao [534 BCE] is really very remote from us now, the archaists need not be overly pessimistic. All the manifestations of peace are still with us: so while we are often afflicted with the ravages of war and drought, who has heard any great outcry? There is fighting and revolt, but are there any high-minded gentlemen flinging accusations against these things? Does not the degree of tyranny toward our own people and obsequiousness toward foreigners resemble the worst features of the tradition? China's old spiritual civilization has not, in fact, been buried by the word *Republic*; the only slight difference with the past is simply that the Manchus have departed the scene.

It is because of this that we still see before our very eyes all manner of feasts: we have barbeque, shark fins, home-style cooking, and Western cuisine. But we also have plain rice consumed under thatched eaves, scraps eaten by the side of the road, and famine stalking the countryside; we have those of immeasurable wealth consuming barbeque even as we have children on the point of starvation selling for eight coppers a pound (see issue number 21 of *Contemporary Review*). What we call our Chinese civilization is actually nothing more than a feast of human flesh prepared for the delectation of the rich, and what we call China is nothing more than the kitchen where these feasts of human flesh are prepared. Those who are unaware of this but still praise the civilization can be forgiven; otherwise, such people should suffer eternal condemnation.

Foreigners who aren't aware of this and praise China can be forgiven, as can those in high positions who praise China as a result of leading charmed lives who have thus become corrupted into insensibility. There are, however, two other types of people: those who take the Chinese as an inferior race, good only for following the ways of the past, and for this reason praise China's relics of the past; and those who wish all people in the world to be different so as to enhance the fascination of their travels, who visit China to see people with queues, visit Japan to see people wearing wooden clogs, and visit Korea to see the bamboo hats. It would be extremely boring if all clothing were alike, so they oppose the Europeanization of Asia. These types are both despicable. As for Bertrand Russell, who praised the Chinese people after seeing the beaming faces of sedan-chair porters at West Lake, he may have been moved by other motives. If, however, those porters had been able to withhold their smiles from their customers, China would long since have ceased to be the China it is today.

This civilization not only intoxicates foreigners, but also has long since intoxicated the Chinese people, to the point they all wear smiles on their faces. Because of numerous distinctions handed down from the past that still exist today and have estranged people from one another, they can no longer feel the suffering of others.

Not only that, but because people all have the hope of enslaving and devouring others, they forget that they, too, face a future in which they may be similarly enslaved and devoured. Thus, since the dawn of civilization, countless feasts of human flesh, big and small, have been continuously prepared up to the present day; people come to these gathering spots to eat others and be eaten; the lamentation of the weak—not to mention those of women and children—are drowned out by the stupid and senseless clamor of the murderers.

The feasts of human flesh are still being prepared, and there are many people who wish to see them continue. The mission of our young people today is to wipe out these eaters of human flesh, upend these feasts, and destroy the kitchen!

April 29, 1925

TRANSLATED BY THEODORE HUTERS

# On Looking at Things with Eyes Wide Open
論睜了眼看

Among Mr. Xusheng's[19] short commentaries on current affairs is one titled "We Should Have the Courage to Face Things Squarely" (*Mengjin*, no. 19). Indeed, only when we have the courage to look squarely at things can we hope to have the courage to think, to speak out, and to take responsibility for our actions. If we don't even dare to look squarely at things, then nothing much can be accomplished. And yet, unfortunately, this is the kind of courage that we Chinese most lack.

However, at the moment, I'm concerned with another aspect of the matter—Chinese literati have never had much courage in looking squarely at life—or at least at the conditions of society. Our sages have long taught: "Do not look at anything not in accordance with propriety."[20] And this "propriety" is very strict: not only are you forbidden from a "square look"; even a "level gaze" or "sideways glance" is not permitted. I don't know about the spirit of the youths nowadays, but judging by the way they carry themselves physically, most have huddled shoulders and hunched backs, lowered brows and obedient eyes, indicating that they are steady sons and submissive subjects of the old school. That they exert a great influence is a new theory that came up just this past month, but it has yet to be tested.

To return to the subject of a "square look": at first, one doesn't dare to look; in time, one is no longer able to look; still later, one will, as a matter of course, neither look nor see. When a car breaks down on the road and a crowd gathers to stare vapidly, what they get in the end is a patch of black grease. And yet, even if one doesn't look squarely at the misery and pain that comes from one's own inner conflicts or society's defects, one still has to suffer them intimately.

Literati men are the sensitive type, and from their works it seems that some have long felt discontent. But at the critical moment when defects are about to be exposed, they will inevitably recite: "There is no such thing" and

---

First published in issue 38 of *Threads of Talk* (Yusi) on August 3, 1925, and later anthologized in *Graves* (Fen, 1927). Lu Xun, *Lu Xun quanji* (Complete works of Lu Xun) (Beijing: Renmin wenxue, 2005), 1: 251–257.

shut their eyes. With their eyes shut, they envision the perfection of everything around them. The current suffering is due to the fact that "When Heaven is about to confer a great office on a man, it first tries his will with suffering, and his sinews and bones with toil. It exposes his body to hunger and subjects him to extreme poverty. It confounds him at every turn."[21] And so no problems, no defects, no injustice exist, and therefore there need be no solutions, reforms, or resistance. As everything will come to a grand and perfect finale, there is no need for us to fret. We can sip our tea with an easy mind and fall asleep happily. If we were to spout any more nonsense, we would be accused of being "unsuited to the times," and inevitably suffer the fate of being corrected by the professors. Pooh!

Although I've never tested them, I've sometimes imagined such scenarios: if we were to throw an old gentleman used to hibernating in his dark room into the blazing noontime sun of the summer, or if we were to drag a high-born lady sequestered in her boudoir into the wilderness one dark night, they would probably just shut their eyes and continue dreaming their old broken dreams. They would see neither the light nor the darkness, though their environment has changed completely. The Chinese literati are similar in this respect: they shut their eyes to whatever they encounter to deceive themselves and others by means of two methods: concealment and deceit.

The defects in the Chinese system of marriage have long been noted by the writers of scholar-beauty romances. They would have a talented scholar write a poem on the wall, and some beautiful girl then writes a poem in reply. From mutual admiration—what we now call "falling in love"—they then form a "life-long commitment." But then there is problem. We all know that "life-long commitment made in private" may be good for poetry, plays, or novels (of course, on the condition that the commitment is made with a man who ultimately places first in the imperial examination); in real life, it is forbidden, and the lovers will inevitably have to part. Writers of the late Ming dynasty shut their eyes and even found a way to salvage the situation: the young scholar gets the highest honors in the examination and marries by imperial decree. Under such pressure, "the parents' orders and the go-between's arrangements"[22] are not worth a cent, and so the problem is solved. If there is any issue, it is only a matter of whether the scholar would place first in the examination, not whether the marriage system is reasonable or not.

(Recently, some people complained that the new-style poets publish their poems to grab the limelight and entice the opposite sex. They even transferred their rage to the newspapers and magazines that indiscriminately print the poems. What they don't know is that even though the ancients had no newspapers, the walls "have been there since antiquity" and have long been a broadcast medium. According to *The Investiture of the Gods*, King Zhou even wrote a poem on the temple wall of the Goddess Nüwa—a very ancient origin indeed.[23] Newspapers may turn down works written in the vernacular or refuse song lyrics, but walls can't all be torn down or kept under close surveillance. Even if you paint them black, people could still scratch on them with a broken shard or write on them with a piece of chalk—there is no way to put a stop to this. Poets no longer carve their works in woodblock and hide them in famous mountains for posterity,[24] but publish them right away. Even though this practice may have problems, it might be rather difficult to stamp out.)

The small tragedy in *Dream of the Red Chamber* is something that happens in the world frequently.[25] The author is also quite daring in depicting reality. The ending isn't bad either, what with the revival of the Jia family fortune, the honors earned by the younger generations, and Baoyu himself appearing as a monk cloaked in a brilliant red cape. There are plenty of monks, but how many could afford a cape like his? No doubt he was "already a sage and had transcended the mortals." As for the other characters, their fates have long been noted one by one in the records; the ends they meet are just a settling of accounts, the resolution of problems, not the start of them. Even if the reader feels a bit uneasy, there is nothing he can do. And yet the sequels and rewrites either revive the dead or make a match in the afterlife—the male and female protagonists must have their "grand reunion" then and there. The sequel writers are so hooked on self-deception and deceiving others that a small deceit cannot satisfy them; they will not rest until they've shut their eyes and made up a bunch of nonsense. Haeckel once said that the difference between one person and another is sometimes greater than the difference between an anthropoid ape and a primitive man.[26] When we compare the sequel writers to the original writer of *Dream of the Red Chamber*, we must acknowledge the truth of this statement.

As early as the Six Dynasties, people began to doubt the truth of the saying "The good will be duly rewarded."[27] One of their epitaphs even says:

"This man accumulated many good deeds but was not rewarded; in the end, we have been deceived."[28] But then muddleheaded latecomers tried to hide the truth again. In the *Records of the Yuan Dynasty*, a certain Liu Xin threw his three-year-old son into the incense burner with the vain hope of obtaining good fortune.[29] But in the dramatic version "Little Zhang Incinerates His Son to Save His Mother" the mother's life is prolonged, and the son doesn't die either.[30] In a tale in *Stories to Awaken the World*, a woman who willingly serves her terminally ill husband is said to have committed suicide together with him in the end.[31] And yet a sequel has a snake fall into the medicine pot, and the husband completely recovers after taking the medicine.[32] If ever things are not perfect, once a writer has whitewashed it, the ending is usually changed and the reader is fooled into believing that the world is indeed bright and rosy. And if anyone encounters misfortune, he must have been asking for it.

If the historical facts are too well known and cannot be covered up, such as the murders of Guan Yu and Yue Fei, then other means of deception are needed. One trick is to say the hero had an unfortunate predestination from a previous life, as in the case of Yue Fei.[33] Another trick is to turn the dead into a deity, as in the case of Guan Yu.[34] Predestination cannot be avoided, while becoming a deity is a most satisfying reward. As such, the killers do not have to be blamed, and the victims do not have to be mourned. It has all been prearranged beyond the human realm. Everyone will get his proper due, and there is no need for anyone to fret.

Afraid to face reality squarely, the Chinese resort to concealment and deceit to design a marvelous escape route, which they believe to be the correct path. This escape route is a clear testimony to the Chinese national character: cowardly, lazy, and cunning. Day after day, they stay contented; day after day, they become more degenerate. And yet they believe their glory grows more visible by the day. In reality, each time the country falls, a few more loyal martyrs are added to the list; afterward, rather than looking to restore their country, people content themselves by eulogizing the martyrs. When war and catastrophe hit, they create a throng of chastity martyrs; afterward, people don't think of punishing the evildoers or improving methods of self-defense, but sing the praises of the chastity martyrs. It is as if the fall of the country and wars were opportunities for the high morality of the Chinese to shine through and as if increasing one's worth depends on these glorious acts; and thus one should do one's utmost to perform these acts rather than worrying or grieving. Naturally, there is nothing more we need to do, since we've achieved the highest glory through the sacrifice of the dead. At the commemoration for the martyrs in Shanghai and Hankou, under a great lofty wooden spirit tablet, the living fought and cursed each other out, going down exactly the same path as our ancestors.[35]

Literature is the spark emitted from the spirit of the people of a nation; it is also the torch that guides the spirit of the people of a nation into the future. The source and the outcome act upon each other, much as sesame oil and sesame seeds do: the oil is extracted from the seeds, but when the oil is used to soak the seeds, the seeds become more oily. If oil is what you want, that's fine. Otherwise, other things should be mixed in, such as water or alkali. Because the Chinese have never dared to look life squarely in the face, we've always resorted to concealment and deceit, from which sprouted a literature of concealment and deceit, which then led the Chinese to sink deeper into a great quagmire of concealment and deceit, to the point where we became quite unconscious of it. The world is changing day by day, and it is high time that our writers take off their masks and look at life with honesty, sincerity, and boldness, and represent it in flesh and blood. It is high time that we have a brand new literary field, high time for a few valiant warriors!

At present, the vogue seems to have changed. We no longer hear the songs about the flowers and the moon that we used to hear everywhere; they have been replaced by praise of iron and blood. But if we harbor deceit in our hearts and speak with deceitful tongues, then whether we are speaking about A and B or Y and Z is equally false. It would only serve to hush up the so-called critics who derided the songs of the flowers and the moon, allowing them to indulge in the belief that China is about to see a revival. Pity that their eyes are closing shut under the great banner of "patriotism"—or perhaps they were already closed to begin with.

Without brave warriors to charge onward and break free of all traditional thinking and devices, China will not have a real new literature.

July 22, 1925

TRANSLATED BY HU YING

# Why "Fair Play" Should Be Deferred

論 "費厄潑賴" 應該緩行

## I. The Solution to the Problem

In issue 57 of *Threads of Talk*, Mr. Lin Yutang speaks of "fair play"; he believes that this kind of spirit is extremely hard to find in China, and so we should actively encourage it.[36] He adds that not "beating a drowning dog" is a good gloss on the meaning of "fair play." I don't understand English, and neither do I understand the deeper meaning behind the phrase; but if not "beating a drowning dog" represents the true spirit of "fair play," then I'm afraid there's more I would like to say on the issue. I have not taken "Beating a Drowning Dog" as my title so as to avoid poking anyone in the eye with my argumentative "antlers."[37] But in the final analysis, my point is merely this: one can indeed beat a drowning dog and usually should.

---

Published in the first issue of the biweekly journal *Wilderness* (Mangyuan) on January 10, 1926, and later anthologized in *Graves* (Fen, 1927). Lu Xun, *Lu Xun quanji* (Complete works of Lu Xun) (Beijing: Renmin wenxue, 2005), 1: 286–297. The immediate context for this essay was a series of protests that unfolded between 1924 and 1925 at the Beijing Women's Normal College, where Lu Xun had lectured until tendering his resignation in 1924. In the fall of 1925, the college president, Yang Yinyu (1884–1938), who was closely affiliated with the conservative Minister of Education Zhang Shizhao (1881–1973), who was himself backed by the Beiyang government of warlord Duan Qirui (1865–1936), expelled a number of activist students, including the young woman, Xu Guangping (1898–1968), with whom Lu Xun had recently initiated a romantic relationship. The students, in turn, demanded Yang Yinyu's resignation. The resultant impasse prompted an executive order from Zhang Shizhao, suspending classes at the college indefinitely and violently evicting the protesters. The subsequent outcry from public intellectuals, Lu Xun prominent among them, eventually cost Yang Yinyu her post. She became, in the terms of the present essay, a "drowning dog." Here, Lu Xun takes up his rhetorical cudgels against those (among them Lin Yutang) who argued that "fair play" and decency demanded refraining from further attacks against Yang and her allies, chief among whom was Lu Xun's nemesis, the academic Chen Xiying.

## II. On the Three Kinds of Drowning Dogs That, By and Large, Should Be Beaten

Modern critics often speak of "flogging a dead tiger" and "beating a drowning dog" in the same breath, considering both to be a form of cowardice. I think there's something quite amusing about those who "flog dead tigers" in a show of strength—they may be cowards, but in a charming way. Beating a drowning dog, however, is not such a simple issue. You need to see what kind of dog it is and how it fell into the water before making an assessment. There are three main reasons for a dog falling into the water:

1. The dog lost its footing and fell into the water.
2. Someone pushed it into the water.
3. You yourself pushed it into the water.

In the first two cases, it would naturally be quite pointless, even cowardly, to join others in beating the dog. But if you had been locked in a fierce fight with the dog and personally knocked it into the water, then even assailing it with a bamboo pole would not seem too excessive, because this is an entirely different case from the first two.

I heard that a brave boxer never hits an enemy when he's down, and this can indeed be held up as a model for us all. I would accede to this only on the additional condition that the opponent is a brave fighter as well, who once beaten, will either be too ashamed to return for another match or will openly come back to seek his revenge. Either option would of course be acceptable. But this example does not apply to dogs, for they can hardly be counted as opponents in the same league, and no matter how loudly they bark, they cannot be expected to understand chivalry. Besides, dogs can tread water and will almost certainly be able to climb up to shore. The moment you let down your guard, the dog will shake itself off, spattering water in your face, and then slink off with its tail between its legs. And its disposition will remain the same afterward. Simple folk may see its immersion as a kind of baptism, after which the dog will certainly repent and never come back to bite again, but this view could hardly be more mistaken.

In short, I believe that all dogs who bite can be beaten, whether they happen to be on shore or in the water.

## III.  Pugs in Particular Must Be Driven into the Water and Given a Beating

Pugs or Pekingese are called "Western dogs" in the south of China, but I hear that they are a special Chinese breed. They often win the gold medal in international dog shows, and among the dogs pictured in the *Encyclopedia Britannica*, you will find quite a few of our Chinese pugs. This too can be considered an honor to our country. But aren't cats and dogs mortal enemies? How is it that, even though a pug is a dog, it resembles nothing so much as a cat—so moderate, affable, and easygoing, with a palpable sense of its own dignity, putting on airs as if saying: "Everyone else goes to such extremes, but I alone practice the Doctrine of the Mean." That is why pugs are such favorites with wealthy men, eunuchs, well-off wives, and their daughters, and why they continue to be bred without interruption to their blood lines. Their ambition is just to be kept on as pets of aristocrats by attracting them with their exquisite grooming, or to follow in the wake of wealthy Chinese or foreign ladies when they go shopping, with a narrow chain around their necks.

These pugs should be driven into the water at the earliest opportunity and then given a sound beating. Even if they have fallen into the water on their own, a good beating would not be out of place. If one has good intentions, you need not beat them, but nor is it necessary to pity their plight. If you can forgive these pugs, there's no reason to beat any dogs at all. For although other dogs also fawn on the rich and powerful, they still have something of the wolf in them, something wild, and are not straddling the fence like these pugs.

But all the above is merely a tangent and doesn't seem particularly relevant to the main theme of the essay.

## IV.  On the Harm Done to Posterity by Not Beating Drowning Dogs

In short, whether or not to beat a drowning dog rests first of all on what their attitude will be once they manage to climb back ashore.

A dog can hardly change its spots. Perhaps in ten thousand years things will be different from how they are now, but I am talking about the present. We may find a drowning dog quite pitiful, but the same can be said of many other harmful animals. Cholera germs proliferate quickly, but they are straightforward, honest creatures. That doesn't stop doctors from treating them without the least bit of mercy.

Today's bureaucrats and gentlemen, be they local or foreign, tend to refer to things that don't suit them as "Red" or "Communist." Before the founding of the Republic in 1911, things were a little different. Back then they objected to "Kang Youwei's Party," and later they called it the "Revolutionary Party" and even went so far as to inform on its members to the *yamen*; they did this not only to maintain their dignity, but also perhaps to "stain the official button on their cap red with blood"—that is, to be rewarded by a promotion for the execution of a revolutionary. But the revolution came nonetheless, and these gentlemen with their high and mighty airs suddenly became— not unlike Confucius himself—"homeless dogs" and tried to conceal their queues by coiling them up atop their heads. The revolutionaries exuded a thoroughly modern air—precisely the sort the gentlemen detested so deeply—and appeared quite "civilized." They said that "the reforms are for all" and that "we do not beat drowning dogs; let them crawl back to shore." And crawl ashore they did, laying low until the second half of 1913 and the "second revolution," when they suddenly reappeared to help Yuan Shikai bite many revolutionaries to death. China fell deeper into darkness day by day, and even today we not only have to contend with the old holdovers, but with their youthful progeny as well. This is the fault of the kind hearts of the martyrs, whose consideration for these snakes in the grass allowed them to proliferate; from here on, enlightened youth will have to expend that much more of their strength, to forfeit many more of their lives, in their struggle to fight against their deceitful schemes.

Ms. Qiu Jin died at the hands of these informers, and while she was referred to for a time after the Revolution as a "female knight-errant," no one really mentions her much anymore.[38] After the revolution began, a general— what we would now call a warlord—came to her district. This was her comrade-in-arms, Wang Jinfa. He arrested the mastermind who plotted her demise and accumulated evidence from the informant to avenge her death. But in the end, the mastermind was released, apparently because it was said that the Republic had already been founded, and we should now let bygone resentments be bygone. When the "second revolution" failed, Wang Jinfa himself was executed by one of Yuan Shikai's running dogs; complicit in the plot was precisely the mastermind behind Qiu Jin's death whom he had released.

Time has passed, and this particular person has enjoyed the privilege of passing away peacefully in his own bed, yet many of his sort are still running rampant; and so year after year Qiu Jin's hometown remains the same sort of place it always was, with no sign of any progress at all. From this perspective, the privilege of growing up, as did Miss Yang Yinyu and Professor Chen Xiying, in what has been termed "China's model district" is really the mark of supreme fortune.[39]

## V. On Why Those Who Have Fallen from Power Are Not to Be Confused with Drowning Dogs

To "bear the trespasses of others without correction" is the path of mercy; "an eye for an eye, a tooth for a tooth" is the path of justice.[40] In China, most paths run crooked: not only won't we beat a drowning dog, but we also get bit by it in return. That's what you get for being good.

"Kindness is just another name for useless," goes the proverb. This is perhaps a touch too harsh, but if you think it over carefully, the intention here is not to lead men into evil, but instead to distill a singular lesson learned from one's bitter experiences into a single homily. There are two possible explanations for the notion that we shouldn't beat a drowning dog: the first is that we're simply not strong enough to beat it; the second is that the analogy is incorrect. We can leave off discussion of the first reason for the moment; as for the second, there are once again two reasons that this might take place. The first is that we have confused someone who has fallen from high position with a drowning dog. The second is that we have mistakenly viewed those who have fallen from high positions as being all the same, drawing no distinctions between the good and the bad. The result is giving free rein to evil. If we look at the present situation, due to the political uncertainty, fortunes are forever rising and falling, like a revolving wheel. An official may have relied on his short-lived power and connections to commit just about any crime he pleased, but once he stumbles, he suddenly mewls for mercy. Even the honest folks who have suffered at his hands suddenly see him as a drowning dog, and not only do they refrain from beating him, they even begin to feel sorry for him. Imagining that justice has already been done and that chivalry is theirs to offer, they fail to realize that he's not really a drowning dog. He may be in the water now, but he's long ago prepared himself a den, laid in with all sorts of delicacies, and it's conveniently located in a foreign concession. Though at times the dog may appear to be injured, it's just a ruse. The dog pretends to limp to elicit sympathy, the better that it might escape into hiding in comfort. When the time comes, it will once again bite the hands of the honest folks who feed it, "throwing stones down a well" and stopping at nothing to get its way.[41] If we want to know the reason for this debacle, we need look no further than those honest folks who would not beat a drowning dog. To put it a bit harshly, it's a case of them digging their own graves, and it would be wrong for them to complain of their fate or blame others for what they have brought down upon themselves.

## VI. On Why We Cannot Yet Be Completely "Fair"

The benevolent will perhaps want to ask: "Does this mean that we don't want fair play at all?" I can provide an immediate reply: Of course we do, but it's still too early. This is a case of giving them a dose of their own medicine, and even if the benevolent aren't willing to take it, the prescription is easy enough to write out. Aren't our gentlemen, be they local or foreign, fond of saying that China is an exceptional case, with its own unique customs, to which foreign notions like freedom, equality, and the like, are inapplicable? I would have thought that "fair play" is another such notion. For if someone is not "fair" to you, but you are "fair" to him, you'll end up losing out all the same. Not only do you have to be fair and not expect to be treated fairly in return, you won't even have the chance to be unfair to someone else even if you wanted to. So if you want to be "fair," it's best to know your opponent ahead of time, and if he is undeserving of fairness, you can quite frankly drop all pretense of politeness. After all, it won't be too late to start talking "fair play" with one's opponent once he himself has started to play "fair."

It may seem like I'm advocating an ethical double standard, but it's really out of necessity. If we don't follow this path, there's no better way for China. China has all sorts of double standards: for masters and their slaves, for men and women. If we were to treat drowning dogs and drowning men exactly the same way, *that* would really be going too far, too quickly. It's like the case the gentlemen make of freedom and equality—they aren't necessarily bad, it's just not quite time yet for them in China. If anyone wants to put the spirit of fair play into practice here in China, then we should first wait until drowning dogs start to become more human. Of course, I don't mean to say that fair play cannot be put into practice in the present; it's just that, as previously mentioned, you need to know your opponent. There are different degrees of fairness, and exactly how fairness should be applied depends on the opponent. No matter how someone falls into the water, if he's a man, we should save him; if it's a dog, we should ignore it; if it's a bad dog, we should beat it. In a word, we need merely to "ally with the like-minded and attack those who are different from ourselves."[42]

We may put aside for the moment the maxims of those gentlemen whose hearts are full of naked self-interest but speak loudly of "justice in the public interest." Even the justice earnestly promoted in today's China by sincere people is powerless to save good folks and often ends up protecting the bad instead. When bad people take power and use that power to abuse good folks, no matter how loudly someone shouts out against the injustice, they will never listen to him. There is nothing he can do but shout as the good continue to suffer. But if for once the good gain a little ground, and it's time for the bad to finally fall into the water, those fine people sincerely interested in the "public interest" will begin to shout in protest: "Don't take revenge!" "Be kind!" "Don't fight evil with evil!" And this time, the shouts yield real results and are no longer just an empty clamor: for the good cannot help but agree, and the bad are spared. But having been spared, they merely congratulate themselves on their good fortune, and of course there's no question of repenting. In any case, they have long ago prepared their secret hideouts, and they are good at getting what they want, and so before long, they are back in power and going about their evil ways. When this happens, the upholders of the "public interest" raise another outcry, but this time no one is listening.

Nevertheless, the "extreme severity" and "overzealous haste" in pursuit of their goals on the part of the Qingliu reformers of the Eastern Han dynasty and the Donglin group in the Ming may indeed have undermined their own efforts. At least, this is the criticism most often rendered by commentators. Yet while the other side may dislike good folks, no one says anything about it. Without a fight to the finish between the forces of light and darkness, honest folks are liable to go on mistaking giving evil free rein for forgiveness and blindly appease evil men, and there will be no end to the current state of chaos.

## VII. On "Treating Them as They Treat Others"

Some Chinese believe in Chinese medicine and others in Western medicine, and these days in most cities you can find both types of doctors, so that people can take their pick. I think this is an excellent state of affairs. If we could apply this principle more generally, perhaps there would be fewer voices of complaint and all under heaven would settle into an orderly state of peace and prosperity. For instance, the most common form of courtesy in our Republic is to bow, but if someone were to disapprove of this, then he can kowtow all on his own instead. The old punishment of flaying is not part of the current legal code, but if someone happened to approve of corporeal punishment, there can be a special provision for flogging his bottom if he commits a crime. People now have bowls, chopsticks, and cooked food for their convenience, but if someone should yearn for the ancient ways before the discovery of fire, they can be treated to raw meat. We could build several thousand thatched huts, and move those esteemed gentlemen who so admire the age of the ancient sages Yao and Shun out of their big houses to live there; and people who oppose "material civilization," it goes without saying, should not be compelled to ride in motorcars. When all of this is done, those "who seek benevolence will have it, and nothing of which to make a plaint," and our ears should hear more sounds of peace and quiet.

But a pity that no one's willing to do this, and instead they measure others by their own standards, and so there is trouble under heaven. "Fair play" is especially flawed in this respect and can even become a real liability, in that it allows evil forces to take an unfair advantage. For instance, when Liu Baizhao beat up and evicted students of the Women's Normal College, there was not so much as a fart from the pages of *Contemporary Review*.[43] Yet as soon as the college resumed normalcy, Professor Chen Xiying then urged students to occupy the school buildings to prevent the resumption of classes: "If they are not willing to leave, what then? Surely you would not be comfortable removing their personal effects by force?" A precedent for beating, dragging, and forcibly removing students had already been set by Liu Baizhao. So what could explain their "discomfort" with these tactics now? I suppose they had gotten a whiff of the "fairness" wafting through the Women's Normal College.[44] Yet in the end, "fairness" once again became a liability, since it was ultimately exploited to protect the elect few who were following the lead of Zhang Shizhao.

## VIII. Conclusion

Some people may suspect that, with the things written above, I am stirring up trouble between the old and the new schools, or between different political factions, intensifying their enmity and sharpening their conflicts. But I daresay that those who oppose reform have never relaxed in their zeal to harm the reformers and have used the sharpest tools at their disposal to do so. Only the reformers continue to sleep and to dream, and to suffer for it. This is why there is no reform in China. From now on, we need to change our attitude and modify our tactics.

TRANSLATED BY ANDREW F. JONES

# Voiceless China

## 無聲的中國

### Presented at the Hong Kong YMCA, February 16 [1927]

I should first express my deep gratitude for such a large audience turning out in the pouring rain to hear this pointless and empty talk of mine.

The topic I am addressing today is "Voiceless China."

There is fighting going on in Zhejiang and Shaanxi, but we don't know whether the people in those places are laughing or crying. Hong Kong seems to be at peace, but outsiders don't know whether the Chinese people living here are contented or not either.

---

First published in a Hong Kong newspaper (name and date unknown) and then published in the supplement of Hankou *Central Daily News* (Zhongyang ribao) on March 23, 1927; later collected in *Three Leisures* (San xian ji, 1932). According to Lu Xun's diary, the speech was delivered on February 18 of that year. Lu Xun, *Lu Xun quanji* (Complete works of Lu Xun) (Beijing: Renmin wenxue, 2005), 4: 11–17.

Making one's ideas and feelings known to a broad audience requires writing, but as things stand now, most Chinese still aren't able to express themselves this way. This is no fault of ours, because our written script is a terrifying legacy passed down to us by our ancestors. Even after years of effort expended at learning it, it's still difficult to use properly. Because of its difficulty, many people don't even bother with it, to the point that some don't even know whether the character for their surname Zhang is written as 張 or 章 or simply don't know how to write it at all but can only say "Zhang." So although people can speak, only a few can hear and those far away have no idea what was said, so it is tantamount to being without a voice. Again, because writing is difficult, there are those who treasure it as if it were some sort of game. The various grammatical particles used in classical Chinese—the "zhi, hu, zhe, ye"—are understood by very few (though it actually isn't even clear whether these few truly understand them), but the vast majority of people don't understand them, so it is tantamount to being without a voice. The primary difference between the civilized and the barbarians is that the civilized have a system of writing and can use it to transmit ideas and feelings both to the masses and to posterity. So although China has a system of writing, it has now become irrelevant to the majority of the people since it uses a difficult to understand archaic language good only for expressing ancient and obsolete ideas. All the sounds in this language are outmoded and are thus tantamount to having none at all. People are therefore unable to understand one another and are like a big platter of loose sand.

It may be amusing to treat writing as an antique—the fewer the people who can recognize or understand it, the better. What, however, is the result? It is that we are no longer able to express what we wish to say. When we are harmed or insulted, we simply are unable to say the things that should be said. Take recent matters as examples: do we have any competent accounts of such significant events as the Sino-Japanese War, the Boxer Rebellion, or the Republican Revolution of 1911 or anything since? Since the founding of the Republic, no one has uttered a sound. On the other hand, there has been much discussion of China in foreign countries, but none of this has been in the voice of the Chinese; it has all been the voice of others.

This inability to speak was not as pronounced in the Ming dynasty; they were, comparatively speaking, more able to say things that needed to be said. But when the Manchus invaded China as an alien tribe, those who discussed history—events of the late Song dynasty in particular—were killed, and naturally, so were those who discussed current events. So by the time of the Qianlong period in the late eighteenth century, people no longer dared to express themselves in writing. Those we refer to as scholars had no choice but to sequester themselves and read the classics, work on the verification of ancient texts, or write essays in an archaic style that had nothing to do with current times. New ideas weren't permitted, either; if writers didn't imitate Han Yu, they imitated Su Shi.[45] It was, of course, quite all right for the likes of Han Yu and Su Shi to use their own styles to express what needed saying at the time. But we are not living in the Tang or Song dynasties, so how did we come to write in a style from a period utterly unrelated to our own? Even if done well, it is still the voice of the Tang and Song, the voice of Han Yu and Su Shi, and not our modern voice. Even down to the present, however, Chinese still play this old game. We have people, but no voices, and feel very lonely. Is it possible for people to go without a voice? If they don't have one, we can say they are dead. If we need to put it in more polite terms, we can say they have become dumb.

It will not be easy to revive China, which has gone without a voice for so many years; it will be like ordering a dead person: "Come back to life!" Although I don't really understand religion, I think that this would resemble what religions refer to as a "miracle."

The first experiment of this sort took place the year before the 1919 May Fourth movement when Mr. Hu Shi advocated a "literary revolution." I don't know if the word *revolution* as I use it here is something frightening or not, but in some places people become frightened as soon as they hear it. *Revolution* combined with *literary*, however, is not as frightening as *revolution* as in the French Revolution, since it simply means "renovation," and by substituting a word the phrase becomes quite mild; so let's just refer to it as the "literary renovation." There are a lot of tricks like this you can play with the Chinese language. There is nothing to be frightened about in the general meaning of this; it is merely to say: we no longer need bend all our efforts toward learning the language of ancient dead people; rather, we should speak the modern language of the living. We do not want to treat language as an antique, but rather write in an easy-to-understand vernacular. Literary renovation alone, however, is not enough; corrupt thinking can be expressed not only in classical Chinese, but in the vernacular as well. So, following that logic, there came along people advocating the renovation of thought. The result of renovating thought was the rise of a movement for social renovation. And once this movement was set in motion, it of course provoked an opposing reaction, which in turn led to struggles. . . .

In China, however, as soon as the call for literary renovation was uttered, there was an opposing reaction. But the vernacular gradually become popular and encountered few obstacles. Why was this? It was because at the time Mr. Qian Xuantong advocated the eradication of the Chinese script in favor of a Romanized alphabet. This was no more than a renovation in script and was thus nothing extraordinary, but when Chinese who were opposed to reform heard it, they thought it a true catastrophe; so they spared the relatively mild literary revolution and expended all their energy on condemning Qian Xuantong. The vernacular availed itself of this opportunity, with the unexpected result of reducing a great number of enemies, and was able to prevail without obstacles in its way.

The Chinese are by nature disposed to compromise and take the middle way. If, for example, you were to say that a room is too dark and needs a window installed, no one would agree to the proposal; but if you suggest tearing off the roof, they would opt for compromise and be willing to put in a window. Without a more extreme proposition, they are unwilling to undertake even moderate reform. The vernacular was able to come into general use at the time due only to the proposition of eradicating the Chinese script in favor of a Romanized alphabet.

In fact, the discussion over the merits and demerits of the classical and the vernacular should have ended long ago, but China is never willing to decide on things promptly, so there are still any number of pointless debates going on. There are those who say, for example, that classical Chinese can be understood in every province, whereas the vernacular differs from place to place and so people wouldn't be able to understand each other. But everyone knows that as soon as we have education and transportation improves, this will be taken care of, and by that time everyone will be able to understand the more readily comprehensible vernacular. As for the classical language, it is in no respect true that people of every province can understand it, because in each province there are very few who actually do understand it. There are also those who say that if we universally adopt the vernacular, people won't be able to read old books, and Chinese culture will meet its demise. In fact, though, there is no need at all for people to read old books even now, and even if there really are things of value in them, they can be translated into the vernacular, which eliminates the need for panic. There are also those who say that even foreigners translate Chinese works, evidence enough of their value, so why would we not read them? But everyone knows that for their own particular purposes foreigners have also translated the books of ancient Egypt as well as the myths of black Africans, so such translations cannot be considered matters that bring any particular glory. There has of late been another idea set forth, namely that it is the renovation of thought that is important, while the reform of writing is secondary. If, therefore, one uses an uncomplicated classical language to write essays conveying new thought, one will incur less opposition. This seems reasonable, but we know that those who refuse even to cut their fingernails will absolutely refuse to cut off their queues.

Because we speak an ancient language that no one understands and no one hears, we have become a platter of loose sand, each one of us no longer able to relate to the suffering of others. If we wish to revive ourselves, the first thing we must do is have young people stop speaking the language of Confucius, Mencius, Han Yu, and Liu Zongyuan. The times are different, and conditions have changed. Hong Kong in the era of Confucius was not like it is now, and we can no longer compose a "Treatise on Hong Kong" in a Confucian style; phrases like "Hark thou splendorous Hong Kong!" would be nothing more than a joke.

We need to speak a modern language of our own, to use a living vernacular to express our thoughts and feelings directly. This will, however, incur the ridicule of gentlemen of the older generation. They say that the vernacular is contemptible and without value; they say that the writings of the young are immature and risible. Just how many people in China can write the classical language? All the rest can only speak the vernacular, so does that mean that all these Chinese are contemptible and without value? As for being immature, this is nothing to be ashamed of, just as children have nothing to be ashamed of when compared to old people. The immature can grow up and become mature, and as long as they avoid senescence and corruption, they will be fine. Even a peasant woman would not be as stupid as to think that one cannot do anything before achieving maturity. When her child is learning to walk and falls down, she would never confine the child to bed and have him or her get up only when he or she has mastered the technique of walking.

Youth must first transform China into a China with a voice. They must speak boldly, move forward courageously, forget all considerations of personal advantage, push aside the ancients, and express their authentic feelings. Authenticity is of course not easy to achieve. It is, for instance, not easy to achieve an authentic manner. When I am speaking publicly, it is not my authentic manner, because when I speak to friends or to children it is not in this manner—but one may still speak with relative authenticity and in a relatively authentic voice. Only an authentic voice will be able to move the Chinese and the world's people; it is necessary to have an authentic voice so that we may live in the world with others.

Let us try to think about which peoples are without voice. Have we heard voices from Egypt? Have we heard the voices of Vietnam and Korea? Aside from Tagore, does India have any other voices?

From this point on, there are only two paths available to us: one is to cling to the classical language and die, and the other is to abandon the classical language and survive.

TRANSLATED BY THEODORE HUTERS

# The Old Tunes Are Finished

老調子已經唱完了

A speech given to the Hong Kong Youth Association, February 19, 1927

At first glance, my topic for today, which is "The Old Tunes Are Finished," might seem a bit strange, but in fact it's nothing of the sort.

Everything that's old, that's ancient, is over! And it should be this way. This kind of talk might disappoint many of our elders, but I've got no choice but to say it.

---

First published in *New Age* (Xin shidai), the literary supplement to the Guangzhou newspaper *National News* (Guomin xinwen), in March 1927 and then reprinted on May 11, 1927, in the Hankou newspaper *Central Daily News* (Zhongyang ribao). Later anthologized in *Supplement to the Collection of the Uncollected* (Ji wai ji shiyi, 1938). Lu Xun, *Lu Xun quanji* (Complete works of Lu Xun) (Beijing: Renmin wenxue, 2005), 7: 321–329.

Chinese people hold a set of contradictory ideas. We want our children and grandchildren to survive, but we also want to live long lives, to live forever; when we realize that all our methods are useless and that we are bound to die, then we hope that our corpses will never rot. But think about it—if nobody in the history of humanity had ever died, the face of the earth would be so densely packed with people that there wouldn't be any space to live in today. If all the corpses in the history of the human race had failed to rot, they would have long ago piled up higher than fish in a fish market. How would we find the space to dig wells or build houses? So what I think is that everything that's old, that's ancient, might just as well go happily to its death.

It's the same in literature. We're done singing everything that is old and ancient, or we soon will be. Russia provides the most recent example. During the reign of the tsars, many writers felt great empathy for the common people, and they cried out with bitter and mournful voices. Then later they saw that the common people had shortcomings, and they became disenchanted, so they were no longer able to sing like this, and no great works of literature appeared until after the revolution. Instead, there were just a few old-style writers who fled abroad and wrote a few pieces, none of which were particularly remarkable. This was because they had left their old surroundings and could no longer speak as they had in the past.

By this time, new voices should have appeared in their nation, but we haven't really heard them yet. I think in the future these voices will assuredly appear. This is because Russia is alive; although it's momentarily silent, its capacity for reform will certainly lead to the appearance of new voices.

And then there are a few countries in Europe and the Americas. Their art and literature had long been a bit old-fashioned, but during the Great War, a kind of war literature arose. When the war ended, the milieu also changed, and the old tunes could no longer be played, so those in the literary world today feel a bit lonely. We can't predict what the future may hold. But I believe that it, too, will definitely include new voices.

Now let's think about how our China operates. China's literary writing is the most unchanging, its tunes are the oldest and the ideas within them the most ancient. The strange thing about this, though, is that China is different from other countries: nobody's stopped singing those old tunes.

How can this be? Some people say that China has a "special national condition."[46] Whether China is "special" in this way, I don't know, but I've heard it said that this is how Chinese people are. If this kind of talk is true, then in my eyes there are probably two ways that China is special.

First, it is because the Chinese have no memory, and because they have no memory, the words they heard yesterday are forgotten today. When they hear them again tomorrow, they'll still find them fresh and new. Our actions are also like this: what you did wrong yesterday is forgotten today, and when you do it again tomorrow, it'll still be the old tune "after the ancient fashion."[47]

Second is that although as individuals we have not yet finished singing the old songs, the nation has been destroyed several times. How can this be? I think that after a certain amount of time has passed, it's right to stop singing all the old-fashioned songs. There comes a time when people with consciences and those who are awakened naturally understand that they shouldn't sing the old tunes anymore, that they should be discarded. The average self-centered person, though, can't bear allowing the masses to act as subjects. Instead, they scheme purely in pursuit of their own interests, such that they never tire of singing their own old tunes, even though the nation's song is finished.

The scholars of the Song dynasty taught Neo-Confucianism and respected Confucius, churning out thousands of completely indistinguishable essays. Although there were a few innovators among them, like Wang Anshi and others who put a new legal code into place, they never gained wide acceptance and therefore failed. After them, everyone started singing the old songs again, songs that had nothing to do with society, and they did it right up until the dynasty was destroyed.

When the Song dynasty had sung its last, the Mongols came in to rule as emperors—the Yuan dynasty. The old tunes of the Song should have been finished along with the dynasty itself, but no. Though the Yuan originally looked down on the Chinese, they later came to feel that our old tunes were actually quite novel, and they slowly became envious. So the Yuan started singing our old tunes along with us, right up until their dynasty was destroyed.

This was when the Ming emperor Taizu appeared on the scene. At this point, the old tunes of the Yuan should have been done with, but they weren't done yet. Taizu felt they still had a bit of charm, and so he again instructed everyone to keep singing them. You had your eight-legged essay, your study of the Way, things that didn't have any relevance to society or common people. They walked right down that old road of the past, right up until the Ming was destroyed.

The Qing rulers were also foreigners. China's old songs, in the eyes of these newly arrived foreign masters, again seemed fresh, and so they were sung yet again. Still with the eight-legged essay, the imperial examination, writings in ancient Chinese, readings in ancient books! As we all know, though, we're now sixteen years since the end of the Qing, which in its last years became ever so slightly awakened and considered studying new methods from abroad as remedies, but it was already too late: time was up.

The old songs have made China fall silent many times, and yet somehow they are still sung. This has provoked a bit of discussion. Some people say, "It's obvious that China's old songs are truly excellent, and there's no harm in continuing to sing them. Consider the Mongols of the Yuan, the Manchus of the Qing. Didn't we assimilate them all? From this perspective, in the future we will be able to assimilate any country in exactly this way." So in the past, our China was like a person with a communicable disease: we'd gotten sick, but we had the ability to transmit our disease into the bodies of others. This is actually quite a special talent.

Little do we know how terribly mistaken this attitude is in today's society. Why was it that we could assimilate the Mongols and the Manchus? It was because their culture was far beneath our own. But if we compare other kinds of cultures against ours to see which is more advanced, the results will be very different. If they're smarter than we are, then in this case we are not only powerless to assimilate them, but they'll also exploit our corrupt culture in order to rule over our corrupt populace. They don't love the Chinese people in the least, so of course they'll allow you to continue being corrupt. These days I hear that there are a lot of people from abroad who respect our ancient culture. But how can it be true respect? It's exploitation!

Long ago there was a Western country whose name I can't remember that wanted to build a railroad in Africa. The stubborn African locals strongly opposed it, so the Westerners used the locals' own myths to cheat them. They said, "Long ago you had a deity among you who built a bridge from earth to the heavens. The railroad we're building now has the same basic intent as that of your ancient sage." The Africans were pleased and impressed, and the railroad was built. China has always excluded outsiders, but now there are those who are gradually coming in and singing the old songs, even saying "Confucius also said that 'If the Way were proved unviable, I would put to sea on a raft . . .' so outsiders are actually quite a good thing." The foreigners also say that "the words of your sages are really not so bad."

If things continue in this way, what are China's prospects? I'm not sure about other places, so I can only use Shanghai as an analogy. Shanghai: where the group with the most power is made up of foreigners, surrounded by a group of Chinese businessmen and so-called scholars, while outside those social circles are a lot of poor and suffering Chinese, the lowest level of slaves. In the future, if we want to keep singing the old tunes, then the situation in Shanghai will spread to the whole country, and the sufferers will multiply. Our age is different from the age of the Yuan and the Qing, when we could count on the old tunes singing themselves silent. Now we can only sing ourselves out of existence. Because today's foreigners aren't like the Mongols or the Manchus—their culture is not in the least beneath ours.

So, what do we do? I think the only solution is to immediately get rid of the old songs. Old literature, old thinking, they're all already irrelevant to today's society. Confucius wandered among the warring states in an oxcart; do we still ride in oxcarts? During the times of Yao and Shun, food was eaten from mud bowls. What do we use now? For those born into modern times, it's completely useless to hold tight onto ancient books.

However, some scholars say, when we read these ancient things, they don't seem to do any particular harm to China, so why must we be so absolute in tossing them out? They're right—but this is exactly the reason these things are so fearsome. If we thought of them as harmful, we would be alert to their danger, and it's exactly because we believe them to be harmless that we can never discern the deadliness of their disease. These books are "soft knives." The name "soft knife" wasn't invented by me: in the Ming dynasty a scholar named Jia Fuxi sang a drum ballad in which he talked about King Zhou of the Shang.[48] It went like this: "Several years after his head had been cut off by a soft household knife, he didn't feel like he was dead; only when they hung the white banner did he finally realize that his fate was bleak."[49] Our old songs are exactly this kind of soft knife.

If China had been sliced apart by somebody's steel sword, it would hurt, but we still might figure out some way forward; with a soft knife, we've truly been "decapitated without realizing that we're dead," and it's all over for us.

China has been attacked many times by people using various weapons. For example, the Mongols and Manchus used the bow and arrow, while the people of other countries used guns and cannons. By the time of the last few attacks with guns and cannons, I had already come into this world, though I was still young. I seem to remember people at that time still feeling a few prickles of pain and having thoughts about resisting, about reforming. When they attacked us with guns and cannons, I heard that it was because we were barbarians; today, by contrast, we are not often attacked with guns and cannons, probably because we are so cultured. There are indeed those who like to say that China's culture is terrific, that we must preserve it. Their evidence is that foreigners also admire it. This is the soft knife. If it were a steel sword, we could feel it, so the tactic has changed to the soft knife. I believe that the moment of being called upon to sing ourselves out of existence has already arrived.

I don't have any idea where Chinese culture resides. The things we call culture, what relationship do they have to the common people, and of what benefit are they? Recently foreigners have also been saying that Chinese ceremonies are good and that Chinese banquets are good. Chinese people parrot all this. But what do these matters have to do with the common people? The cart driver has no money to make ceremonial robes, and the best food available to most peasants in the north is grain. What do these things have to do with one another?

Chinese culture is a culture of servitude to the master. It trades on the suffering of many people. Whether they are Chinese or foreigners, all those who praise Chinese culture are simply seeing themselves in the role of the master.

In the past, most books written by foreigners hurled abuse at China's corruption; now they're not quite so abusive; indeed, they even praise Chinese culture. I often hear them say, "I lived quite the comfortable life in China!"

This is evidence that the Chinese people are gradually giving our own happiness to the foreigners to enjoy. The more they praise it, the deeper the suffering of our China will be!

That is to say: to preserve ancient culture is to force Chinese people to forever serve as raw material for masters and to make them suffer and suffer. Although the well-to-do are affluent right now, their children and grandchildren won't be able to escape. I once wrote a short essay, the gist of which is this: "Most of those who praise ancient Chinese culture are rich people who live in the foreign concessions or in secure areas. Because they have money and haven't suffered from the civil war, they're able to utter such praise. They can't imagine that in the future their children and grandchildren's professions will be even lower than that of today's unfortunates, and the mine pits they'll have to dig will be much deeper. . . ."[50] This means that in the future they'll be poor too, just a little bit later. But as for the descendants of the unfortunate ones who were poor before, who dug the shallow pits, they will have to dig deeper. Nobody paid any attention to my words. They still sing the old song, still sing it in the foreign concessions and abroad. But from this day forward we can't do as we did in the Yuan and Qing dynasties: we can't sing other people silent. We can only sing until we ourselves are done for.

What can we do about it, though? First, I think we must ask them to walk out of their foreign offices, their bedrooms, and their studies and look at things around them, look at society and the world. Then they should think: once they come up with something to do, they should do it. "It's dangerous to walk out your front door"—naturally, this is what gentlemen who sing the old songs will say. But it is always a bit dangerous to be a human being. If hiding in your room meant you'd live a long life for sure, then we should see a lot of old men with white beards. But how many have we met? Though their lives aren't dangerous, these people also often die young, and they die in a muddled state.

If you want to avoid danger, I've found a truly suitable place to do it: jail. In jail, people aren't looking to cause any further trouble or to commit more crimes; the firefighting equipment is always fully stocked, so there's no need to fear fire; you don't fear robbery, because no strong-arm bandit has ever gone to prison to commit theft. Imprisonment is really the safest and most secure kind of life.

However, life in prison lacks one thing: freedom. If you want security, then you'll have no freedom; if you want freedom, you'll always have to face some danger. There are only these two paths. It is crystal clear which of them is the better one, and you don't need to listen to me say it.

Now I would like to express my gratitude for your generosity in coming here today.

TRANSLATED BY NICK ADMUSSEN

# Tablet

扁

A frightening development in the Chinese literary scene is the widespread importation of terms with no explanations of what these terms mean.

So people interpret them as they please. A work mostly about oneself is referred to as "expressionism"; a work mostly about others is "realism"; writing poetry after seeing a woman's bare calf is "romanticism"; banning poems written after seeing a woman's bare calf is "classicism"; "a head drops down from the sky, on top of the head is an ox, oh, blue thunderbolts at sea" . . . this is futurism . . . etc.

And still more discussions ensue from all this. This "ism" is good, that "ism" is bad . . . etc.

For a time there was a running joke in the countryside. Two nearsighted men wanted to compare whose vision was better, but had no means of verification. So they arranged to go to the Temple of Guandi to look at the tablet newly hung that day. They each went to the painter ahead of time to find out what characters had been written on the tablet. But each obtained different information. The one who knew of the large characters refused to give in and started wrangling, claiming that the other, who had seen the small characters, was lying. Again they had no means of verification, so they asked

---

First published in volume 4, issue 17, in the "Random Thoughts" column in *Threads of Talk* (*Yusi*) on April 23, 1928, and later anthologized in *Three Leisures* (*San xian ji*, 1932). Lu Xun, *Lu Xun quanji* (Complete works of Lu Xun) (Beijing: Renmin wenxue, 2005), 4: 88–89.

a passerby. The person took a glance and replied: "there's nothing there, the tablet hasn't been hung yet."

I feel that before literary critics compare visions, a tablet must first be hung. Such futile wrangling, no one other than the two parties involved can understand the point.

April 10, 1928

TRANSLATED BY EILEEN J. CHENG

# The Evolution of Men

男人的進化

To say that the copulation of birds and beasts is a kind of romantic love is a bit blasphemous. However, animals have sex lives, too: this fact is incontrovertible. During their spring rut, the female and the male come together, and inevitably they get all lovey-dovey and have a go at it. It's also true that sometimes a female puts on a little show, running a couple of steps away and then turning back to look, even calling out a few times, right up until she's successfully "shacked up." Although there are many types of animals, and although their methods of "romance" are complex, one thing is true without a doubt: the male has no guaranteed privileges.

That humans are the cleverest of all creations is, first of all, a credit to the capabilities of men. In the beginning, everything was carelessly thrown together, but because children "knew their mothers and not their fathers," there was a period of time when women ruled. Our ancestral foremothers from that time were probably much more awe-inspiring than the clan patriarchs that followed. Who knows what happened next—women hit a streak of truly bad luck. Their necks, hands, and feet all got locked up in chains, encircled by rings and hoops—although over the course of thousands of years, these changed into gold and silver and were inlaid with diamonds and

---

First published in the "Free Talk" (Ziyou tan) column of *Shen bao* on September 16, 1933, under the pen name Lü Sun and later anthologized in *Quasi Discourses on the Wind and Moon* (Zhun feng yue tan, 1934). Lu Xun, *Lu Xun quanji* (Complete works of Lu Xun) (Beijing: Renmin wenxue, 2005), 5: 300–302.

pearls. Still, though, these necklaces, bracelets, and rings remain symbols of female slavery. Now that women have become slaves, men no longer need to solicit their consent before "loving" them. After ancient tribal warfare, captives would be made into slaves, and the female captives would be raped. Back then, it's likely that the spring rut was canceled, as men could rape female captives and slaves whenever and wherever they pleased. The way that today's bullies and bandits dehumanize women is actually a faithful inheritance of the warrior code of the tribal headman.

Although humans' ability to rape is one "evolutionary" step past the ability of beasts, it is, however, only halfway to civilization. Think about it—women wailing and screaming, wriggling and struggling with their hands and feet, how much fun is that? After the appearance of the dearly beloved thing called money, the evolution of men progressed to an enviable degree. Everything under heaven can be bought and sold, and sex is naturally no exception. For a few coins of dirty money, a man can obtain anything he wants from the body of a woman. Plus, he can tell her this: I'm certainly not raping you, you willingly went along, if you're willing to take the money then you need to do this and that, you've got to be docile and obedient, we're engaging in fair trade! After he violates her, he even wants her to say, "Thank you, young master." Could a beast get away with this? Prostitution is therefore a sign of a rather advanced stage in male evolution.

At the same time, though, old-style marriage that is ordered by parents and arranged by matchmakers is even cleverer than prostitution. Under this system, men obtain a perpetual, lifelong piece of living property. When the bride is placed into the bed of the groom, she has only her duty and lacks even the freedom to negotiate a price, to say nothing of love. Whether you're in love or not, in the name of the duke of Zhou and the sage Confucius, you must stay faithful all your life, you must protect your chastity. The man can use her at his whim, but she must comply with the code of the Confucian sages, even though "evil thoughts appearing only in the mind must still be judged as criminal fornication."[51] If a male dog used such an ingenious and severe tactic against a female dog, the female would certainly jump the fence in panic. Humans, by contrast, know only how to jump into wells and assume the roles of chaste widows, honored virgins, or martyrs to virtue. The evolutionary significance of arranged marriages should be obvious to those who think about it.

Some men are able to use the "most scientific" theories to induce women to happily stay faithful unto death; they believe that sexual desire is itself bestial, and should not be a fundamental precondition for romantic love. They've therefore invented "scientific chastity"[52]—this is of course the pinnacle of the evolution of civilization.

Alas, this is how humans—men—differ from the beasts!

Author's note: this is an essay in defense of traditional values.

September 3

TRANSLATED BY NICK ADMUSSEN

# Thinking of the Past Again

## 重三感舊

I'd like to say a few words in praise of some men of the past, though perhaps not out of an "infatuation with dead bones."[53]

What I mean by men of the past are those who were known as the "new clique" at the end of the reign of Emperor Guangxu and later known as "the old new clique" in the early years of the Republic.[54] Stunned by the 1895 defeat, they wanted "reform."[55] Even middle-aged men in their thirties and forties started to read *On Learning Mathematics* and *Principles of Chemistry*.[56] Trying to learn English or Japanese, they recited their lessons with stiff tongues and were not ashamed of their weird intonations. Their goal was to read "foreign books," and the reason they wanted to do so was because that would help make China "wealthy and powerful." At stalls that sell used books, one can still find volumes from the "Wealth and Power" series, the products of a historical moment, just like today's *Dictionary of Descriptive*

First published in the "Free Talk" (Ziyou tan) column of *Shen bao* on October 6, 1933, under the pseudonym Feng Zhiyu and later anthologized in *Quasi Discourses on the Wind and Moon* (Zhun feng yue tan, 1934) with a subtitle added: "1933 Recalling the Last Years of the Guangxu Reign." The Emperor Guangxu reigned between 1875 and 1908. Lu Xun, *Lu Xun quanji* (Complete works of Lu Xun) (Beijing: Renmin wenxue, 2005), 5: 342–345.

*Phrases* and *Basic English*. Even Zhang Zhidong, who came from the tradition of the eight-legged essay, made sure to incorporate a good many translated books in the *Guidebook to Bibliography*, which he asked Miao Quansun to compose for him.[57] From this, one can get a sense of just how powerful the tide of "reform" was then.

But now there is a different phenomenon. There are some new young men whose experience is just the opposite of "the old new clique." Although they haven't been poisoned by the eight-legged essays, graduated from new schools, and aren't experts in the Chinese classics, they have now turned to studying the ancient seal script and composing song lyrics, advising others to read such books as *Zhuangzi* and *Selections of Refined Literature* (Wen xuan).[58] They make their own hand-printed stationery and arrange their modern poems in regulated squares.[59] But for their penchant for making modern verse, they are no different from the literati of the early Guangxu reign. The only difference is that they have no queues and sometimes wear Western suits.

These days, we often hear that "old bottles cannot hold new wine."[60] This isn't, in fact, true. Old bottles can hold new wine, just as new bottles can hold old wine. If you have any doubts, try switching a bottle of Wujiapi with a bottle of brandy—the Wujiapi in a brandy bottle is still Wujiapi.[61] This simple experiment shows that old tune patterns like "Wugeng diao" and "Zuan shizi" can indeed be fitted with new content;[62] but even more, it confirms that the "Tongcheng lackeys" and "Metaphysics evildoers" can also inhabit the bodies of modern youths.[63]

Although people of "the old new clique" were limited in their knowledge, they had a goal: to make China wealthy and powerful. And so they were determined and pragmatic. Although they had a funny accent when they spoke in foreign tongues, they had a goal: to find the way to wealth and power. And so they were serious and passionate. After the spread of anti-Manchu ideas, many became revolutionaries, because they still wanted China to become wealthy and powerful; they believed that the first step to accomplishing this was to expel the Manchus.

Expelling the Manchus has long since been accomplished, and the May Fourth movement has long since passed. So now we have the seal script, the song lyric, *Zhuangzi*, *Selections of Refined Literature*, antique stationery, and regulated modern poetry. For now we have a new goal: to establish a place for ourselves in the world with our "ancient culture." If indeed we can really establish a foothold for ourselves in this way, then we would have added a new example of "the survival of the fittest."

October 1

TRANSLATED BY HU YING

# Curiosities

奇怪

Were it not for the fact that they appear in the historical record, there are many things in this world that even geniuses would be unable to imagine. There is an African tribe among which the taboos regarding the sexes are especially strict. If a man encounters his mother-in-law, he must immediately prostrate himself on the ground. Not only that, he must also bury his face in the dirt as well. Even the ancestors of our propriety-bound land who proclaimed that "boys and girls may no longer sit on the same mat from the age of seven"[64] don't come anywhere close to matching them in this regard.

What our ancestors prescribed regarding the segregation of the sexes is rather dimwitted by comparison; that we are unable to escape our ancestors' strictures shows how even more dim-witted we are. No integrated swimming, no integrated walking, no integrated dining, no integrated acting in films—these are simply variations of the old taboo against men and women sitting together. But even at its height such dimwittedness fails to consider that men and women still breathe the same air. The air that a man exhales out his nostrils is inhaled through that woman's nostrils. This must surely unleash chaos in heaven and earth, and it is far more serious a problem than the

First published in *China Daily* (Zhonghua ribao) on August 17, 1934, and later anthologized in *Fringed Literature* (Huabian wenxue, 1936). Lu Xun mocks the Nationalist government's efforts to promulgate ordinances forbidding the mixing of the sexes in public places. Lu Xun, *Lu Xun quanji* (Complete works of Lu Xun) (Beijing: Renmin wenxue, 2005), 5: 571–573.

ocean's waters merely touching the skin of both male and female swimmers. There will never be a clear division between the sexes if we do not devise a solution to this grave problem.

I believe we have no choice but to adopt Western methods. While Western methods do not stem from our native traditions, they can still be of benefit to our native culture. For example, while the wireless is a modern invention, we can still hear Buddhist monks chanting through the morning broadcasts—not at all a bad thing. While cars are foreign imports, we can still ride them to our mahjong games; you can get there far quicker than wasting half the day in a palanquin and play a couple of extra rounds. By the same token, we can use hygienic masks to prevent men and women from breathing the same air. Each person can breathe oxygen directly into their nostrils through a tube attached to a canister on his or her back. Moreover, the masks will prevent men and women from revealing their faces and can also be used in air raid drills. This is a clear case of using "Chinese learning for the essence, Western learning for practical application."[65] The veil that Turkish women before Atatürk had to wear does not come anywhere close to matching this in effectiveness.

If we had someone like the Englishman Jonathan Swift to author a satirical novel similar to *Gulliver's Travels*, he might describe his arrival in a civilized nation in the twentieth century where he observed inhabitants burning incense and worshiping dragons, praying for rain, admiring fat ladies, and forbidding the killing of turtles.[66] Another group of people might be assiduously researching the dance customs of ancient times, promoting the segregation of the sexes, and forbidding women from exposing their legs.[67] People from distant countries or some future time would likely think that these occurrences are nothing more than the author's tall tales conjured at whim to irritate those who displeased him.

But in actuality these are all facts. If they did not exist in reality, then it is unlikely that any genius writer, no matter how sardonic his wit, could have ever conjured them up. No hallucination could be so marvelous. So when people happen upon such things, they immediately declare them to be "curiosities."

August 14

TRANSLATED BY ROY BING CHAN

# Confucius in Modern China

## 在現代中國的孔夫子

It was reported in a recent Shanghai paper that to mark the occasion of the completion of a temple to Confucius in Yushima, Japan, General He Jian, Governor of Hunan Province, has donated a hitherto jealously treasured portrait of Confucius.[68] One has to point out that the Chinese man in the street has practically no idea what Confucius looked like. From time immemorial, every county without exception has had a Confucian temple or, as it is known, a Temple of Culture, but they have hardly ever contained a likeness of the sage. Whenever portraits or statues of venerable personages are made, the rule is that they should be made to look very grand, but when it comes to the most venerable personages, saintly people like Confucius, it would seem that even images are a form of profanation, and it is really better to do without them. As a matter of fact, this is not unreasonable. Confucius left behind no photograph of himself, so naturally we cannot know his true appearance: though in the literature there are references to it, they may be just bunkum. If a figure were to be sculpted from scratch, then one would have even less confidence in it, as it would have no other basis than the unfettered imagination of the sculptor. This being so, Confucians are in the end thrown back on adopting the attitude of Ibsen's Brand: "All or nothing."

Still if we are talking about portraits, those may indeed be occasionally encountered. I have seen three such: the first was an illustration in *Sayings of the Kong Family*;[69] the second was a frontispiece to *The China Discussion*, published by Liang Qichao in Yokohama after he took refuge in Japan and imported back into China;[70] and another was a relief of Confucius meeting Laozi carved on a Han dynasty tomb. As regards the impression I got of Confucius's appearance from these pictures, it was that this gentleman was a very thin old codger who wore a long gown with loose sleeves and had a

This essay was originally composed in Japanese for publication in the June 1935 edition of *Kaizo* magazine. It was translated into Chinese by Yiguang and appeared in *Zawen* in July. This translation is from the version revised by the author that was printed in volume 2 of *Essays from the Semi-Concessions, Volume Two* (Qiejie ting zawen er ji, 1935). Lu Xun, *Lu Xun quanji* (Complete works of Lu Xun) (Beijing: Renmin wenxue, 2005), 6: 324–333.

sword stuck in his belt, or a staff under his arm, but had never a trace of a smile and was extremely intimidating. Seated at his feet one would have had to have kept one's back as straight as a ramrod; after a couple of hours the pain in one's joints would have been killing, and any ordinary person could hardly have been anything other than desperate in his desire for deliverance.

Afterward, I went traveling in Shandong. As I was suffering misery from the bumpiness of the roads, our Confucius suddenly came into my mind. At the thought of the Sage wearing his sanctimonious expression and sitting in olden days in a rudimentary cart, jolting and lurching along as he hurried about his business thereabouts, I was struck by the comicality of it. Naturally, this feeling was not a proper one; to put it bluntly, it was nigh on irreverent. Had I been a follower of Confucius, I suppose it should never have occurred to me, but at that time there were lots of young people who were of the same impertinent mind as myself.

I came into the world in the last years of the Qing dynasty, when Confucius had already acquired the frighteningly imposing title of Perfect and Saintly King of Letters: needless to say, this was an age when the Saintly Way held sway over the whole country. The government required that all educated people should study certain books, that is the Four Books and Five Classics; should abide by a certain exegesis of them; should write a certain kind of composition, that is the so-called "eight-legged essay"; and should produce a certain kind of disquisition. However, these Confucians, all stamped in the same mold, while very much at home with a square world, were quite at sea with a round one; consequently, when they waged war against France and England, countries that went unrecorded in the Four Books, they were defeated. I don't know if it was because they thought that to die in the service of Confucius was not as masterly a strategy as self-preservation, or what, but the long and the short of it is that this government and these bureaucrats who were so dead set on venerating Confucius were the first to break ranks. Out of government funds they paid for heaps of books of the foreign devils to be translated. Such scientific classics as Herschel's *Outlines of Astronomy*, Lyell's *Principles of Geology*, and Dana's *Manual of Mineralogy* still survive as relics of that era: from time to time they may be found lying around in some second-hand bookshop.

However, there was bound to be a reaction. Grand Secretary Xu Tong, described as the epitome and apostle of Confucianism at the end of the Qing dynasty, emerged. His dismissal of mathematics as the learning of the foreign devils was not the worst of it: though he acknowledged that there were states like France and England on earth, he adamantly refused to believe in the existence of Spain and Portugal, maintaining that these were countries dreamed up by France and England out of embarrassment at their own appetite for spoils. He was also a covert instigator and director of the famous Boxer Rebellion in 1900. But the Boxers were completely routed, and Xu Tong committed suicide. The government then once more took the view that there was quite a lot in the politics, law, learning, and skills of foreign countries. It was at that time that I had the yearning to go to Japan to study. This objective attained, the place where I started my schooling was the Kobun Academy in Tokyo founded by Mr. Kano.[71] There Mr. Mitsu Rikitaro taught me that water was made up of oxygen and hydrogen, and Mr. Yamauchi taught me that there was somewhere inside a shell something called a "mantle." Then it happened one day that the dean of students, Mr. Okubo, gathered everyone together and said: "As you are all disciples of Confucius, today you shall go and make your obeisances at the Confucian temple in Ochanomizu."[72] To this day I still remember thinking to myself then that it was precisely because I despaired of Confucius and his disciples that I came to Japan; was I supposed to bow down all over again? For a while I was quite perturbed. I think I was far from the only one who had this feeling.

But Confucius's being without honor in his own country did not begin in the twentieth century. Mencius judged him "the sage whose actions were timely."[73] There is really no other way of translating this into present-day language except as "fashionable guru." From his own point of view, this is no doubt a harmless honorific, though as a title it is not a wholly welcome one. But perhaps it was not like this in reality. Confucius's establishment as a "fashionable guru" was something that happened after his death; in his lifetime, he had a pretty rough ride. Always running from pillar to post, he did once achieve eminence as commissioner of police, but in no time he was out in the cold again and unemployed. Furthermore, he was despised by the high and mighty ministers, ridiculed by the common folk, even menaced by a pack of ruffians; and his belly went empty. Though he collected three thousand disciples, only seventy-two were of any use, and there was only one of them he could really trust. One day Confucius cried out in exasperation: "If the Way were proved unviable, and I were to put to sea on a raft, I suspect only Zilu would be with me."[74] From this forlorn conclusion we may gather that such was the case. Yet this same Zilu later on had his hat string cut in a fight for his life, and being the estimable Zilu that he was, still mindful even at this pass of the precept learned from Confucius, he declared, "The gentleman does not doff his cap when he meets his end,"[75] and as he set about retying his hatstring, he was chopped up into little pieces. At the loss of this one and only trustworthy disciple, Confucius was naturally grief-stricken; it is said that when he got the news, he ordered that the mincemeat in the kitchen be thrown away.[76]

I think one can fairly say that Confucius's fortune after his death was somewhat better. As his tiresome nagging was buried with him, all kinds of wielders of power used all kinds of whitening cosmetics to make him up, and raised him all the way to awesome heights. But compare him with the later import, Sakyamuni, and you can't help being sorry for him. True, every county had its Temple of the Sage, or Temple of Culture, as we have said, but what cheerless and depressing places they are: the average commoner would never dream of offering prayers there; if he went anywhere, it would be to the Buddhist temple or some local shrine. If you asked the ordinary person who Confucius was, he would naturally answer that he was a sage, but in that way he would only be acting as a gramophone for the wielders of power. The ordinary person also treasures the written word, but that is because of the superstition that the Thunder God would strike him dead if he didn't. Admittedly, the Temple of Confucius in Nanjing is a very lively place, but that's because of its other attractions—the entertainers and teahouses. Though Mencius said turbulent ministers and treacherous sons were sore afraid when Confucius wrote *The Spring and Autumn Annals*,[77] nowadays practically no one could tell you the names of those turbulent ministers and treacherous sons who fell to that verbal foray. Mention of "turbulent ministers and treacherous sons" would probably suggest Cao Cao to most people, but that view of him was formed by anonymous authors of novels and plays, not by the sage.

To sum up, Confucius owes his exalted position in China to the wielders of power. He is the sage of the wielders of power or those who would be wielders of power; it has nothing to do with the mass of common people. But with regard to the Temples of the Sage, the enthusiasm of the wielders of power has been a passing one. As they already had other aims in mind when they did reverence to the sage, once the aims were attained this instrument ceased to be useful, and if they were not attained it was even less useful. Thirty or forty years ago, those intent on achieving power—that is, those who wanted to become officials—all studied the Four Books and Five Classics and wrote "eight-legged essays." A separate few gave these books and compositions the general name of "bricks to bang at the door." That is to say, as soon as success in the examination for civil officials was gained, from that moment these things were forgotten, just like the brick that is used to bang on the door: when the door is opened, the brick is thrown away. In fact from the time he died and ever after, old Confucius served this office of "bricks to bang on the door."

A look at some recent examples makes the case even more apparent. From the beginning of the twentieth century, Confucius's fortune had been very bad, but in Yuan Shikai's time he was remembered again: not only were the sacrifices restored, weird sacrificial robes were also created for those offering the sacrifices.[78] What was supposed to follow these exercises was the revival of monarchy. However, in the end that door resisted banging, and Yuan died on the outside. He left behind the Northern Warlords. When they felt they were nearing the end of their road, they used this brick to bang on other doors to fortune. Entrenched in Jiangsu and Zhejiang, General Sun Chuanfang, who slaughtered ordinary civilians by the roadside without a second thought, restored the "arrow tossing" ceremony.[79] Holed up in Shandong, General Zhang Zongchang, who couldn't even count the money or soldiers or concubines he had, for his part printed the Thirteen Classics;[80] and looking on Confucianism as something akin to syphilis that can be transmitted through physical relations, he made one or other descendant of Confucius his son-in-law. Still the door to fortune opened to neither of them.

All three used Confucius as a brick, but times had changed and they failed conspicuously. Not only did they meet with failure themselves, indeed they also reduced Confucius to an even sorrier state. The perversity of these barely literate characters holding forth on the Thirteen Classics and the like, people found a joke; the blatant discrepancy between their deeds and words, people viewed with greater loathing. Revulsion for the monk leads to distaste for the habit, and the exploitation of Confucius as an instrument to gain a certain end becoming once more transparently obvious, the desire to dethrone him grew the more potent. Therefore, when Confucius is dressed in perfect dignity, articles and works exposing his flaws are bound to appear. Confucius though he be, he must have his flaws. In normal times no one would pay them any heed, because a sage is still a man, and as such they may be forgiven him. Yet if the disciples of the Sage come forth and start prating, telling us that the Sage was this and was that, and therefore you must be likewise, people will not be able to keep from laughing out loud. Five or six years ago, the staging of the play *Confucius Saw Nancy* caused some trouble.[81] In that play, Confucius appears on stage in person: viewed as a sage, one must admit that in some respects he is somewhat lacking in gravity and rather slow-witted, but seen as a human being he is actually a likeable sort of fellow. Nevertheless, the descendants of the Sage got very hot under the collar and took the dispute right up to the courts, the reason being that the place where the play was put on happened to be Confucius's birthplace. There the descendants of the Sage had multiplied exceedingly, forming a privileged class that would make Sakyamuni and Socrates blush from inferiority. However, that might be precisely the reason why the local youths who were not descendants of Confucius were driven to put on *Confucius Saw Nancy*.

The mass of ordinary folk in China, especially the so-called "ignorant commoners," may call Confucius a sage, but they do not believe he is a sage. They show respect for him, but do not feel close to him. I think, though, there is no one in the world for understanding Confucius like the ignorant Chinese commoners. True, Confucius did devise an outstanding scheme for ruling the state, but that was a scheme made in the interests of those who ruled the masses—that is, those who wielded power; it gave no thought to the interests of the masses themselves. This is summed up in the sentence "The rites do not extend to the common people."[82] That he became the sage of the wielders of power, and finally "a brick for banging on doors," should give Confucius no grounds for complaint. One cannot say he had nothing to do with the masses, but I would have thought that to say he was in no way close to the masses would have been the politest way of putting it. It is only natural that they should not approach the wholly unapproachable Sage. You can put the matter to the test any time you like; try going barefoot and in rags into the Grand Hall of a Confucian temple to look around; in just the same way as if you had strayed into a posh Shanghai cinema or the first-class compartment of a tram, I'm afraid in no time at all you'd be out on your neck. Everyone knows that is the domain of the big shots: the masses may be "ignorant," but they aren't ignorant to that extent.

April 29, 1935

TRANSLATED BY DAVID E. POLLARD

# SECTION IV

*On Art and Literature*

# Impromptu Reflections No. 43

## 隨感錄四十三

Progressive Artists—this is what I demand of the Chinese art world.

Artists should, of course, be highly skilled technically, but even more importantly, they ought to be noble in character and possess progressive ideas. Their works may appear on the surface to be a mere painting or sculpture, but they are, in fact, expressions of the artist's thought and character. When we look at the works, we not only like and delight in them, but, more importantly, we are moved and affected spiritually.

The artists we need are enlightened ones who can lead us forward, not leaders of a thuggish "citizen corps."[1] The works of art we need are specimens reflecting the highest intellect of the Chinese people, not the mediocrity of subpar thinking.

I recently came across "Puck," a supplement to some Shanghai newspaper, which contained several satirical cartoons. The technique does indeed mimic a Western style, but I was puzzled as to how the artist could be so bigoted and so vile in character; it was as if he were some uneducated kid scribbling the phrase "so-and-so is my sun"[2] over and over again on an otherwise perfectly clean white wall. What a pity that when things foreign arrive in China, it is as if they all fall into a vat of black dye, losing their original color. Art is a case in point: having studied nude portraits without learning to paint bodies in proper proportion, "artists" paint pornography; having studied still-life without mastering proper chiaroscuro, they can only paint shop signs. Such are the results of superficial reforms driven by old ways of thinking. That satirical cartoons have turned into tools for character assassination is not surprising in the least.

Speaking of satirical cartoons, I can't help but think of the American artist L. D. Bradley (1853–1917). He drew satirical cartoons exclusively, and his works depicting the European war are particularly well known. A pity

First published in volume 6, issue 1, of *New Youth* (Xin qingnian) on January 15, 1919, and later anthologized in *Hot Wind* (Re feng, 1925). Lu Xun, *Lu Xun quanji* (Complete works of Lu Xun) (Beijing: Renmin wenxue, 2005), 1: 346–347.

"The Harvest Moon," by L. D. Bradley (August 31, 1914)

he died the year before last. I saw a cartoon of his entitled "The Harvest Moon." Above is a moon in the shape of a skull, shining over a barren field; on the barren field are row upon row of soldiers' corpses. Ah, ah! Only works like this can be considered satirical cartoons of a truly progressive artist. I hope in the future there will come a day when China, too, will be able to produce such a progressive satirical artist.

TRANSLATED BY EILEEN J. CHENG

# My Hopes for the Critics
## 對於批評家的希望

For the past two or three years, our periodicals, as far as literature is concerned, have run only a few creative works (let's use this term for the moment) and translations, so that readers started to demand that critics make an appearance. These critics have now appeared, and there are actually more and more of them by the day.

First published in *Morning Post Supplement* (Chenbao fukan) on November 9, 1922, under the pen name Fengsheng and later anthologized in *Hot Wind* (Re feng, 1925). Lu Xun, *Lu Xun quanji* (Complete works of Lu Xun) (Beijing: Renmin wenxue, 2005), 1: 423–424.

At a time when our literature is so immature, we are much obliged to these critics for their good intentions in unearthing its merits to fan the literary flames. Otherwise, however, they lament the superficiality of modern works in the hope that authors will become more profound, or bewail the lack of blood and tears for fear that writers revert to frivolity. Although it may seem their veiled criticism is excessive, it is in fact due to their fervent goodwill toward literature, for which we are truly much obliged.

However, there are others who (relying solely on one or two old books of "Western" literary criticism) either dredge up some dull-brained scholars' spittle or else trample over the literary world on the basis of some kind of heaven-ordained principles that have long existed in China. These people I do indeed regard as abusing their critical authority. Let me draw a crude analogy: if a chef prepares a meal that a customer finds fault with, there would be no justification for the chef to hand over his kitchen knife and cauldron to his critic, saying, "Here, see if you can make something better." However, he may well entertain the hope that his customers don't suffer from abnormal food addictions, or aren't drunk or running a fever with a coated tongue two or three times thicker than usual.

My hopes for literary critics are more modest than this. I don't dare hope that before dissecting and judging other people's work, they first dissect and judge their own mentality to see if they are free of superficiality, meanness, or absurdity, because this would be expecting too much. All I hope for is just for them to have a modicum of common sense. For example, I would hope that they know the difference between nude studies and pornography, kissing and copulation, autopsies and corpse mutilation, study abroad and banishment, bamboo shoots and bamboo stems, cats and tigers, tigers and foreign restaurants. . . . To take it a step further, critics are naturally entirely free to base themselves on the doctrines of elderly British and American scholars, but I do hope they bear in mind that there are more than two countries in the world. They are free to despise Tolstoy, but I would hope they first investigate his life's work and read a few of his books seriously.

Some critics, when reviewing translations, are given to slandering translation as a waste of effort and fault the translator for not writing an original work. The honorable status of creative writing is, I should imagine, something that translators are well aware of, but in the end they remain translators either because it is all they can do or because they happen to enjoy it. So for critics not to accept this and to claim it should be otherwise is to overstep their authority: it amounts to advice or lecturing, not criticism. To return to the analogy of the chef, it's fine for a customer to comment as long as he confines himself to how the food tastes; otherwise, if he blames a chef for not being a tailor or a builder, even the thickest chef would be bound to say this customer is a nincompoop.

November 9

TRANSLATED BY BONNIE S. MCDOUGALL

# Must-Read Books for Young People

青年必讀書 —— 應《京報副刊》的征求

In response to a request from the *Capitol News Supplement*

| | |
|---|---|
| Must-Read Books for Young People | I have never paid much attention to this question, and so I have nothing much to say about it now. |
| Supplemental Note | But I would like to take this opportunity to share my own experience for the reference of some of your readers. Whenever I read Chinese books, I feel myself settling into quietude, leaving real life behind; when I read foreign books—with the exception of those from India—I often come into contact with real life and want to do something about it. |
| | Although there are Chinese books that urge readers to engage with the world, they offer the optimism of the living dead; whereas when foreign books are decadent or cynical, theirs is the decadence and cynicism of a living, breathing people. |
| | I think that we ought to read fewer Chinese books—if at all—and read more foreign books. |

First published in the *Supplement to Capital News* (Jingbao fukan) on February 21, 1925, and later anthologized in *Inauspicious Star* (Huagai ji, 1926). Lu Xun, *Lu Xun quanji* (Complete works of Lu Xun) (Beijing: Renmin wenxue, 2005), 3: 12–13.

The only problem with reading Chinese books less often is being unable to write well. But the priority for today's young people is to act, not to talk. As long as they are living, breathing beings, what does it matter if they can't write essays?

(February 10)

TRANSLATED BY ANDREW F. JONES

# This Is What I Meant
## 這是這麼一個意思

From Mr. Zhao Xueyang's letter (published here on March 31), I learned that in response to my "Must-Read Books for Young People," one scholar opined to students that I "had read a great deal of Chinese books. . . . And yet now he won't let other people read them. . . . What's the meaning of this!"[3]

I have in fact read a few Chinese books, but not "a great deal" of them; and it's not at all the case that I "won't let other people read them." Whoever wants to read them can of course do as they please. But if you're asking for my opinion, it's this: read fewer Chinese books—if at all—and read more foreign books.

What do I mean by that?

I was never a drinker, but a number of years ago, abandoning myself to a kind of despair, I started drinking, and actually found it rather comforting. I started by drinking a little and then I drank a lot, and the more I drank, the worse my appetite became. I knew that the spirits had already damaged my digestion. Nowadays I sometimes abstain and sometimes still drink, just like I still leaf through some Chinese books. If I were to speak of dietary matters with young people, of course I would tell them: don't drink. And if those listening to me knew that I used to indulge in drink, they would still understand what I mean.

---

First published in the *Supplement to Capital News* (Jingbao fukan) on April 3, 1925, and later anthologized in *Supplement to the Collection of the Uncollected* (Ji wai ji shiyi, 1938). Lu Xun, *Lu Xun quanji* (Complete works of Lu Xun) (Beijing: Renmin wenxue, 2005), 7: 274–276.

Even if I was suffering from smallpox, I would not on that account be opposed to cowpox; even if I owned a coffin shop, I would not sing the praises of the plague.

That is pretty much what I meant.

Let me add a statement on an unrelated matter while I am at it. A friend told me that there was an article in the *Supplement to Morning News* criticizing Yujun that mentioned my essay from *Mass Literary Arts Weekly*, "Warriors and Flies."[4] Actually the idea behind that piece did not pertain to the contemporary literary scene. The warriors I was talking about were Sun Yatsen and the martyrs who sacrificed themselves for the country right around the founding of the Republic, only to meet with sneers and derision from flunkies. The flies obviously referred to those flunkies. And as far as the literary scene goes, there are still no warriors to speak of; as for critics, while some of them may well have made a name for themselves despite having accomplished little of substance, they are hardly annoying enough to qualify as "flies." I mention all of this here merely to avoid any misunderstandings.

TRANSLATED BY ANDREW F. JONES

# Old Books and the Vernacular
## 古書與白話

I remember that when the vernacular was being advocated, it was subjected to a great many imprecations and much slander; but when it didn't take a tumble in the end, some people changed their tune, saying: if one doesn't read old books, one can't write the vernacular well. We should of course pardon these protectors of the past for the pains they have taken, but neither can we fail to entertain a bit of derisory pity for their use of ancestral precedent. All those who have read a few old books play this familiar trick: any new idea—that is, "heterodoxy"—must be wiped out. But after it has struggled

---

First published in *Supplement to Citizen's News* (Guomin xinbao fukan) on February 2, 1926, and later anthologized in *Sequel to Inauspicious Star* (Huagai ji xubian, 1927). Lu Xun, *Lu Xun quanji* (Complete works of Lu Xun) (Beijing: Renmin wenxue, 2005), 3: 227–231.

and established a foothold, only then do they discover that its origins are "from the same source as the sacred teachings of China": all things from abroad that "use barbarian ways to change China" must be removed, but when these barbarians become the masters of China, their textual research suddenly reveals that these "barbarians" have all along also been the descendants of the Yellow Emperor. Does any of this come as a surprise? For no matter what, there isn't anything that can't be encompassed in our notion of "antiquity"!

There can of course be no progress when these old tricks are used, so even now they maintain that if one hasn't "pored over several hundreds of books," one cannot produce decent vernacular, so they are determined to invoke the precedent of Mr. Wu Zhihui. But that we can have such nauseating spectacles told with such relish just goes to show the myriad of odd things under the sun. In fact, how is Mr. Wu's "use of the spoken language for writing" and the form that it takes in any way the same as that of "an immature child"? Was he not "setting free his pen and unleashing a vast array of words"? Contained therein, of course, were allusions to past writing that an "immature child" would not know, and there are even new allusions that "a callow youth" would not know. At the end of the Guangxu reign, when I had first arrived in Tokyo, this Mr. Wu Zhihui was already in the midst of a great battle with the Qing minister to Japan, Cai Jun; the length of the battle, along with plethora of things he experienced, was, needless to say, not something that an "immature child" could hope to match. So much of the rhetoric and the allusions he used would have been intelligible only to those familiar with the stories, great and small, of that time.

From a young person's perspective, the first thing of note would be surprise at the tremendous fluency of his wording. This is perhaps what prominent scholars would consider its strong point, but its life force did not reside there. It might even be precisely the opposite of what the prominent scholars tried to align themselves with and praised obsequiously. It was that he did not intentionally show off these strong points, nor could he eradicate what scholars regarded as his strong points; all he did was to take what he wrote and what he said as a bridge toward reform, or even did so without the intention of serving as a bridge toward reform.

The more pointless and unpromising one's role in life, the longer one wishes to live; and the greater the wish for immortality, the more photographs one wants of oneself, the more one wishes to occupy the minds of others, and the better one is at putting on airs. In the end, however, it is as if one's "unconscious" senses one's own pointlessness and the only recourse is to cling onto an "antiquity" that has not yet fully rotted away, with the intent of becoming a parasite in its gut and being passed down to posterity along with it; or to seek a bit of the ancient in things such as the vernacular to in turn add a bit of glory to these antiques. If the "enduring enterprise of writing" amounts to nothing more than this, how utterly pathetic. Moreover, it is a miserable prospect to think that by the year 2929 "immature children" will still be reading the likes of *The Tiger*, even if "the journal has gradually shown signs of reviving, since Mr. Gutong[5] stepped down."

It is true enough that only those who have read old books can most powerfully disparage them. Since they are familiar with their flaws, they can turn their spears against their own shields, just as only those who have smoked opium themselves are most profoundly and painfully aware of how to explain its harmful effects. Yet even so, how can we say that a "callow youth" must first smoke several hundred ounces of opium before he can write an essay on quitting opium?

Ancient prose is now dead; the vernacular is still the bridge to reform, because humanity is still in the process of evolving. Even writing doesn't necessarily possess uniquely inalterable principles. Although it has been said that certain places in the United States have already prohibited the theory of evolution, in fact, the ban will probably be ineffective in the end.

January 25, 1926

TRANSLATED BY THEODORE HUTERS

# Literature in Times of Revolution

## 革命時代的文學

A speech delivered April 8, 1927, at the Whampoa Military Academy

Today I would like to say a few things on the topic of "Literature in Times of Revolution." This academy has invited me on a number of occasions, but I have always put off coming. Why? Because I thought that the reason you gentlemen invited me was probably because I have written several works of fiction and am a man of letters, and so you would like to hear something about literature from me. In truth, that's not who I am, and I really don't understand much about literature. My formal studies were first in mining, so the results might be somewhat better if you asked me to speak on the mining of coal than on literature. Naturally, because of my own interests, I also read some literature from time to time, but I never learned anything that might be of use to you gentlemen. Added to that, my experience in Beijing over these past few years gradually led me to start doubting all the old literary discourses I am familiar with. That was when they opened fire and murdered students[6] and censorship was especially tight. I thought: Literature, oh literature, you are a most useless thing. Only those without power talk about you; no one with real strength bothers to talk, they just murder people. Oppressed people who say a few things or write a few words will be killed. Even if they are fortunate enough not to be killed, and shout out, complain of their suffering, and cry out against injustices every day, those with real strength will still continue to oppress, abuse, and kill; there is no way to deal with them. What value does this literature have for people, then?

The natural world also works this way. When a hawk hunts a sparrow, it is the hawk that is silent while the sparrow squawks. When a cat preys on a mouse, it is the cat that is silent while the mouse squeals. The result is still

First published in the Whampoa Military Academy weekly paper *Whampoa Life* on June 12, 1927, and later anthologized in *Sequel to Inauspicious Star* (Huagai ji xubian, 1927). Lu Xun, *Lu Xun quanji* (Complete works of Lu Xun) (Beijing: Renmin wenxue, 2005), 3: 436–443. The speech reflects a profound ambivalence on Lu Xun's part between his conviction of China's need for revolution, on the one hand, and his recognition of the necessity of violent means to effect that revolution, on the other.

that those who cry out are eaten by those who remain silent. If a writer does well and writes a few essays, he might garner some fame for himself in his time or earn a reputation for a few years. This is like how after a memorial service, no one mentions the feats of the martyr; rather, everyone discusses whose elegiac couplets are best. What a stable business this is.

However, I'm afraid that the literary specialists in this revolutionary place are always fond of saying how close the connection between literature and revolution is. For example, they say literature can be used to publicize, promote, incite, and advance the revolutionary cause, and thus bring about revolution. Still, it seems to me that this sort of literature has no strength because good literature has never been about following orders and has no regard for its effects. It is something that flows naturally from the heart. If we write literature according to a preselected topic, how is that any different from the formal prose of an imperial examination? It has no value as literature, not to mention no ability to move people.

For revolution to occur, what is needed are revolutionaries; there is no need to be overly anxious about "revolutionary literature." Only when revolutionaries start writing will there be revolutionary literature. Still, it seems to me that, after all, there is a relationship between revolution and writing. The literature in times of revolution is not at all the same as literature in times of peace. When there is revolution, the contours of literature itself change. However, only real revolution can change literature; a small revolution won't because it doesn't revolutionize anything, so neither can it change literature. Everyone here is used to hearing the term *revolution*. But when the term is mentioned in Jiangsu or Zhejiang, the people who hear it become fearful, and those who speak it are put in danger. In truth, though, there's nothing special about revolution; only with it can society reform and humanity progress. That humans were able to evolve from protozoans and civilizations to evolve from barbarism is precisely because there is never a moment without revolution. Biologists tell us: "There is no great difference between humans and monkeys; humans and monkeys are cousins." But why have humans come to be humans, while monkeys remained monkeys? The reason is that monkeys refuse change—they insist on walking with their four limbs. Perhaps there was once a monkey who stood up and attempted to walk on two legs. But many other monkeys said: "Our ancestors have always crawled. We forbid you to stand!" And then they bit the monkey to death. Not only did they refuse to stand, they also refused to speak, all because they had to follow old behaviors. Humans are different. They finally came to stand and speak, and they emerged victorious as a result. Now, things are not finished yet. So I say that revolution is nothing special. Every race that has not yet gone extinct is earnestly engaged in revolution on a daily basis, even if it is only a small revolution.

What influence does real revolution have on literature, then? We can roughly divide things into three periods.

(1) Before the revolution, all literature is, in the main, attuned to the inequities and suffering in various social conditions. So this literature complains of suffering and cries out against inequities. There is no dearth of examples of this sort of writing in world literature. However, this literature that complains of suffering and cries out against inequities has no influence on the revolution because it has absolutely no power to it; the oppressor pays it no mind. Even if the mouse were to produce excellent literature from its squeals, the cat would still unceremoniously devour it. Therefore, at a time when literature merely complains of suffering and cries out against inequities, the race will have yet to find hope because it remains limited to complaining of suffering and crying out against inequities. This is similar to the situation in a court case when the defeated is reduced to asserting that an injustice is being rendered—his opponent then knows that he no longer has power to fight anymore and that the case is closed. Similarly, literature that complains of suffering and cries out against inequities amounts to such an assertion of injustice and makes the oppressor feel at ease. Some races simply don't bother to complain of suffering or cry out against inequities since doing so is futile, and they become silent and gradually fall into decline: the Egyptians, the Arabs, the Persians, and the Indians have all lost their voices! As far as races that are defiant and powerful are concerned, since complaining of suffering and crying out against inequities is useless, they see the light and progress from sorrowful laments to shouts of anger. Once this angry literature arrives on the scene, resistance is soon to follow. They are already enraged, so works of literature from this period when the revolution is about to erupt are often accompanied by sounds of rage. This literature wants to resist, and it wants revenge. There was quite a bit of such literature just before

the Russian Revolution. Of course, there are also exceptions, for example, Poland. Although the Poles early on had a literature of revenge, it took the Great War in Europe for Poland to become independent.

(2) When revolution arrives, there will be no literature, no voice anymore. This is because, under the influence of the revolutionary tide, everyone has shifted from shouting to action, everyone is busy with revolution, and there is no leisure for discussing literature. Seen from another angle, when life is destitute and people think only of finding nonexistent food to eat, who would be in the frame of mind to discuss literature? Because they have taken a blow from the revolutionary tide, those who long for the past are furious and can no longer indulge in their sort of literature. Some say, "literature is written in times of misery," but this is not necessarily true; it may be that in times of misery there is no literary output. In Beijing, whenever I was in dire straits, I went all over looking to borrow money and couldn't write a single word. It was only once my salary was paid that I could sit down and write. It is also impossible to write when you are busy: a porter with a load must put it down first before he can write; a rickshaw puller must park his rickshaw first before he can write. Revolution is an extremely busy state. At the same time, poverty is widespread during a revolution. This faction is fighting that faction. It is absolutely necessary to first change the social conditions. No one has the time or the mind to write literature. So in times of revolution, literature must temporarily fall silent.

(3) When the revolution is successful, social conditions have improved, and there is abundance in people's lives, then literature can be produced again. There are two kinds of literature in this period. The first kind acclaims and lauds the revolution. It sings the praises of revolution because progressive writers find it meaningful when they reflect on how society has changed, and progress will contribute to the collapse of the old society and the establishment of the new. On the one hand, they are pleased to see the collapse of the old system; on the other hand, they praise the establishment of the new one. The second kind of literature, which mourns the eradication of the old society—the elegy—is also a kind of literature you find after a revolution. Some feel that this is "counterrevolutionary literature," but it seems to me that there is no need to label it as such a serious crime.

Although the revolution is in progress, there are still a great many old-style people in society who can't possibly be converted right away into new-style people. Their minds are full of old thoughts and things. As their environment gradually changes, affecting everything about them, they then recall the comfort of the old times and become nostalgic for the old society. Accordingly, they will create a sort of literature using ancient and stale language. This sort of literature is tragic in tone, expressing the unease in their hearts, witnessing the victorious establishment of the new alongside the destruction of the old system, so they start singing elegies. But this nostalgia and elegiac literature shows that revolution is in progress. If there were no revolution, these old-style people would be ascendant and would not, therefore, sing elegies.

Nonetheless, China has neither of these two types of literature: elegies for the old system or songs lauding the new system. This is because the revolution has not yet succeeded, and we are still engaged in it. However, the old literature remains quite prevalent: nearly everything in the papers is in the old style. I think this is indicative of the fact that the revolution in China has not had a great effect on society and has had no great influence on old-style people, so they can transcend world matters. The literature discussed in Guangdong's papers is all in the old style; very rarely is new literature taken up. This is evidence of the fact that Guangdong's society has not been influenced by the revolution. There are no songs lauding the new, no elegies for the old. Guangdong today remains the same as the Guangdong of ten years ago. Not only is this the case, there isn't even any literature that complains of suffering or cries out against inequities. All we ever see are reports of unions marching in protest, but even this is limited to what has been permitted by the government; it isn't resistance to oppression but rather revolution by imperial order. There has been no change in Chinese society, so there are no nostalgic laments, nor are there any battle hymns for the new. These two types of literature exist only in Soviet Russia. The majority of the literary works written by their old-style writers who have fled to foreign lands are mournful and nostalgic laments. The new literature, by contrast, is vigorously moving forward. While there are no great masterpieces yet, even now there are a large number of new works that have already left angry shouts behind and transitioned to the period of singing in praise. It is impossible to know now exactly what the effect this literature extolling the establishment of a progressive, revolutionary society will be, but we may conjecture that it likely will be a people's literature, since a world for the masses is the goal of revolution.

Of course, there is no people's literature in China; indeed, there is no people's literature anywhere in the world yet. All literature that exists now—songs, poetry, and whatnot—in the main is written for the elite. With full bellies, they recline on a couch and read. A scholar encounters a beauty, and the two fall in love. A scoundrel appears causing mischief and creating misunderstandings, but it's happily ever after in the end. It's so pleasant to read such things. If the literature doesn't describe such elite pleasures, then it ridicules the lower classes. A few years ago, *New Youth* published a few stories describing the life of a criminal in the barren north. A number of college professors were displeased on reading them since they don't like reading about this sort of low-class person. If a poem describes a rickshaw puller, then it is lowbrow; if a play includes criminal events, then it is lowbrow. For these professors, the characters in a play should be restricted to scholars and beauties: the scholar is ranked highest among imperial examinees, the beauty is ennobled as a lord's wife. They like the idea of scholars and beauties, so they are fond of reading such literature and are filled with delight after reading it. The lower classes have no choice but to share in their delight. If today someone writes a novel or poem about the people—workers or peasants—we call it people's literature. But in truth this is not people's literature for the reason that the people have not yet begun to speak. This is the writing of someone else observing the life of the people and adopting the people's manner of speaking. There are some writers before us who, although poor, are still better off than workers or peasants, otherwise they couldn't afford to read or write. On first glance it seems that this is the people's voice. But this is not the case; these are not true stories of the people. Nowadays there are also people who transcribe the mountain songs and folk ballads that the people sing. They imagine that this is the true voice of the people since this is what ordinary folks sing. But the fact of the matter is that they have to a large extent been indirectly influenced by ancient books. The ordinary folks greatly admire the immense holdings of land of the local gentry; and so they often model their own thoughts on that of the gentry. The gentry recite poetry of regulated verse in either five- or seven-character lines. Accordingly, the majority of the mountain songs and folk ballads sung by the ordinary folk also have five or seven characters per line. This is to speak merely of form; in terms of plot and theme, it's all very hackneyed and worn out, and we can't call this a true people's literature. Chinese fiction and poetry today just isn't comparable to that of other countries. Since nothing can be done, all we can do is call it literature, but it doesn't qualify as literature in times of revolution, let alone people's literature. The writers today are all scholars. If workers and peasants are not liberated, their thought patterns will remain the same as those of the scholars. We must await the true liberation of the workers and peasants before there can be a true people's literature. Some say, "China already has a people's literature," but this is wrong.

You, gentlemen, are true fighters, are warriors of the revolution. For now, I think, it is best not to hold literature in overly high regard. Studying literature doesn't benefit the war. At best, a war song, if written well, can be read while resting between battles and may provide some amusement. To put it somewhat more grandly, it's like planting a willow tree: once it has grown tall, providing broad and dense shade from the sun, the farmers, having plowed until noon, might sit under the tree to eat their meal and rest. The present state of affairs in China is that we are in the midst of a revolutionary war. A poem will not scare off Sun Chuanfang,[7] but a cannon shot might send him scurrying for cover. Of course, some say that literature gives strength to the revolution, but personally I have my doubts. Literature has always been a product of leisure. To be sure, though, it can reflect a nation's culture.

For the most part, people aren't satisfied with their present occupations. I have no abilities other than writing some essays, and I have grown tired of doing it. But you, gentlemen, grasping your rifles, want to hear a speech on literature.

For myself, I'd naturally prefer to hear the sound of artillery. It seems to me that the sound of artillery is a much finer thing than the sound of literature. This is the end of my speech; thank you, gentlemen, for listening to the end.

TRANSLATED BY ANDREW STUCKEY

# Miscellaneous Thoughts

小雜感

Once a bee uses its sting, it loses its life immediately. Once a cynic uses his sting, he drags out his life momentarily. This is how they differ.

John Stuart Mill said: Tyranny makes people cynical.
But he didn't realize that a republic makes people silent.

If one enters the battlefield, it's best to be a combat doctor; if one joins the revolution, it's best to be behind the lines; if one wants to kill, there's nothing better than being an executioner. All heroic and stable professions.

When discussing matters with an eminent scholar, pretend, at times, not to understand some of the things he says. Understand too little and you will be despised; understand too much and you will incur disgust. If you pretend not to understand things at times, you will get on well.

Most people know only that the sword is wielded to command soldiers, not giving a thought to how the sword can also be wielded to command intellectuals.

Yet another collection of speeches, yet another collection of speeches published.
But a pity that there's no explanation of why the speechmaker's thoughts changed drastically from the past, nor clarification of whether he truly believes his own words.

Wealthy people who are smart can pretend everything is a thing of the past.

---

First published in volume 4, issue 1, of *Threads of Talk* (Yusi) on December 17, 1927, and later anthologized in *And That's All* (Eryi ji, 1928). Lu Xun, *Lu Xun quanji* (Complete works of Lu Xun) (Beijing: Renmin wenxue, 2005), 3: 554–558.

For fools who are poor, everything is, in fact, a thing of the past.

The once wealthy want to revive the past, the now wealthy want to maintain the status quo, and the never been wealthy want reform.

This is generally the case. Generally!

What is referred to as reviving the past means going a few years back to a time one can still recall, not going back to the times of Yu, Xia, Shang, and Zhou.

It is in women's nature to have motherly and daughterly instincts, but not wifely instincts.

Wifely instincts came about as a result of forced circumstances; it is nothing more than a combination of motherly and daughterly instincts.

Beware of being deceived.

There's no need to beware of those who call themselves thieves; to the contrary, they may, in fact, be good people. One must beware of those who call themselves estimable gentleman, for they may, in fact, be thieves.

A man downstairs is sick and on the verge of death. The neighbor next door is playing his gramophone; the neighbor across is playing with the children. Upstairs two people are laughing maniacally to the sound of shuffling mahjong tiles. In a boat on the river, a woman cries over her dead mother.

People are unable to empathize with each other's joys and sorrows; I just feel that they are all making a ruckus.

Whenever a person in tattered clothes walks by, the lapdog starts barking, not necessarily on the orders or urging of its masters.

Lapdogs are often more harsh than their masters.

I'm afraid a day may come when people aren't allowed to wear tattered clothes, lest they be mistaken for communists.

Revolutionaries, counterrevolutionaries, those apathetic to the revolution.

Revolutionaries are killed by those who are counterrevolutionaries. Counterrevolutionaries are killed by revolutionaries. Those apathetic to the revolution or mistakenly identified as revolutionaries are killed by counterrevolutionaries; or they aren't mistaken for anything at all and are killed by revolutionaries or counterrevolutionaries.

Revolution, re-revolution, re-re-revolution, re-re . . . [8]

When a person feels lonely, he will create. When he is empty of feeling, he will no longer create and will have reached a point where there is nothing left in the world that he loves.

The root of creativity is love.

Yang Zhu left no writing behind.

Though writing is a way of releasing one's own thoughts, one still hopes for readers.

Writing has a social dimension.

But sometimes, you derive satisfaction even if only one person, such as a good friend or a lover, reads it.

People often despise monks, nuns, Muslims, disciples of Jesus, but don't despise Daoists.

Those who understand this principle have a good understanding of the Chinese.

A man who wants to commit suicide may be afraid of the vast expanse of the ocean, afraid of how easily corpses rot in the summer.

But when he encounters the clear and placid pond and the refreshing air of the autumn night, he usually will still commit suicide.

Those who are executed by those in power are all "guilty" of crimes.

Liu Bang wanted to eradicate the violent ways of Qin and made a pledge to the elders that there would only be three rules.[9]

Afterward they still executed clans and banned books, all of which were the laws of the Qin. "Rules" are just empty words.

On seeing a woman in short sleeves, they immediately think of white arms, naked bodies, genitals, sexual intercourse, promiscuity, and bastards—Chinese people's imaginations are capable of such great advances only in matters such as these.

September 24, 1927

TRANSLATED BY EILEEN J. CHENG

# The Divergence of Art and Politics
文藝與政治的歧途

A talk given at Jinan University, Shanghai, December 21, 1927

I don't often come out to make speeches; I'm here today only because I had said I would many times. So here I am and that should settle it. The reason I don't give public lectures is, for one thing, I have no opinions to speak of, and for another, as this gentleman has just said, many of you have read my books, which means there's not much for me to talk about. People in books are probably a little nicer than the genuine article: characters in *Dream of the Red Chamber* like Jia Baoyu and Lin Daiyu made me feel an unusual sympathy; later on, after looking into some of the facts of that era, I saw them both, performed by the opera stars Mei Lanfang and Jiang Miaoxiang in Beijing, and didn't find them that brilliant.

I have no grand comprehensive theory and no brilliant views, so I'll just talk about something I recently thought of. I have often felt that art and politics are in constant conflict; art and revolution are not actually opposites, and in fact are both unhappy with the status quo. But politics wants to maintain the status quo, and naturally its direction is different from art, which is unhappy with the status quo. And yet art dissatisfied with the

Transcribed by Liu Shuaizhen (also known as Cao Juren) and published in two parts in 1928 in issues 182 and 183 of the *Academic Journal* (Xue bao) of the *News* (Xinwen bao) on January 29 and January 30 and later anthologized in *Collection of the Uncollected* (Ji wai ji, 1935). Lu Xun, *Lu Xun quanji* (Complete works of Lu Xun) (Beijing: Renmin wenxue, 2005), 7: 115–123.

status quo only arose after the nineteenth century and has a very short history. What politicians dislike most is for anyone to oppose their opinions, for anyone to think or speak out. In earlier societies, no one ever thought or spoke out. Among animals, just look at monkeys: they have their leaders, and they do whatever their leaders tell them to. Similarly, in a tribal society, people followed a chief, whose word was law. If the chief wanted them to die, all they could do was die. In those days there was no art, or at best nothing more than an art praising God (not yet as mystifying as the *Domine* coined by later generations)! How could there be any free thought? Then these tribes began swallowing each other up until, having devoured a vast number of small tribes, some gradually grew into big nations. When it came to big nations, internal affairs got more complex, blending many different ideas and many different problems. This was when art emerged in ceaseless conflict with politics. Politics wanted to keep the status quo to hold the nation together, but art pushed society to evolve, thus leading to its gradual disintegration. Although art made it fall apart, that was how society progressed. Since art is a thorn in politicians' flesh, it can't avoid being driven out. Many foreign writers, unable to hang on in their own land, sought refuge one after another in other countries. This method is called "escape." If they don't make it, they're executed, beheaded. Beheading is the best method, since they'll neither speak out nor think anymore. This is what happened to many Russian writers, while many others were exiled to ice-bound Siberia.

There's a clique in favor of art that stays away from real life and talks about, oh, . . . the moon, or flowers, or birds (here I won't even mention our National Essence moral code, which doesn't permit talk of moon and flowers—things are different in China), or talks exclusively of dreams, or future societies—nothing too close at hand. All writers like this hide in an ivory tower, but, you know, you can't live very long in ivory towers. After all, you can only build ivory towers in the real world, where political oppression is unavoidable. When war breaks out, what can you do but flee? One literary bunch in Beijing has utter contempt for writers who describe society. In their view, admitting the lives of rickshaw men into fiction violates the formula for fiction that it be a lyrical account of love between a scholar and a beauty. Ah, but now they themselves can no longer be noble writers and have to flee to the south. After all, handouts of bread did not keep coming in through the windows of the ivory tower!

By the time this bunch finally fled, other writers were long gone or dead. They had been dissatisfied with the status quo for a long time, had felt compelled to protest, to speak out, and that was their undoing. I believe that what writers feel personally in real life will leave an imprint on their art. There's a writer in Norway who describes hunger in a book based on his own experience. Let's set aside other life experiences for the moment and talk about the matter of hunger. If you think it's pleasurable, then give it a try. It only takes a couple of days without food for its aroma to become a distinct temptation. If you find yourself walking past the door of an eatery, you'll feel the aroma assail your nose in waves. We don't think twice about spending money when we have it, but when it's gone, a single coin becomes significant. The book describing hunger tells how a man who goes hungry for a long time comes to see everyone on the street as an enemy and even someone wearing thin clothes strikes him as arrogant. It reminds me that I myself wrote about someone like that, he had run out of everything, yet kept opening the drawers to see if he could find anything in the corners and along the edges; he'd search everywhere up and down the street to see what he could find. This is something I've gone through myself.

When someone who's led a life of poverty becomes rich, one of two things can easily develop: he can live in an ideal world where compassion for those in the same predicament turns into humanitarianism; or, having earned everything on his own, his former hard times make him feel the world is a heartless place, a feeling that sours into individualism. Our China will likely have a majority of individualists. The advocates of humanitarianism want to find a way out for the poor, to change the status quo, which strikes the politician as a fate decidedly worse than what the individualists promise. So there's a conflict between humanitarians and politicians. The Russian writer Tolstoy spoke for humanitarianism, opposed war, and wrote a thick three-volume novel, *War and Peace*. An aristocrat himself, he had experienced life on the battlefield and had felt the misery of war. How much more piercing the pain was when he stood facing the shields of officers (top officers on the battlefield each had a shield as protection against bullets). He had seen many friends sacrificed on the battlefield. War, too, can result in the development of two attitudes: one is held by the hero, who sees that others have died or been wounded, but as long as he's in one piece, he considers himself terrific and tries every which way to magnify his prowess on the battlefield. The other is held by those who've turned against war and hope the world will never again take up arms. Tolstoy was the latter, advocating nonresistance as a means to eliminate war. Naturally the government couldn't stand him. Opposing war conflicted with the tsarist lust for aggression. His nonresistance would have men in the ranks not fight for the tsar, police not enforce law for the tsar, judges not pass sentences for the tsar, the public not sing praises of the tsar. All rulers want praise, for what sort of ruler would one be without it. All this provoked further conflicts with the government. With the appearance of such writers dissatisfied with the status quo, always criticizing this and that until everyone in society became personally aware of it and grew uneasy because of it, the only solution was for heads to roll.

But the language of the writer is the language of society. His sensibilities are keen, quick to feel and quick to express (too quickly, at times, so even society opposes and rejects him). Take military drill, for example: in presenting arms, the regulation command is "pres-seeeent arms," and you damn well can't present them until the word *arms* is called. Yet some people raise the rifle as soon as they hear the word *present*, causing the sergeant to punish them for their error. That's exactly how it is with the writer in society; he speaks a little too soon, and the public hates him for it. Politicians are convinced that the writer is an instigator of social disorder and think killing him off will bring society some peace. Little do they know that kill him or not, society still wants revolution. The number of Russian writers killed or exiled isn't small, but the fires of revolution flared up everywhere, didn't they? Throughout his life, a writer will likely get no sympathy from society and will lead a life of frustration. Then four or five decades after his death, he's discovered by society, and the public really acts up. For this, politicians detest him all the more, realizing the writer had long ago sown the seeds of trouble. Politicians would like to bar the public from thinking, but that savage age is long gone. I don't know the views of all of you sitting here, but I figure they are not the same as the politicians'. Since politicians always blame the writer for ruining their social unity, such a biased view makes me unwilling to talk to them ever.

Time passes and society eventually changes. The public gradually recalls what the artist said before, and however much he suffered their taunts during his lifetime, everyone now approves of and compliments his foresight. Just now as I came up to speak, you gave a sudden round of applause, but this applause shows that I'm not so great.

Applause is a dangerous thing: it might make me believe that I'm great and no longer need to go any further. So better not to applaud. As I said earlier, the writer has keener sensibilities; many concepts strike him before society has any awareness of them. For example, today someone is wearing a leather coat, whereas I'm still in cotton. That man's sense of the cold is more acute than mine. Another month maybe and I, too, will feel I have to put on a leather coat. If one can be a month off in his sense of the weather, he can be thirty to forty years off in his sense of ideas. When I say things like this, many writers will object. In Guangdong I once criticized a revolutionary writer—currently in Guangdong, unrevolutionary literature doesn't count as literature, and nothing counts as *revolutionary* literature without "strike, strike, strike, kill, kill, kill, re, re, re, volt, volt, volt"—I simply didn't think revolution can be linked with literature, although in literature there are *literary* revolutions. People writing literature simply have to have the time for it. Who has time to write literature in the midst of a revolution? Imagine in hard times how cumbersome it would be to pull a rickshaw while polishing prose. There were some ancients who did manage to write poems while farming, but they sure didn't farm with their own hands. Only after hiring people to farm on their behalf could they chant their poems. If you actually have to farm, then there wouldn't be time to write poems. And so it is in times of revolution, no one has time to write poems. During the fight against the warlord Chen Jiongming, several students of mine were on the battlefield, and I read what they wrote to me; I could see their language getting rustier with each succeeding letter. After the Russian Revolution, people lined up for bread with bread coupons in hand. In those days the nation no longer cared if one was a writer, painter, or sculptor. If getting bread took up all one's time, when could one think of literature? And when literature did reappear, the revolution had already succeeded. After which, things relaxed a bit, and some people flattered the revolution and others sang its praises, but none of this was revolutionary literature. To flatter and praise the revolution is to praise those in power, and what does that have to do with revolution?

Writers of keen sensibility may once again be dissatisfied with the status quo and again be ready to speak out. The political revolutionaries had previously endorsed the writers' words, but when the revolution succeeded, its politicians began to adopt the methods they originally opposed. And the artists, inevitably dissatisfied, had to be barred or beheaded. Cutting off heads, as I have said, is the best method—from the nineteenth century to the present, that has been the trend in world art.

Art from the nineteenth century on bears little resemblance to art prior to the eighteenth. The aim of eighteenth-century English fiction was to provide wives and young women with pleasant and entertaining pastimes. The last half of the nineteenth century saw a complete change, as the problems of life took on immediacy in literature. It is sheer agony to read it, yet we read on compulsively. The reason is that earlier art seems to describe a different society that we can appreciate only from a distance. Contemporary art describes our own society, and even we are written into it. Society can be found in this fiction, and so can we. Previous art, like a fire across the river, had little to do with us. In contemporary art, even we ourselves are burning; we definitely feel it deeply. And once we feel it, we definitely want to take part in society!

The nineteenth century can be called an age of revolution, revolution meaning unhappiness with the present, discontent with the status quo. Art that hastens the gradual elimination of the old is also revolution (the new can only emerge with the elimination of the old), but the writer's fate doesn't go through the same transformations simply because he himself takes part in revolution. Instead, there are brick walls to face at every turn. The revolutionary forces have already made their way north to Xuzhou. North of Xuzhou, writers had never been able to hold their ground; south of Xuzhou, writers still can't hold their ground; even when communized, writers still won't be able to hold their ground.

Revolutionary writers and revolutionaries, it's fair to say, are two totally different things. Denouncing the irrationality of warlords, that's revolutionary writers for you; overthrowing warlords, that's revolutionaries for you. Sun Chuanfang was sent packing, blasted out by artillery in revolutionaries' hands, and not driven out by a few words in a revolutionary writer's essay: "Hey, Sun Chuanfang, we'll get rid of you, you know." During a revolution, writers are busy dreaming of what kind of world it will be when the revolution succeeds; after the revolution, the reality they see is not what they had in mind at all, and once again they suffer. To go by their weeping and wailing, nothing has succeeded, neither going forward nor backward leads to success. It's just fate that reality doesn't match up to the ideal, just as the Lu Xun on the podium doesn't match up to the Lu Xun of *Outcry*. Maybe you all imagined I'd part my hair and wear a Western suit, but I am not wearing a Western suit, and you see how close-cropped my hair is. And so, self-proclaimed revolutionary literature certainly isn't revolutionary literature—where in the world is there a revolutionary literature pleased with the status quo? Unless it's been etherized! There were two writers before the Russian Revolution, Yesenin and Sobol, who sang the praises of revolution, but they later died crashing into the solid monument of reality, the very revolution they had sung of and hoped for. The Soviets were established then.

But society is so desolate that only such people can give it a little more appeal. Humanity likes to see a little theater, writers volunteer to perform, getting bound or dispatched to the headsman or else to the nearest wall facing a firing squad, all of which livens things up. It's just like the Shanghai Concession police clubbing people. The public gathers round, and although they themselves don't want to be clubbed, seeing someone else clubbed is mighty amusing. So writers are the ones who take the clubbing on their own hides!

It's not very much, but that's today's talk. Give it a title, call it . . . "The Divergence of Art and Politics."

TRANSLATED BY DONALD HOLOCH AND SHU-YING TSAU

# Literature and Revolution: A Reply

## 文藝與革命: 回信

Dear Mr. Dongfen:

I am no critic, neither am I an artist. These days, if you want to be a professional something-or-another, it is categorically necessary that either you or your friends also perform the role of the critic. It will never do to be without a clique; at least this is the case in Shanghai presently. Since I am

First published in volume 4, issue 16, of *Threads of Talk* (Yusi) on April 16, 1928, and later anthologized in *Three Leisures* (San xian ji, 1932). Lu Xun, *Lu Xun quanji* (Complete works of Lu Xun) (Beijing: Renmin wenxue, 2005), 4: 83–87. Lu Xun's letter is a response to a letter dated March 25, 1928, written by Dongfen, a pseudonym for Dong Qiufang (1897–1977), who was a student in Beijing at the time and later became a noted translator. Lu Xun notes that unlike Dongfen and the "estimable gentlemen" of the Crescent Moon Society, he insists that literature not be placed above social concerns; but he agrees that much of "revolutionary literature," such as that by members of the Creation and Sun Societies, is abysmal in quality and thus cannot truly be considered art.

not a professional artist, I have never thought of art as something particularly lofty. This follows the same logic that since I do not sell poultices, neither do I shadow box to promote their benefits. It seems to me that literature is merely a social phenomenon, a record of life in this era. If humanity progresses, then no matter whether literature describes the external world or an interior psychological state, it is destined to become outmoded, to the point of dying out. Nevertheless, recently professional critics seem especially fearful of these two words: *literature* and *revolution*; their only hope is to gain immortality on the back of literature.

Likewise, it is inevitable that the repute of various philosophies will rise and fall. At all times there is revolution in the world, so naturally there will also be revolutionary literature. There are some people in the world who have been awakened, though many still suffer oppression. Still, a certain number have gained power, and so naturally there will also be a people's literature—more specifically, a literature of the fourth estate.[10]

As for the current state of Chinese criticism, I neither understand it very well nor pay it much attention. From what I see and hear, the standards deployed by various experts are incredibly numerous: British and American standards, German standards, Japanese standards, and naturally there are also Chinese standards; some experts deploy more than one simultaneously. Some insist we need to be accurate, some insist that we need to struggle, while some insist on transcending the age, and still others make snide remarks while hiding behind other people's backs. And there are also those who pose as literary critics and excoriate others who support creative works. But what I simply cannot fathom about this last group is, if there are no creative works, what can they possibly criticize?

But let's leave all this aside for the moment. Presently, there are two types of people claiming to write revolutionary literature: those calling for struggle and those wanting to "transcend the age." Transcending the age, in fact, is merely escapism. Those who do not have the courage to look squarely at reality and yet still wish to claim an identity as a revolutionary, consciously or unconsciously, end up walking this path. Being part of this world, how can one depart from it? This is as deceptive a claim as that of one who says he can levitate by pulling himself up by the ears. When society has stagnated, there is absolutely no way for literature to leap ahead by itself; if it actually continues to develop in this stagnating society, then it means that it has become part of this society and has already parted ways with revolution. The result is merely selling a few more journals or else increasing opportunities for publication in journals put out by large commercial presses.

As for struggle, to me this seems the correct approach. When people are oppressed, why shouldn't they struggle? The clique of estimable gentlemen deeply fears this and detests it as "extreme." They feel everyone should love each other, only nowadays people have been corrupted by a few bad apples. Those with full bellies probably do love the hungry people, but hungry people do not love those with full bellies. In the time of Huang Chao,[11] people ate each other. At that time, hungry people did not even love other hungry people. Surely this is not the fault of the literature of struggle. I don't believe in the power of literature to shake heaven and earth, but if others want to use it for other purposes, I think it's fine. "Propaganda" is one example.

The American Upton Sinclair has said: "All art is propaganda." Our writers of revolutionary literature previously held this saying dear, printing it in bold letters. The serious critics, however, said he was a "shallow socialist." Yet I—myself shallow—believe Sinclair. All art, as long as it is shown to someone, is propaganda. Even an individualist piece, once it is written, has the potential to be propaganda, unless you refrain from writing and keep your mouth shut. It is naturally also possible, then, for literature to serve as a tool to be used in the course of revolution.

Nevertheless, it seems to me that we should first require solid content and technique of the highest caliber; we do not need to busy ourselves with how it is labeled. Fragrant Rice Village and Lu's Straw Mat[12] have already lost their luster. In my judgment, the number of customers at Empress Dowager Shoes is no greater than at Empress Shoes. Writers of revolutionary literature hate it as soon as anyone mentions "technique." But although I believe all art is certainly propaganda, not all propaganda is art. This follows the same logic that all flowers have color (I include white here), but something with color is not necessarily a flower. The reason revolution, besides relying on slogans, posters, proclamations, bulletins, textbooks, and so on, needs to employ literature is precisely because it is art.

Nevertheless, the so-called revolutionary literature in China seems to follow a different logic; while the placard of revolution has already been hung, all people do is write essays lavishing praise on their own clique; they do not dare to look squarely at the present violence and darkness in society. Although a few of these pieces are published, inevitably they are so inferior that they cannot compare even to newspaper reports. Or else they push the responsibility for the script's plot and phrases onto the actors or "yesterday's littérateurs."[13] Then the content of the remaining thought must be very revolutionary, right? I will give you the example of the lines ending Feng Naichao's script:

Prostitute: I don't fear the dark anymore.

Thief: Let's resist![14]

April 4

TRANSLATED BY ANDREW STUCKEY

# An Overview of the Present State of New Literature
## 現今的新文學的概觀

A speech delivered to the National Literature Studies Association of Yenching University, May 22, 1929

For the past year or more, I have not had much to say to you esteemed youth. The reason is that since the advent of the revolution, the room for discourse has been very narrow—if it's not too radical, then it's reactionary—which doesn't benefit anyone. On my return to Beiping this time, several people whom I have known for a long time invited me to come here to say a few words. On the strength of our friendship I could not refuse, so here I have come to say a few things. Yet after all, for a variety of reasons, I wasn't able to settle on what I would come to speak on—I didn't even have a topic.

---

First published in volume 2, issue 8, of *Weiming* on May 25, 1929, and later anthologized in *Three Leisures* (San xian ji, 1932). Lu Xun, *Lu Xun quanji* (Complete works of Lu Xun) (Beijing: Renmin wenxue, 2005), 4: 136–42. Lu Xun deplores the contemporary state of Chinese literature in this speech. Though he derides "conservatives" such as Hu Shi (1891–1962) and Xu Zhimo (1897–1931), he saves his most severe criticisms for the revolutionary writers of the Creation Society such as Guo Moruo (1892–1978).

I was originally planning to decide on a topic during the car ride over here, but the road was so bad that the car bounced up over a foot off the road, and I could think of nothing else. It then occurred to me that it is never enough to adopt foreign things in isolation: if you want to use automobiles, you must also have good roads. Nothing can escape the influence of its environment. Literature—in China the so-called new literature or so-called revolutionary literature—is no different.

Chinese culture, one must admit, no matter how patriotic you are, is somewhat backward. New things have intruded from the outside. New forces have arrived, but still the majority of the people remain at a loss for how to respond. Things haven't yet come to this in Beiping. Take as an example the foreign concessions in Shanghai, where foreigners take center stage. Surrounding them are a herd of translators, detectives, policemen, boys serving as foreign servants ... and so on, who understand foreign languages and are familiar with the regulations of the concessions. Outside this circle, there is the multitude of ordinary people, who never understand the true situation when they arrive in the concessions. The foreigner says "yes," and the translation is "He said to slap your face"; the foreigner says "no,"[15] but the translation is that he said "have him shot." If one wishes to avoid such pointless injustice, the first thing to do is to know a bit more and break out of this circle. It is the same in the literary world. We know so little, and the materials we have for enhancing our knowledge are too few. Liang Shiqiu has Irving Babbitt; Xu Zhimo has Rabindranath Tagore; Hu Shi has John Dewey—oh yes, Xu Zhimo also has Katherine Mansfield,[16] he even once went to her grave and wept—the Creation Society has revolutionary literature and literature of the times. But those who chime in mostly write, very few actually engage in study. Even to this day, debates are still monopolized by the tight circle of people who raise the issues.

Every form of literature is produced in accordance with environmental pressures. Although those who hold literature in high esteem like to claim that literature can make waves in society, in truth, it is politics that acts first, and only later does literature adjust. It is simply "idealism" to presume that literature can alter its environment, but reality never turns out as the writers predict. Thus, in the wake of a great revolution, even the former so-called revolutionary literature must be eradicated; only after the revolution has borne some small fruits, when there is space to breathe, can new revolutionary writers be born. Why is this? Because whenever an old society is on the brink of collapse, literary works that seem to have a revolutionary flavor often appear. Yet in truth, these aren't actually works of revolutionary literature. A few examples: Some may loathe the old society, but they merely loathe it and have no ideals for the future to speak of. Some may clamor loudly for social reform, but if you ask what sort of society they desire, it's some unrealizable utopia. Some are bored and vainly hope for some major transformation for stimulation. This is just like people who have eaten and drunk their fill yet still wish for something spicy to stimulate their tongue. The lowest of these are really old-style people who have failed in society and wish to start afresh, so they throw in with the rising power to raise their status.

Examples of writers who once had hoped for revolution but who fall silent once the revolution arrives exist in China. There was the Southern Society[17] at the end of the Qing dynasty, which advocated revolutionary literature. Its members bemoaned the oppression of the Han, raged at the arrogance of the Manchu, and desired "to recover what had been lost." But there was nary a peep from them once the Republic was established. It seems to me that this is because after the revolution their ideal became "restoration of the impressive manner of the Han"[18] and wearing a tall cap and wide belt.[19] But reality certainly didn't live up to this, and so instead they felt listless and found no motivation to write. The Russian example is especially clear. A good number of revolutionary writers were overjoyed in the early stages of the October Revolution. They welcomed this tempest hoping to be tested in the tumult. But afterward the poet Sergei Yesenin and the fiction writer Andrei Sobol committed suicide, and recently I have even heard that Ilya Ehrenburg has become somewhat reactionary. Why is this? For the simple reason that they were assaulted by neither tempest nor tumult, but by a genuine "revolution." They could no longer live on when their empty dreams were shattered. They died even before achieving their goals, which is a far cry from the fortune enjoyed by the ancient poets who believed their souls would ascend to heaven and that they would enjoy tasty treats by God's side after death.

China has reportedly already had a revolution—perhaps this is true in terms of politics, but for literature there has been no change. Some say, "Petit bourgeois literature has lifted its head," but the truth is that petit bourgeois literature doesn't even have a head to lift. The hypothesis I presented above that there has been no change or flourishing of literature—loath as the revolutionaries are to hear this—reflects the fact that there has been no revolution or progress.

As for what the Creation Society promotes, an even more thoroughgoing revolutionary literature—proletarian literature—well, naturally, this is nothing but a name. "Pong Pong Pong"—Wang Duqing's poem commemorating the violence in Guangzhou as witnessed from the Shanghai concessions—banned here and there and whose type size gradually enlarges, signifies merely that Wang was once moved by movie subtitles and pickle shop signs; he has the ambition to imitate Alexander Blok's "The Twelve" without the latter's strength or talent. Many people promote Guo Moruo's "Only One Hand"[20] as an excellent piece. The story speaks of a revolutionary who loses a hand in the course of making revolution but is still able to clasp his lover's hand with the one remaining. This "loss" seems a little too convenient. Of the four limbs and head, if you must lose one, what could be better than a hand? A leg would be so inconvenient, and naturally the head all the more so. If one were only prepared to lose just one hand, it surely diminishes the spirit of advancing bravely into the struggle. It seems to me that a revolutionary would not hesitate to sacrifice much more than this. "One Hand" still sings the old tune of a poor scholar who encounters troubles but in the end places first in the imperial exam and marries a beauty.

Still, these are true reflections of China's current state. A steel trident appears on the cover of a book of revolutionary literature recently published in Shanghai. The trident is taken from the cover of *Symbols of Suffering*[21] with the addition of an iron hammer in the style of the Soviet flag set on the trident's middle prong. Nevertheless, this arrangement prevents the trident from piercing through and the hammer from striking. All it does is show the author's mediocrity and vulgarity—and so it serves as an appropriate badge for those writers. Naturally it is possible to move from one class to another, but it is best to acknowledge your consciousness and speak frankly so that the masses can clearly distinguish friend from foe. It will not do to intentionally conceal the dregs of old thought remaining in your mind and then point at your own nose saying, "Only I am proletarian!" People today are all neurotic; if they were to hear the word *Russian*, they would expire from rage. Soon it won't be permissible even for lips to be red. As for publications, they're afraid of this and afraid of that. On the other hand, revolutionary writers are unwilling to introduce more theories or works from other countries; instead, they just point at their own noses and in the end appear like they are giving "a rebuke by imperial edict" of the former Qing dynasty—no one knows what any of this is about.

"A rebuke by imperial edict" may require a few words of explanation for the assembled gentlemen here today. This is a custom from imperial times. When an official committed a grave error, he was made to kneel outside a certain door, and the emperor would send a palace eunuch to reproach him. At this time it was convenient to have a small bribe ready, in which case there would be just a few words of scolding and that would be the end of it. If there was no bribe, then the official would be cursed from his forefathers all the way down to his grandchildren. This was considered an "imperial" scolding, but who would ever ask the emperor if this was how he would conduct the scolding? According to a Japanese magazine, Cheng Fangwu[22] was selected by the Chinese peasant and working masses to go to Germany to study drama last year. We have no way of verifying whether he was really selected in this manner or not.

So I believe that if we want to arrive at a deeper understanding, we can only fall back on my old motto, "Read more foreign books,"[23] to break through the encircling group monopolizing the debates. This should not require much effort from you gentlemen. Even if there are not many examples of new literature in English or English translation, still, those that exist are certainly more truthful and reliable. Once you have read more of the theories and literature of other countries, you will be able to see much more clearly when you come back to judge China's new literature. It would be even better if you introduced them to China; translation is not as easy as carelessly writing original works, and it is an even greater contribution to the development of new literature and more beneficial to everyone.

TRANSLATED BY ANDREW STUCKEY

# A Glimpse at Shanghai Literature

上海文藝之一瞥

Shanghai literature began with the newspaper *Shen bao*.[24] To discuss *Shen bao*, you need to go back sixty years, but I have no knowledge of those matters; all I can recall is that the *Shen bao* of thirty years ago was still only printed on one side of traditional bamboo paper. Those who wrote for that venue were mostly the "talented scholars" who flocked to Shanghai from various locales.

The educated people of that time can be roughly divided into two camps, the "gentlemen" and the "talented scholars." The "gentlemen" were those who only read the Four Books and Five Classics, composed eight-legged essays, and were extremely scrupulous with regard to the rules. The "talented scholars" did the same, but in addition also read vernacular novels, such as *Dream of the Red Chamber*, and composed old- and new-style verse that was not permitted on the civil service examinations. In short, the talented scholars openly read *Dream of the Red Chamber*, but whether the gentlemen may have also read it in secret, I have no way of knowing. Once Shanghai's foreign concessions appeared, talented scholars flocked to Shanghai. (At that time, the foreign concessions were also called "Westerners' Square" and "Barbarians' Square" [*Yi chang*]. Later, because people feared violating the taboo against the word *barbarian*, the character *yi* was replaced by a homophone.)[25] Since they were open-minded, the talented scholars roamed about everywhere. The gentlemen, however, regarded foreign things with some disgust. Moreover, they sought the fame that came with following the proper career path, so they most certainly didn't roam about so freely. Confucius once said, "If the Way were proved unviable, I would put to sea on a raft."[26] From the talented scholars' perspective, this captures something of the

---

Based on a lecture delivered to the Social Science Research Association. First published in two parts on July 27 and August 3, 1931, in *Literary News* (Wenyi xinwen) and later anthologized in *Two Hearts* (Er xin ji, 1932). The lecture is erroneously dated August 12 in the written essay; Lu Xun's diary notes that it was delivered on July 20. Lu Xun, *Lu Xun quanji* (Complete works of Lu Xun) (Beijing: Renmin wenxue, 2005), 4: 298–315.

spirit of talent. The talented scholars thus thought of the gentlemen's behavior as outdated pedantry.

Talented scholars have always been filled with worries and ailments; they get worked up at the call of a crow or melancholy upon seeing the moon. Once they arrived in Shanghai, they encountered prostitutes. When going about his whoring, a talented scholar could call upon ten or twenty maidens to gather together, a scene that much resembled something from *Dream of the Red Chamber*. He thereupon saw himself as a Jia Baoyu, and since he was a talented scholar, these whores had to be beauties—like that, the scholar-beauty romance genre was born. These tales for the most part described how only talented scholars could pity forlorn, fallen beauties, and how only those beauties could appreciate these frustrated scholars. After undergoing myriad trials, they finally become happily married couples or transcend the world to become immortals.

The talented scholars assisted the Shenbao Press in producing and selling volumes of Ming-Qing short essays. They also established their own literary clubs and invited members to submit lantern riddles. Those whose riddles were deemed excellent were then rewarded with these small volumes, which as a result became known far and wide. There were also volumes of long works, such as *The Scholars, Eunuch Sanbao's Voyage to the West*, and *Stories to Delight the Heart*.[27] When we visit old bookstalls today we can still find on the first page of some thin volumes a stamp that says "Shanghai Shenbao Press Collected Treasures Edition." It is these books I'm referring to.

The scholar-beauty romances were best sellers for a number of years. But the thinking of the next generation of talented scholars gradually changed. They realized that beauties were not turning to prostitution because they were thirsting to appreciate talent, but only because they were after money. That the whores only wanted money didn't seem proper, so talented scholars devised all kinds of ingenious methods for subduing them. Not only did they avoid being deceived, they were even able to con the whores in turn. Novels detailing such methods thus appeared and were quite popular in society because people could read them as textbooks for whoring. The protagonists of these novels were no longer scholar-idiots; as they were now heroes who had achieved victory over the whore, they became scholar-thugs.

Well before this, an illustrated magazine titled *Dianshi Studio Pictorial*, whose main illustrator was Wu Youru, had already appeared. Immortals and humans, domestic and foreign news—he would illustrate them all. But when it came to foreign affairs, there was much he didn't understand. For example, when illustrating a battleship, he actually drew a merchant ship instead, but with movable cannons added to the ship's cabins. Illustrating a final duel, he featured two well-dressed soldiers crossing swords in a living room, with flower vases that had been knocked down and shattered on the floor. However, when he illustrated scenes of a "madam abusing her prostitutes" or "ruffians extorting money," he drew them very well. I think this was because he had seen many of these occurrences all too often in real life; even today I often can see faces in Shanghai resembling the ones he depicted. The *Dianshi Studio Pictorial* was quite popular at that time, reaching every province and the eyes and ears of those who sought to know "current trends" (what we now call "new learning"). A few years ago these illustrations were reissued in a new volume titled *Wu Youru's Treasured Prints*, which had a tremendous influence on later times. It goes without saying that we see this style in illustrations for novels; but even in illustrations for textbooks we can see kids donning a crooked cap with their slanted eyes and fleshy faces, the very picture of a thug. Today the new thug-illustrators include Mr. Ye Lingfeng. Mr Ye's illustrations are derived from the style of the English artist Aubrey Beardsley. Beardsley was a proponent of "art for art's sake," and his paintings bore a considerable influence from Japanese "floating world" (*ukiyo-e*) art. Although *ukiyo-e* is folk art, much of it depicts geishas and entertainers, who had voluptuous bodies and slanted eyes—"erotic" eyes. But the characters Beardsley drew were emaciated because he was a follower of the Decadents. The Decadents tended to be thin and listless and felt a little ashamed of themselves next to such robust, healthy women, so they didn't like them. As our Mr. Ye's new pictures of slanted eyes were just like Wu Youru's old pictures of slanted eyes, they naturally proved quite popular for a number of years. But Mr. Ye didn't just draw hoodlums; there was a period when he also drew proletarians. But the eyes of the workers he drew had the same slant as they stretched out their oversized fists. But I feel that depictions of the proletariat should be realistic and reflect the actual image of workers—there's no need to make their fists even larger than their heads.

Chinese films today also continue to bear the strong influence of the "scholar-thug" figure. The heroes, or the "good guys," are all shallow and resemble the slick young men who are accustomed to living in Shanghai and know how to extort money, harass women, and seduce girls. After watching such films, one is led to think that in order to become a hero or a good guy these days, one must be a thug.

But the "scholar-thug" novel slowly receded from view. I believe the reasons are twofold: for one, it always follows the old plot—a whore wants money, the john employs methods to avoid paying her, and the storyline inevitably exhausts itself. The second reason is because it tends to use Suzhou vernacular, with *ni* standing for "I" (*wo*), and *nai* for "you" (*ni*), *ashi* for "whether or not" (*shifou*), etc. With the exception of natives of Shanghai, Zhejiang, and Jiangsu, no one can understand these novels. But among the scholar-beauty novels there appeared one that at the time caused quite a stir. It was the Chinese translation of the English novel *Joan Haste* by H. R. Haggard. But only the first half appeared. According to the translator, he found the original at a used bookstand and thought it exceptionally good; unfortunately, he couldn't find the second volume, so nothing could be done about it. As expected, it struck the hearts of scholars and beauties alike and became very popular. Later it also moved Mr. Lin Qinnan, and he translated the whole novel and kept the original title. But it quickly evoked the ire of the first translator, who said that he shouldn't have done the complete translation, for by doing so he debased Joan's value, thus upsetting readers. I then realized why the previous translator had only rendered half the novel, and it wasn't because he had an incomplete version; rather, it was because he knew that Joan gives birth to a child out of wedlock, and he purposely chose not to include this episode. In fact, this kind of book, which isn't long, would never have been published in two volumes in foreign countries. And yet, through this episode, we can see Chinese attitudes at that time toward marriage.

At this time a new kind of scholar-beauty novel became popular. However, the beauty was a girl of a respectable family who falls deeply in love with a scholar. They are inseparable, and under the flowers of the willow tree, they appear like a pair of butterflies or mandarin ducks. But sometimes, because of their family's disapproval or an unlucky fate, they might on occasion actually meet a tragic end—no longer do they transform into immortals. One can't say that this isn't a big improvement. With the appearance of the monthly periodical *Eyebrow Talk*, edited by Chen Diexian, who also manufactured a brand of toothpaste that could be used simultaneously as a facial cleanser, the Mandarin Ducks and Butterflies genre reached its peak. Afterward, *Eyebrow Talk* faced censorship, but its influence did not recede. It was only when *New Youth* appeared that the genre became the butt of attacks. During that time, Ibsen's drama was introduced, and Hu Shi's new-style *Greatest Event in Life* made an appearance. While not deliberate, the effect of these works was that the Mandarin Ducks and Butterflies genre, which had the issue of marriage as its very raison d'être, fled from view just like Nora.[28]

Later, the Creation Society, founded by a camp of new talented scholars, appeared on the scene. The Creation Society revered genius and believed in art for art's sake. They emphasized subjective expression, worshipped creation, detested translation, and especially hated indirect translations via an intermediary language. The Society stood in opposition to the Shanghai Literary Research Association. In the Society's initial announcement proclaiming its establishment, its members claimed that there were people who "monopolized" the literary scene; they had in mind the Literary Research Association. The Literary Research Association was quite the opposite of the Creation Society: its members emphasized art for life's sake. They emphasized original creation while also respecting translation, focusing in particular on introducing the literature of oppressed nations. These nations were all minor countries, and no one understood their languages, so their literature almost always appeared via indirect translation. Moreover, because the Literary Research Association had supported *New Youth* at one time, new grudges combined with old ones, and the Literary Research Association underwent attacks on three fronts.

First, because the Creation Society upheld artworks of genius, its members thought that the Literary Research Association, with its promotion of "art for life's sake," did nothing more than meddle in other people's business and had an air of the vulgar about it. They also regarded the association's works as technically deficient; therefore, if a mistake in translation happened to occur, a society member would compose a long critique devoted to that single error. Another front of attack came from the camp of gentry who had once studied abroad in the United States. They believed that literature was meant only for gentlemen and ladies to read. For this camp, the only kinds of people who were fit to serve as literary characters, besides gentlemen and ladies, were literati, scholars, artists, academics, maidens, etc. Only those who knew how to use the English "yes" and "no" possessed the dignity of the gentry.

At that time, Mr. Wu Mi published an article in which he expressed his sheer incomprehension as to why some writers enjoyed describing the lower social orders.[29] The third front came from the Mandarin Ducks and Butterflies school previously mentioned. I don't know what methods they used, but they were able to force the publisher of Commercial Press to replace the editor of *Fiction Monthly*, a member of the Literary Research Association. Moreover, the Commercial Press established the magazine *Fiction World* in order to publish articles from the Creation Society.[30] The magazine stopped publication only last year.

On the surface, the Creation Society's battle ended in victory. Many of its works were compatible with the tastes of those who declared themselves talented scholars and benefited from the help of publishers. The society's influence grew. As its influence widened, big publishing houses like the Commercial Press began putting out translations from Creation Society members—that is, the works of Messrs. Guo Moruo and Zhang Ziping. As I recall, that was the moment when the Creation Society ceased to inspect Commercial Press publications for translation errors and then write up essays about them. I think these things bear a little of the "scholar + thug" style. However, the "new Shanghai" camp ultimately couldn't triumph over the "old Shanghai" camp. While in the middle of singing their victory song, the Creation Society members finally realized that they were merely producing commodities for their publishers. After all their effort, their bosses viewed them just like the paper figurines with winking eyes featured in the window displays of eyeglass shops: nothing more than a marketing ploy to attract customers. When Creation Society members sought to publish independently, the old bosses would take them to court. They eventually achieved independence and claimed that all of their publications had been heavily revised, published under new imprints, and issued in brand-new editions. The old publishers, however, could always just use their old editions, but offer huge discounts both in printing costs and sale price, and market these discounted books each year as some kind of anniversary or commemorative edition.

No longer wanting to produce commodities and unable to survive independently, the only exit strategy for the Creation Society members was to head to the somewhat more hopeful province of Guangdong, "cradle of the revolution." While the term *revolutionary literature* appeared in Guangdong, no such works actually existed. The term didn't even appear in Shanghai.

Only two years ago did the term *revolutionary literature* begin to flourish. Its champions were the senior statesmen of the Creation Society who had just returned from the "cradle of revolution," as well as some new figures. The reason for the flourishing of revolutionary literature lies in the social context—the masses and youth in general demanded it. When the Northern Expedition was launched from Guangdong, enthusiastic youths immersed themselves in practical work. At the time there was still no noticeable movement for revolutionary literature. But the political atmosphere suddenly changed. The revolution encountered setbacks, and the widening gap between classes became very clear. Under the pretext of "cleansing the party," the Guomindang slaughtered Communists and revolutionary masses. The youth who escaped death once again entered oppressive circumstances. Only at this point did revolutionary literature become extremely active in Shanghai. Thus the flourishing of revolutionary literature in China appears quite different from the situation in other countries: it wasn't due at all to a tide in the revolutionary, but rather to a setback in the revolution. Although some were old literati who laid down their sabers and returned to writing as a profession and some were young people pushed out of practical work with no choice but to write to survive, there was enough of a social foundation to produce among the new figures some with exceptional fortitude and propriety. But in my opinion, the revolutionary literature movement of that time was never well organized and had its problems. For one, it never engaged in a thorough analysis of Chinese society and merely sought to mechanically apply measures that could only be adopted under a Soviet political system. Second, its proponents—especially Mr. Cheng Fangwu—made revolution into something people in general found extremely frightening. They put on the menacing guise of the extreme left and seemed to suggest that once the revolution arrived, all nonrevolutionaries would be put to death, which led people to harbor nothing but terror toward revolution. But in fact revolution is not about teaching people how to die, but teaching people how to live. This method of "putting a little fear of the revolution" in people was about adopting an air of speaking freely and boldly, and thus was again poisoned by the "scholar + thug" style.

Revolutionary literature heated up quickly but then settled down and degenerated just as quickly. An educated person will always have a reason for defending a change and will cite some theory as his authority for making that change. For example, when he is in need of assistance, he will point to Kropotkin's theory of mutual aid, but when he is in fighting mood, he will cite Darwin's theory of the survival of the fittest. There are those who don't hold any definite principles or those who change their opinions without any apparent reason; they adopt any theory from whatever camp as their weapons. These people, past or present, can all be considered hoodlums. For example, when a Shanghai hoodlum sees a man and woman from the countryside walking together, he'll employ Chinese law and say: "Hey! The way you're acting is an offense against decency. You're breaking the law!" When he sees a man from the countryside urinating by the street and says, "Hey, that's not allowed. You're breaking the law and should be sent to jail," he is using foreign law. But the result has nothing to do with the law; as long as he extorts some cash, the matter is over.

In China, the revolutionary writers of last year were quite different from those of the year before. This is certainly due to a change in circumstances, but some "revolutionary writers" still retained old flaws that easily resurface. "Revolution" and "literature," whether separated or linked together, are like two boats floating side-by-side, one marked "revolution," the other marked "literature." A writer stands with each foot in separate boats. When the environment is relatively good, an author will step more firmly on the boat of revolution and make it clear that he is a revolutionary. But once the revolution is suppressed, then he'll step a bit more firmly on the boat of literature and transform to being just a writer. The opinions of two years ago were so fervent. But those who believed that people who wrote nonrevolutionary literature should all be wiped out last year began to recall the story of how Lenin loved reading the works of Ivan Goncharov[31] and began to believe that nonrevolutionary literature could actually bear deep significance. Moreover, there was that committed revolutionary Mr. Ye Lingfeng; he once depicted a character who was so revolutionary that he would use pages of my *Call to Arms* to wipe his ass when he went to the toilet. Now, for some inexplicable reason, Ye Lingfeng trails behind the asses of the so-called "nationalist writers."[32]

For a similar example, we can bring up Mr. Xiang Peiliang.[33] When the tide of revolution was gradually rising, he was very revolutionary. He once even said that the youth should not only howl, but also bare their wolves' teeth. Of course this isn't bad at all, but one should still be careful, because the wolf is the dog's ancestor. Once a wolf is tamed, it becomes a dog. Mr. Xiang now advocates humanistic art and opposes the existence of class-conscious art. As humanity can be divided between good and evil people, humanistic art thus becomes a weapon in the battle between good and evil. Dogs also divide people into two sorts—the sort of owners who raise dogs are good people; the poor and beggars are, in the dog's eyes, evil people that it will bark at or bite. But even this is not altogether a bad thing, because at least they still retain some of their wild nature. If they change further into docile dogs and pay no mind to anything but devoting themselves to their masters' service, they are just like today's well-known art-for-art's-sake figures who openly refuse to get involved in everyday matters. They're only good as a decoration for a college classroom.

This somersaulting petit bourgeoisie all too easily distorts revolution when writing revolutionary literature, and in distorting revolution, they bring harm to it. Thus it is hardly worth pitying when they change from being revolutionary. When the revolutionary literature movement was surging forward, many petit bourgeois writers suddenly changed sides. At the time, the explanation given for this phenomenon was the theory of sudden change. But we know that in order for this so-called sudden change to occur, for A to become B, several variables have to be present. When one variable is lacking and then finally appears, A can become B. For example, for water to crystallize, the temperature must reach zero, but at the same time there must also be a vibration in the surrounding atmosphere—if there is no such vibration, then even if the temperature reaches zero, it still won't crystallize. But once a vibration passes through the air, the water will then suddenly become ice. Thus while it appears as a sudden change, in fact it was not sudden at all. But if the right variables are not present, then even if one claims to have changed, he hasn't really changed at all. Thus there are petit bourgeois revolutionary writers who claim to have suddenly changed overnight and who not long afterward suddenly change right back to what they were. The founding of the League of Left-Wing Writers in Shanghai last year was an important event. Because they had already adopted the ideas of Georgi Plekhanov, Anatoly Lunacharsky, and others, everyone had a chance to exchange views. This exchange helped them to become stronger and more powerful. But precisely because the league was stronger and more powerful, it suffered oppression and devastation rarely seen the world over. However, this oppression and devastation unmasked some of these so-called revolutionary writers who had previously thought that once left-wing literature entered the limelight, they would soon enjoy the buttered bread offered by workers as a tribute. Some of these writers wrote statements of repentance, and some even turned around and attacked the league in order to demonstrate how their knowledge had made great progress in the past year. Although the league certainly didn't take active part in this exposure, it constituted a kind of purging of its ranks. Whether they've changed or not, these writers aren't able to produce good works anyway.

But can the left-wing writers who remain write good proletarian literature? I think this is also a difficult task. The reason is because today's left-wing writers are still educated people—that is, they are of the intellectual class, which is why it would be very difficult for them to write about the actual circumstances of revolution. The Japanese literary critic Kuriyagawa Hakuson once asked, "Must a writer only describe that which he has himself experienced?" He answered, not necessarily, because a writer can go out and observe. Therefore, if he wished to write about stealing, he needn't become a thief, and to write about adultery, he needn't go out and personally commit the act. However, I believe that because such writers were raised in the old society, were familiar with its mores and used to its people, they were able to observe this world. As for the proletariat and its world, which have no relationship whatsoever to their own lives, they would either be unable to depict them or would depict them inaccurately. Therefore, revolutionary writers must, at the very least, either live alongside revolution or deeply internalize the pulse of revolution. (The league's recently proposed slogan, "The Proletarianization of Writers," reflects an accurate understanding of this point.)

In the kind of society we have in China today, what we can most readily hope to see are works of exposure or resistance by rebellious elements of the petit bourgeoisie. Because they live in a class that is undergoing extinction, they therefore acquire a deep understanding of society and harbor great disgust toward it. The blow they deliver on society with their swords is, thus, the most powerful and fatal. While there are some works that appear to be revolutionary, they don't seek to overturn either their own class or that of the bourgeoisie. Instead, these works express how their authors lament or resign themselves to their inability to either improve their station or preserve their present status for much longer. Thus, from the proletariat's view, these works express nothing more than a sibling rivalry between the petit bourgeois and the capitalists, and both parties are to be regarded as enemies. But these works can nevertheless be caught up in the tide of revolution and form a single bubble of foam in its midst. I believe there is really no need to call these works proletarian literature; nor should such writers, in hopes of gaining future fame, call themselves proletarian writers.

Although these works attack the old society, unless they clearly recognize society's faults and diagnose the roots of its illness, then they will also bring harm to revolution. A pity that today's writers, including revolutionary writers and critics, are either completely unable or unwilling to directly confront society as it is now. They fail to recognize how society works and in particular how the enemy works. To casually bring up one example, in the formerly published *Leninist Youth*,[34] there was an essay that reviewed the Chinese literary scene and divided it into three camps. The first was the Creation Society, which represented the proletarian literary camp, and it was discussed at length. The next was the *Threads of Talk* (Yusi) group, which represented the petit bourgeois literary camp, but it was discussed rather briefly. The third was the Crescent Moon Society, which represented the capitalist literary camp; this discussion was even shorter, not even filling a whole page. This demonstrates the young critic's logic: the more something is recognized as belonging to the enemy camp, the less it's discussed and the less it is carefully observed. Naturally, when we read, it seems far more comfortable, pleasurable, and interesting to come across something we agree with than something we oppose. But when engaged in battle, I believe that in evaluating both revolution and the enemy, it is more important for us to dissect the enemy standing in front of us. Writing a literary work is the same; one should not only know the reality of revolution, but also have a deep and multisided understanding of the enemy's condition and the current situation. Only then can one determine the path of revolution. Only by understanding the old can one take note of the new; knowledge of what has passed will help us deduce what is to come. Only then will there be hope for our literature's development. I believe that, as long as writers work hard at it, they can still achieve this in the current conditions of our society.

As mentioned earlier, today's literature suffers a rarely seen oppression and devastation, and desperate conditions are prevalent. Not only revolutionary literature, but even literature that is just a little bit critical, suffers persecution. The same goes not just for literature that censures the present situation, but that attacks long-standing bad habits. This situation clearly demonstrates that revolution coming from the powers above has always constituted nothing more than the seizure of an old chair. When one wishes to push it aside, the chair appears loathsome, but the moment one grasps it, it suddenly feels like a treasure. At the same time, one will feel that he and this "old thing" are meant for each other. Twenty years ago, everyone said that Zhu Yuanzhang was a national revolutionary, but in fact he was nothing of the sort. After he became emperor, he declared the preceding Mongol dynasty "the Great Yuan Dynasty," and he went on to kill more Han Chinese than the Mongols did. When a slave becomes a master, he becomes utterly unable to do away with the title "master." His airs are even more ostentatious and ridiculous than those of his master. This is just like the Shanghai worker who earns a bit of money, opens a small factory, and then treats his workers in turn with utmost cruelty.

In an old work of *biji* fiction—I forget the title—there is a story of how in the Ming dynasty a certain general invited a storyteller to tell a story. The storyteller went on to recount a tale about Tan Daoji, a general of the Jin dynasty. After the storyteller finished his tale, the general ordered him beaten, and people asked the reason. He said, "He told me a story about Tan Daoji. Well, in mentioning Tan Daoji, he was obviously talking about me." The psyches of today's rulers are just as frail as that of this general; they fear everything. The reason is because there are hoodlums in the publishing world who are even cleverer than those of the past. Their presence is unseen, but their hoodlum techniques are even more underhanded: they employ advertisements, entrapment, and intimidation. There are even some writers who worship these hoodlums as godfathers in hopes of gaining a stable life and other benefits. Therefore, a revolutionary writer must not only watch out for the enemies in front of him, but also defend himself from secret agents who lurk all around. Compared to a battle merely confined to the world of letters, this battle is far more arduous, but it also affects literature greatly.

Although there are piles and piles of so-called literary journals in Shanghai today, they are all nothing but a bunch of hot air. Motivated by profit, the publishers are afraid of stirring up trouble; they do their utmost to select essays of no consequence. These essays say things like "while life (*ming*) cannot thrive without some kind of change (*ge*), such change cannot be taken too far."[35] People read them from beginning to end, but it's the same as not reading anything at all. As for government-sponsored journals or magazines that curry favor from officials, the authors are a bunch of rabble whose shared goal is to earn fees for their writing. They thus produce random pieces such as "Victorian English Literature" and "Sinclair Lewis Wins the Nobel" in addition to commentaries whose opinions they themselves don't hold and articles they themselves don't take seriously. And so I say that Shanghai's literary magazines are nothing but a bunch of hot air; though the literature of revolutionaries remains suppressed, there isn't anything noticeably literary about the magazines produced by the oppressors. Does that mean the oppressors don't have their own literature? Sure they do, just not the usual kind. Their literature consists of telegrams, official notices, the press, "nationalist literature,"[36] court judgments, etc.

For example, a few days ago *Shen bao* reported the case of a woman who sued her husband for committing sodomy by force, as well as beating her black and blue. But the court decided that according to the law there was no written prohibition against a man sodomizing his wife. As for the beating, the court decided that as long as no vital functions were harmed, then the charges could not stand. Now the man is countersuing his wife for false accusation. I don't know the law, but I have studied a bit of biology. When skin is beaten until bruised, the vital functions of the lungs, liver, or digestive tract are not harmed. But the vital functions of that patch of bruised skin have certainly been harmed. Although we encounter things like this all the time in China now, we don't think of it as anything unusual. But I believe such things allow us to understand certain aspects of society in a way that far surpasses an ordinary novel or poem. In addition to what I've discussed above, we should also analyze carefully the so-called nationalist literature and the long-debated martial arts novel. But the time allotted today isn't enough, and we must wait for a future opportunity to discuss it. I'll stop here for now.

TRANSLATED BY ROY BING CHAN AND YU CHIH CHOU

# On the "Third Type of Person"

## 論第三種人

For the past three years, there's been silence in the debates on the literary arts. Nobody can open their mouths, except for the "theorists" protected by generals' sabers who parade under the "leftist" banner, find arguments for artistic freedom in Marxism, and discover Leninist rationales for slaughtering all the rebel Communists. However, even if it's "art for art's sake," it's still "free," because these artists have never been suspected of accepting rubles. But the "third type of person"—that is to say, "a person who keeps a death grip on literature"—is unable to escape a stabbing premonition: that the leftist literary circle is going to brand them "running dogs of the bourgeoisie."

Representing this "third type of person," Mr. Su Wen cries out in *Les contemporains* magazine numbers 3 and 6 against the injustices they've faced (here I should first make a clarification: for convenience's sake, I will for the time being use words like *represent* and "third type of person," though I know full well that Su Wen's "group of writers" don't want to fix the meanings of words, because once fixed, they lose their coveted freedom; this is much like refusing to use words that aren't firmly defined, such as *perhaps, somewhat,* or *influence*). He's under the impression that leftist critics are prone to labeling writers "running dogs of the bourgeoisie." He says leftists will even take neutral parties as the opposition so that they can then be considered "running dogs of the bourgeoisie," and for this reason he calls left-wing writers "ideologues who never write anything." The "third type of person" wants to write but doesn't dare, and as a result the literary scene is devoid of artworks. However, the claim is that there's a small proportion of literary art that transcends

---

First published in volume 2, issue 1, of *Les contemporains* (Xiandai) on November 1, 1932, and later anthologized in *Southern Tunes in Northern Tones* (Nan qiang bei diao ji, 1934). Lu Xun, *Lu Xun quanji* (Complete works of Lu Xun) (Beijing: Renmin wenxue, 2005), 4: 450–456. This piece responds to an essay by Su Wen called "On 'Renewing Literature' and the Aesthetic Debates of Hu Qiuyuan" (Guanyu 'wenxin' yu Hu Qiuyuan de wenyi lunbian); quotations in the piece, with some exceptions, are from this essay. The debate at hand is whether the reformist literary world is divided entirely into proletarian leftists and bourgeois rightists, or whether there can be some desirable "third type" of writer.

class struggle and serves the future, a true and eternal literary art, and this is what the "third type of person" clings to so tightly. What a shame that the left-wing theorists have made it so that they don't dare write, because they have the premonition they're going to be criticized even before they begin.

I believe that writers can have such premonitions, but writers who consider themselves the "third type of person" are particularly prone to them. I also believe the author when he says that there are a lot of writers nowadays who have a good understanding of theory but haven't been swayed by it at an emotional level. But if one's feelings haven't changed, then one's understanding of theory will unavoidably be different from those whose feelings have already changed or whose feelings have undergone slight changes; these are therefore two different types of viewpoint. Mr. Su Wen's views, in my eyes, are completely incorrect.

Of course, since the formation of the left-wing literary scene, theorists have indeed made mistakes. Not only are there writers who resemble Mr. Su Wen's description of "ideologues who never write anything," but also those who are leftists on the outside and rightists on the inside. They go so far as to become foot soldiers for nationalist literature, bookstore owners, and anti-party spies. These writers loathe the leftist literary scene, but after they've abandoned it, it survives without them. It's done more than survive; it's still developing, overcoming its own evils, urging its troops forward toward the sacred terrain of literature. Mr. Su Wen has asked: After fighting for three years, isn't the victory already won? The answer is yes, we must continue to fight, and there's no saying whether it'll last another thirty years. But while we are fighting, while we are urging the troops forward, we shouldn't do anything so stupid as to wait until all obstacles are removed before advancing. However, Mr. Su Wen has made the following "joke": left-wing writers receive royalties for their literary work from capitalists. Here I want to say something honest, which is that left-wing writers are still oppressed, fettered, and slaughtered by the laws of this feudalist-capitalist society. So left-wing magazines have all been ruined and today are very few in number. Even if they occasionally manage to get an issue printed, they very rarely include critical works. When they do occasionally have critical works, they never identify writers as "running dogs of the bourgeoisie," and they don't refuse "fellow travelers." The leftist writer is not a divine soldier fallen from heaven, and he is not an enemy invader on a murderous rampage. Not only does he want the "fellow traveler" to take a couple of steps alongside him, he wants to recruit the onlookers watching from the roadside to come along too.

At this point we have to ask: Since the leftist literary scene is currently suppressed and can't publish many critical works, if there is a day in the future when they can be published, will they refrain from endlessly referring to the "third type of person" as "running dogs of the bourgeoisie"? Provided that the leftist critics haven't sworn not to, this possibility seems to exist when I look at it from an exclusively negative perspective. I can even imagine much worse. But I think that this kind of prediction is much like committing suicide because you believe the world will perhaps one day split in two—it's completely unnecessary. We hear, though, that Mr. Su Wen's "third kind of person" has, out of fear of this future, completely stopped writing. In all my life, I've never seen any writers put down their pen on account of a phantom conjured up in the mind. How could the strength of the writers "who keep a death grip on literature" be so weak? Would two lovers decline to embrace one another out of a fear of potential social reprimand?

In reality, the reason the "third type of person" has stopped writing has nothing to do with the cutting power of leftist criticism. The real reason is that it's just not possible to become a "third type of person," and because that's not possible, a third kind of pen can't be said to exist, so there's no point in discussing whether or not to put it down.

To be born into a class-based society and attempt to be a writer who transcends class, to be born into an age of struggle and attempt to avoid struggle through independence, to live today and attempt to give your works to the future, this kind of person is truly a phantom conjured up in the mind. In the real world, they don't exist. To be this type of person is like trying to leave the world by yanking upward on your own hair.[37] When it doesn't work, they get impatient, but it's not because anyone's shaking their head in disapproval that they give up.

So though there may be a "third type of person," they still haven't transcended economic class. Mr. Su Wen himself predicts an onslaught of class criticism, so how can writing cast off the force of class? There is also no escape from struggle: Mr. Su Wen has created the name "third type of person" as a form of resistance, although *resistance* is another one of those words he isn't willing to use. They can't extricate themselves from our modern times, either: before they've even composed the works that will transcend class and serve the future, they first have to attend to the criticism of leftist writers.

These truly are dire straits. But the dire straits are caused by the impossibility of turning fantasy into fact. Even if the obstacle of leftist writers didn't exist, there still wouldn't be any "third type of person," to say nothing of their literary works. Mr. Su Wen has invented a fantasy of a violent leftist literary scene that prevents the fantasy of his "third kind of person" from coming true. He has cast upon it the sin of preventing the literature of the future from appearing.

Left-wing writers are indeed less than superlative, with their comic strips and their folk operas, but they're not quite as devoid of future prospects as Mr. Su Wen has concluded. They also want Tolstoys and Flauberts, but they don't want Tolstoys and Flauberts who "strive to create works that belong to the future (because they don't care for *now*)." Both these authors wrote for their present time—the future is, after all, the future of the present, and things are meaningful to the future only after they have been meaningful in the present. Tolstoy in particular wrote little stories for rural people without calling himself a "third type of person," and the many bourgeois attacks on him never caused him to put down his pen. If the left wing really is as Mr. Su Wen says, it's not so stupid as to be ignorant of the fact that "comic strips can't produce a Tolstoy or a Flaubert," but it *does* believe that it can produce a painter as great as Michelangelo or da Vinci. What's more, I believe that the writing of folk operas can produce a Tolstoy or Flaubert. When we talk about Michelangelo or da Vinci's paintings today, nobody criticizes them, but weren't they in fact propaganda posters for religion, comic strips of the Old Testament? Furthermore, they were in service of the "modern day" of those times.

In summation, Mr. Su Wen claims that the "third type of person" is better off diligently writing literature than engaging in deception or producing fake goods. This is quite correct. "You must have the courage to believe in yourself, and then you'll have the courage to work!" This is especially true.

A speech given at Beijing Normal University, November 27, 1932

But Mr. Su Wen has also said that many of the "third type of person," great and small, have divined an inauspicious future—and have put down their pens out of fear of criticism from leftist theorists!

"Whatever shall we do?"

October 10

TRANSLATED BY NICK ADMUSSEN

# The Most Artistic Country
最藝術的國家

In our China, the greatest, most eternal and universal form of "art" is men impersonating women.[38] What's most admirable about this art form is its ability to appeal to all sides, otherwise known as adhering to the "middle way"[39]—men see the "woman" being impersonated, and women see the "man" impersonating. On the surface, the performer appears androgynous, but is, of course, still male to his very bones. But if it weren't for the disguise, would it still be art?

For example, things like the examination system and circumventing exams by purchasing official posts have been essential components of Chinese culture. When people started saying that such things did not at all resemble democratic rights and went against the tide of the times, the country then assumed the disguise of the Republic of China; yet this Republic of China has gone through years of disrepair, and its original facade has just about completely flaked off like the rouge and powder on the face of an old female impersonator. At that same time, the honest masses began to demand political rights for real; they even wanted to strip the voting rights of those who attained status through the examination system or by purchasing official posts. This is disloyal to our race and unfilial to our ancestors and is, indeed, reactionary to the extreme. Now that the "tide of the times" has long

---

First published in the "Free Talk" column of *Shen bao* on April 2, 1933, under the pseudonym He Jiagan and later anthologized in the essay collection *Fake Liberty* (Wei ziyou shu, 1933). Lu Xun, *Lu Xun quanji* (Complete works of Lu Xun) (Beijing: Renmin wenxue, 2005), 5: 91–94.

since reverted to reviving what is essential to our culture, how can we tolerate such rampant disloyalty and unfilial behavior?

And so we had no choice but to adopt a new disguise again, passing preliminary regulations like the following: first, those with the qualifications to represent the people will be selected through an examination; second, after the successful examinees have been selected, there will be another process of selection, called *xuan juren*, or electing *provincial candidates*.[40] Candidates selected on this basis are naturally those voted into office. Based on grammar alone, the representatives of the national assembly should be called "electors" (*xuanju ren zhe*) and those who are selected should be called "the elected" (*bei xuanju zhi ren*). But if it weren't for the disguise, would it still be art? And so they had to perform the roles of the electorate and the elected of a country governed by a constitution, even though in principle they were, in fact, still *xiucai*[41] and *juren* from the old examination system.

Here lies the deeper significance of these regulations: to let the masses see what appears to be democratic rights and to let one's race and ancestors see what appears to be loyalty and filiality—loyalty to the race that produced the examination system, filiality to the ancestors who instituted that system. Other than this example, there's the democratic rights already in place in Shanghai, where only those who pay taxes have the right to elect and be elected, making it so that the vast area of Shanghai is left with only 4,465 citizens. Though this is like purchasing an official post, the majority of them doing so being wealthy, they most certainly will be selected as *juren*; even without making it to the following exam, some would still be granted the status of a low-level *jinshi*,[42] because one ought to follow the model of the Western masters. Not to mention, isn't this an example of something that doesn't violate what is essential to our culture and yet also maintains the facade of a constitutional government and democratic rights? This is just one example.

A second example is that one can engage and resist at the same time.[43] Seen from this angle, it's resistance; seen from that angle, it's engagement. A third is that one can be an entrepreneur or a banker and still call oneself "modestly poor."[44] A fourth is that when sales of Japanese goods are brisk, one can still say it's "national products year."[45] There are too many examples to raise here, almost all of the disguises done quite cleverly, appealing to all sides.

Oh, China is indeed the most artistic country and the race that most adheres to the middle way.

And yet the masses still insist on being disgruntled. Alas, gentlemen follow the middle way, petty men oppose it!

March 30

TRANSLATED BY EILEEN J. CHENG

# The Crisis of the Small Essay
## 小品文的危機

I seem to recall a month or two ago reading in some sort of daily paper an article that recorded the death of a famous collector of "curios" and ended with a vague lament that the passing of this person would mark the demise of "curio" collecting in China.

A pity, however, that I wasn't paying much attention at the time and have now forgotten the name of the daily and the name of the collector.

On the whole, the new youth of today, I'm afraid, don't know what a "curio" is. But if he happens to have been born into an old family whose members once dabbled with brush and ink and that hadn't fallen too badly on hard times and hadn't yet sold off its knick-knacks to a secondhand store, then perhaps he might find among a pile of dusty discarded things a miniature free-standing mirror, an exquisitely carved stone, a figurine whittled from bamboo roots, an animal sculpted of old jade, or a three-legged toad made of patina bronze—so-called "curios." Before, when they were displayed in literati studios, each had its own elegant name; the three-legged toad, for example, would be called "water well in a toad inkstone" or the like. The last

---

First published in volume 3, issue 6, of *Les contemporains* (Xiandai) on October 1, 1933, and later anthologized in *Southern Tunes in Northern Tones* (Nan qiang bei diao ji, 1934). Lu Xun, *Lu Xun quanji* (Complete works of Lu Xun) (Beijing: Renmin wenxue, 2005), 4: 590–593. This essay was written in response to the emergence of a style of essay writing, promoted by Lin Yutang (1895–1976) and others, that emphasized humor and taste. Lu Xun considered this style of essay to be frivolous, like curios.

collector mentioned above would certainly know all these names, and now they will disappear along with the glory of the objects themselves.

Those objects were of course decidedly not possessions of the poor, though they were also not displayed by powerful officials or wealthy families; what these latter preferred were bonsai trees made of pearl and jade or porcelain with polychromatic illustrations—the "refined objects" of the so-called literati, for whom, at the very least, a dozen acres of fertile land and, in the home, several elegant studios were de rigueur. Even when they sojourned to Shanghai, they still had to live a relatively leisurely life; leasing from a guest house a long-term room with an escritoire and an opium couch, they would smoke themselves into a state of insouciance and fondle their curios in appreciation. However, this world has now been flushed away by a global tide of peril, like a small boat caught among raging waves.

Yet even in times of peace and prosperity, these "curios" were never terribly important. Etching a copy of the "Preface to the Orchid Pavilion" on an inch-long piece of ivory might be called a objet d'art, but if you hang it on the Great Wall or place it at the feet of an eighty-foot-high Buddha at the Yungang Grottoes, it would appear tiny to the point of being invisible; even if someone passionate about curios eagerly pointed it out, it would merely leave the onlooker with a feeling of amusement. Furthermore, at a time when we are buffeted by biting winds and surrounded by wolves and tigers, who has that much idle time to fool around with amber fan pendants or jade rings? If they want to feast their eyes on something, a grand building is better, one that soars high in the biting winds, solid and imposing, not refined. To satisfy them, it should be daggers and spears, incisiveness and conscientiousness, no need for anything elegant.

The illusion of the demand for "curios" in the art world has already been shattered, something the author of that daily paper article already knew intuitively. But the demand for "curios" in the literary world—the small essay—is getting more vigorous by the day. Those making the demands believe they can rely on soft laments and gentle moans to gradually refine the coarse and unruly minds of men. The thinking is that if someone reads the *Literary Collection of the Six Dynasties* with all their heart, they will forget that they are clutching the tops of a tree flooded by the waters of the Yellow River after it burst its banks.

But in times like these, the only things we need are struggle and combativeness.

Indeed, the very existence of the essay relies on struggle and combativeness. The pure talk of the Jin dynasty disappeared long ago with the dynasty itself. By the end of the Tang, poetry had begun to decline, and the small essay emerged with luster. Luo Yin's (833–910) *Book of Slander* consists almost entirely of words of struggle and anger; Pi Rixiu and Lu Guimeng saw themselves as hermits and others called them such, but when you read the essays in their *Master Pi's Literary Anthology* and the *Lize Collectaneum,* you can see that they by no means forgot the affairs of the world; their essays were a bit of brightness and clarity in a confused and muddy world. Although by the end of the Ming the small essay had degenerated, it was more than just sentimental gush about the wind and the moon; there were among them expressions of injustice, satire, attack, and destruction. This kind of style provoked anxiety among the Manchu rulers, and with the aid of many swords of evil-abetting generals and pens of idle literati, it was suppressed by the time of the Qianlong Emperor. What followed were "curios."

These "curios," of course, would never have thrived broadly. But when the May Fourth movement came, another expansion occurred, and the success of the prose essay and the small essay almost surpassed that of fiction, drama, and poetry. Naturally, they contain elements of struggle and combativeness, but because they are often modeled after the English "essay," they also contain some humor and grace; their writing style, with its charm and precision, was a show of force against the old literature to demonstrate that the strengths associated with the old literature are just as possible in the vernacular. And because it grew out of the "literary revolution" and the "revolution in thought," its later development was most certainly one of even sharper struggle and combativeness. But the tendency today is instead to advocate for points of commonality between it and the old literature—grace, charm, and precision—which is to say that those promoting this kind of essay want it to become a "curio" for sophisticated people to fondle. The idea is that if young people fondle these "curios," their coarseness and brutish ways will become elegant and refined.

But now there are no longer any more escritoires. Although opium is already sold publicly, opium pipes have been banned, so it's really not that easy to partake. To think that someone on a battlefield or in a disaster zone would want to appreciate "curios"—everyone knows that's an even stranger illusion. These kinds of small essays are rife in Shanghai, hot topics in tea-houses and taverns and filling the tabloid-selling kiosks, but their authors are just like prostitutes who can no longer ply their trade in the alleyways and can only put on some makeup and shuffle along the main streets at night.

This is how the small essay has reached a state of crisis. What I mean by crisis is something like the term *Krisis* in medicine, the intersection point between life and death that can lead, on the one hand, to demise or, on the other, to recovery. Works that anesthetize will die out along with those who anesthetize and those who are anesthetized. The essays that live on will be daggers and spears, things that are able to hack out, along with their readers, a bloody path for survival. But naturally they will also be able to offer people happiness and respite, though they are not "curios" and, even more, will neither console nor numb; the happiness and respite they offer are a form of cultivation, to prepare them for future labor and combat.

October 1, 1933

TRANSLATED BY KIRK A. DENTON

Portrait of Lu Xun, May 1, 1933

# SECTION V

*On Modern Culture*

# Impromptu Reflections No. 48
## 隨感錄四十八

The Chinese have had, throughout the ages, only two terms of address for other races: either "beasts" or "royal highnesses." They have never been called friends, nor said to have anything in common with us.

We have been deceived by accounts in ancient books of treacherous seas that cannot be crossed: the foreigners we had never heard of arrived. After battling with them a few times, we gradually found that the sayings of Confucius and verses from the *Book of Odes* didn't seem very useful, so we sought reform.

After the reforms, China became wealthy and powerful. It used the new things learned from abroad to expel the new things from abroad and closed its large doors, once again observing the old ways.

A pity that the reforms were but superficial and closing the doors was just a dream. Newer and increasingly superior theories from abroad proliferated. The more we tried to squeeze out of the sayings of Confucius and verses from the *Book of Odes*, the more we suffered; the more we read them, the more useless they seemed. So other than those two old terms of address for other races, we came up with a new nickname: the "Western sage," sometimes referred to as the "Western Confucian."

Although the terms of address were new, our opinions were the same as before. Although it was necessary to learn the skills of the "Western sages," it became all the more important that the sayings of Confucius and verses from the *Book of Odes* flourish. In other words, it was necessary to both learn foreign skills and preserve old Chinese customs. Skills had to be new, but thought old. It is like expecting the new folks of the new-skills-and-old-thought persuasion to carry on their backs the old folks of the old-skills-and-old-thought mentality, while asking the old folks to make full use of their well-seasoned old skills. In short, what was called "Chinese learning for the

First published in volume 6, issue 2, of *New Youth* (Xin qingnian) on February 15, 1919, under the pseudonym Si and later anthologized in *Hot Wind* (Re feng, 1925). Lu Xun, *Lu Xun quanji* (Complete works of Lu Xun) (Beijing: Renmin wenxue, 2005), 1: 352–353.

essence, Western learning for practical use" a few years ago has in recent years been referred to as "adopting suitable measures according to the times; the middle way is the most appropriate course."

But there are really no such happy compromises in the world. It is like the case of a sacrificed cow: it can no longer plow the field if it's placed as an offering to Confucius; it can no longer be milked once its meat has been eaten. How much more the case of someone who not only has to keep himself alive, but to do so while carrying his elders on his back and having to respectfully obey the elders' instructions on the middle way: bow in the morning, and shake hands in the evening; use Western technology and skills in the morning, and cite the Confucian classics in the afternoon.

The people who are most superstitious about gods and ghosts can, after all, only carry the sedan chair of the gods on the day of the temple fair.[1] I wonder if those "progressive sages" studying Western skills and technology will be able to make happy compromises in their lifetimes while carrying the hermits living in the wild and old loyalists living by the sea on their backs?

The "Western sage" Ibsen probably felt this wasn't possible, so he borrowed Brand's mouth to say: "All or nothing!"[2]

TRANSLATED BY EILEEN J. CHENG

# Untitled

無題

On the second day of the charity gala for a private school, I went along with a few friends on a stroll in Central Park.

I stood by the entrance of a building displaying a sign on the wall that read "Kunqu Opera." Someone squeezed past me from behind, pressing me into the wall so hard that I could hardly draw a breath. He seemed to think

---

First published in the *Supplement to the Morning Post* (Chenbao fukan) on April 12, 1922, and later anthologized in *Hot Wind* (Re feng, 1925). Lu Xun, *Lu Xun quanji* (Complete works of Lu Xun) (Beijing: Renmin wenxue, 2005), 1: 405–406.

I was merely a soul without physical substance. It must be said that he was not entirely correct in this assumption.

I wanted to share some snacks with the children when I returned home, and it was thus that I stopped in at a confectionary to do some shopping. I ended up getting some 黃枚朱古律三文治 (*huangmei zhugulü sanwenzhi*).

This, at least, is what it said on the label. Characters with a rather enigmatic flavor to them, but no, in English it was just "Chocolate Apricot Sandwich." I purchased eight chocolate apricot sandwiches, handed over my money, and began to stuff them into my pockets. Unfortunately, I happened to gaze sideways, taking in the counter clerk, whose five fingers were splayed out so as to guard the rest of the chocolate apricot sandwiches I had not bought.

This was obviously an insult to me! And yet, in truth, I should not have felt it as such, because I could hardly guarantee that if he had not covered the rest of the sandwiches, they would never be stolen in the confusion. Nor could I prove to him with absolute certainty that I was not a thief, let alone guarantee, even to myself, that I had never stolen anything in the past, was not now stealing, and would never steal anything in the future.

But at the time I was very displeased and, putting on a fake smile, I slapped the clerk's shoulders and said: "There's no need for that. I wouldn't go so far as to take an extra."

He demurred, "Of course not, of course not . . ." and retracted his hand, ashamed. This was a shock—I had expected him to argue with me—and so I, too, felt ashamed.

This kind of shame was like cold water flung in the face of my suspicion of human beings, and harmful to me as such.

At night, I sat all alone in my room, at a remove of at least several yards from all other people. I ate a left-over chocolate apricot sandwich, leafed through a few pages of a book by Tolstoy, and gradually began to feel that the space around me held a distant hope for humankind.

TRANSLATED BY ANDREW F. JONES

# What Happens after Nora Walks Out

娜拉走後怎樣

A talk given to the Literature and Arts Society at Beijing Women's
Normal College, December 26, 1923

My talk today is on the subject "What Happens after Nora Walks Out."

Henrik Ibsen was a Norwegian writer in the second half of the nine-teenth century. Apart from a few dozen poems, his work was mostly in drama. At one period in his life he wrote plays that were mainly on social problems, known to the world at large as "social drama," and among them was the play known in China as *Nuola* (Nora).[3]

The play's title in German is *Ein Puppenheim* (A puppet's home).[4] How-ever, the word *Puppe* refers not only to a puppet or marionette but also to a doll that children play with; more broadly, it also refers to people whose ac-tions are controlled by others. At the outset, Nora is living contentedly in a supposedly happy household, but eventually she is awakened: she is her hus-band's puppet, and her children are her puppets. So she walks out, and the play ends with the sound of the front door slamming shut.

What would have prevented Nora from leaving? Ibsen may have sup-plied the answer himself in *Die Frau vom Meer* (The lady from the sea), translated into Chinese as *Hai shang furen* (The lady at the sea). The heroine is married, and her former lover lives across the sea, but one day he seeks her out to ask her to elope with him. She tells her husband that she wants to meet her visitor. Her husband finally says, "I give you complete freedom. You can decide for yourself (whether to leave or not) and take sole responsi-bility for your decision." This changes the whole situation, and she doesn't

This talk was first published in a slightly edited version in 1924 in volume 6 of the *Journal of the Literary Association* (Wenyi hui kan) of the Women's Normal College and later antholo-gized in *Graves* (Fen, 1927). It was inspired by two of Ibsen's plays, *Et Dukkehjem* (A doll's house, 1879) and *Fruen fra Havet* (The lady from the sea, 1888). I am deeply indebted to Elisa-beth Eide, formerly of the University of Oslo and the National Library of Norway, Jens-Morten Hanssen of the Centre for Ibsen Studies, University of Oslo, and Anders Hansson for their generous assistance. Lu Xun, *Lu Xun quanji* (Complete works of Lu Xun) (Beijing: Renmin wenxue, 2005), 1: 165–173.

leave. Judging from this, if Nora had been given this kind of freedom, she might have stayed too.

However, Nora ends up walking out. What happens to her afterward? Ibsen gave no answer, and now he's dead. Even if he weren't dead, it wouldn't be his responsibility to answer the question. For Ibsen was writing poetry, not raising a problem for society and providing an answer to it. It's like the golden oriole, which sings for itself and not for the amusement or benefit of human beings. Ibsen was a rather unworldly type of person. It's said that when he was invited to a banquet in his honor by a group of women, and their representative rose and thanked him for having written *A Doll's House* and giving people new insight into women's consciousness and emancipation, he replied, "That was not what I had in mind when I wrote the play. I was just writing poetry."[5]

What happens after Nora walks out? A few people have given their opinions on this. An English playwright wrote a version in which a modern woman leaves home, but as she has nowhere to go, she becomes degraded and enters a brothel. There's also a Chinese man—what shall I call him? Let's just say a Shanghai writer—who claims to have seen a version, which differs from the Chinese translation, in which Nora eventually returns home. Unfortunately, this version hasn't been seen by anyone else, unless Ibsen himself sent it to him. Logically, however, Nora really has only two options: to fall into degradation or to return home. A bird in a cage lacks any kind of freedom, no doubt, but should it leave its cage, dangers lurk outside: hawks, cats, and so on; and if it has been shut up for so long that its wings have atrophied or it has forgotten how to fly, then truly it has no way out. There is another possibility—that is, to starve to death—but since starving means departing from life, it's no solution to the problem and so is not a way out either.

The most painful thing in life is to wake from a dream and find there is no way out. People who dream are fortunate. If there isn't a way out in sight, it is important not to wake them. Take the Tang poet Li He, who died at the age of twenty-six after being poor and wretched the whole of his life. As he lay near death, he said to his mother, "The Emperor of Heaven has built a white jade palace, Mother, and summoned me to write a poem on its completion." Wasn't this surely a falsehood, a dream? But for the young man who was dying and the elderly woman who survived him, it allowed a dying man to go happily to his death, while his survivor was able to live in peace. Falsehoods and dreams at such times may be magnificent. It therefore seems to me that dreams are what we need if we cannot find a way out.

Nevertheless, it's not a good idea to dream about the future. The Russian novelist Mikhail Artsybashev made use of one of his novels to challenge idealists who dream of a future golden age, since they call up misery for the many in order to build that world. "You promise their sons and grandsons a golden age," he said, "but what do you have to give them?" There is, of course, something to be given: it is hope for the future. The cost is too great, however: for the sake of this hope, people are made more sensitive to the depths of their own suffering, while their souls are summoned to witness their own rotting corpses. These times appear to be splendid only in falsehoods and dreaming. To me, therefore, dreams are what we need if we can't find a way out, but not dreams of the future, just dreams of the present.

And yet once Nora had awakened, it was not easy for her to return to dreamland, so her only recourse was to leave; but after she'd left, she soon faced the inevitable choice between degradation and returning home. Otherwise, we are obliged to ask, what did Nora take with her apart from her awakened mind? If she had nothing but a crimson woolen shawl like you young ladies, it would be completely useless, whether it was two feet wide or three feet wide. She would still need something more substantial that could go in her purse; to be blunt, she would need money.

Dreams are fine, but otherwise money is essential.

The word *money* sounds ugly, or even ridiculous to superior folk, but generally it's my belief that people's opinions vary, not just from one day to another but even before and after they've had a meal. People who readily admit that a meal costs money and yet still maintain that money is dirty would, I'm afraid, if you could check their stomachs, probably still have some undigested scraps of fish or pork inside them—but just let them fast for a day and then see what they have to say.

So for Nora, money (or to put it more elegantly, economic means) is crucial. It is true that freedom cannot be bought, but it can be sold. Human beings have one major defect: they are apt to get hungry. To compensate for this defect and avoid acting like puppets, economic rights seem to be the most important factor in present-day society. First, there must be a fair division of property between men and women in the family; second, there must be an equal division of power between men and women in society at large. Unfortunately, I have no idea how to obtain these rights, other than that we will have to fight for them, perhaps with even more violence than we have to fight for our political rights.

Demanding economic rights is no doubt a very commonplace sort of thing, but it may turn out to be more troublesome than demanding elevated political rights or broadly based women's emancipation. There are plenty of examples everywhere of how it's more troublesome to get small things done than big things. For example, if it's a winter like the present one and all we have is a single padded jacket, we are obliged to choose between saving a poor man who is freezing to death or sitting under a Tree of Enlightenment meditating on ways of saving all of mankind. The difference in degree between saving all mankind and saving one poor man is actually immense, but if you were to ask me to choose, I would instantly go and sit under a Tree of Enlightenment, because it would save me from taking off my only jacket and freezing to death. So it won't meet with heated opposition in the family if you talk about a division of political power, but just mention equal shares of economic resources and you'll inevitably find yourself confronted by enemies, which of course leads to ferocious battles.

Fighting isn't very nice, and we can't expect everyone to be a fighter, so peaceful methods will come to be prized: that is, for parents in the future to exercise their authority to liberate their own children. Parental authority in China is absolute, so it should be possible at that point to divide up the family property and share it evenly between sons and daughters so that they receive equal economic rights in peace and without conflict. Afterward, they may do as they please, and whether they go on to study, start up a business, have a fine old time enjoying themselves, work for the betterment of society, or squander the lot, it's all their own responsibility.

Although this is also a rather distant dream, it is much closer than the dream of a golden age. However, the first requirement is memory. Poor memory benefits ourselves but harms our descendants. The ability to forget allows people to leave behind step by step the suffering they once knew; but the ability to forget also leads people to repeat the mistakes of their predecessors. When a daughter-in-law who has been mistreated becomes a mother-in-law, she will still mistreat her own daughter-in-law; an official who detests students may have been a student who used to denounce officials; parents who now oppress their children may ten years earlier have been family rebels. This probably relates to age and status, but poor memory is also a major factor. The remedy is for everyone to go and buy a notebook and jot down what they are now thinking and doing, so that they can refer to it in the future when their age and status have changed. If you get irritated because your child wants to go to the park, take a look through your notebook until you see the entry, "I want to go to Central Park," and you'll immediately calm down. It's the same with everything else too.

There is a kind of low-level criminality at large these days whose chief characteristic is tenacity. It's said that the petty criminals in Tianjin after the Boxer Rebellion were very tough. For example, if you asked someone to take your luggage, he would demand two dollars; if you said it was a small case, he would say it was two dollars; and if you said it wasn't far to go, he would say it was two dollars; and if you said you didn't want it carried, he would say it was two dollars. Petty criminals can't, of course, be considered good role models, but there is something admirable in their tenacity. It's the same with demanding your economic rights. When someone tells you this is too old-fashioned, the response should be that you want your economic rights; when they say it's too petty, the response should be that you want your economic rights; when they say the economic system is about to change and there's no need to worry, the response should still be that you want your economic rights.

Actually, Nora would not necessarily find herself in trouble if she were to leave home at present, because people like her are very unusual and her conduct would appear fresh and novel, so there would be sympathetic people who would help her survive. Survival thanks to others' sympathy is already a loss of freedom, but even this sympathy would be stretched thin if a hundred Noras were to leave home while a thousand or a million Noras would only be met with disgust. Certainly it would be far more reliable to have economic rights in your own hands.

Are you no longer a puppet once you have won economic freedom? No, you are still a puppet. It's just that you are less subject to others' control and more in control of other puppets. In present-day society, it's not only the case that women are men's puppets, but men are other men's puppets, women are other women's puppets, and some men are even women's puppets. This is not something that can be remedied by a few women gaining economic rights.

Nevertheless, people cannot wait quietly with empty stomachs for the arrival of an ideal world. At the very least they must reserve a last breath, like a perch in a dry riverbed desperately seeking a drop of water; they need this economic power—which is relatively close at hand—before devising other methods.

(Of course, this is all empty talk should the economic system actually be reformed.)

However, I have so far discussed Nora as if she were an ordinary person, but it would be a different matter if she were exceptional and had rushed off willingly to sacrifice herself. We have no right to encourage people toward self-sacrifice, nor to prevent them from doing so. There are, moreover, many people in the world who take pleasure in self-sacrifice and suffering. There is a legend in Europe that when Jesus was on his way to crucifixion, he stopped for a rest under the eaves of Ahasvar's house, but Ahasvar refused to let him rest there.[6] For this he was cursed, doomed to roam the world without being able to rest until the Day of Judgment. Ahasvar is still roaming around the world today, unable to stop and rest. Roaming is painful and rest is pleasurable, so why doesn't he take a rest? Although he is under a curse, he most likely still feels that roaming is preferable to resting, and so he continues his frantic roaming.

His preference for such sacrifice is personal to him, however, and has nothing to do with the social aims professed by revolutionaries. The masses (especially in China) have always been spectators at a play. If the sacrificial victim is bold and brave when he takes the stage, they are watching a tragedy; if he cringes and cowers, they are watching a farce. You'll often find people standing outside a Beijing mutton shop watching open-mouthed as a sheep is being skinned. They seem to enjoy the sight, and what they gain from human sacrifice is little more than this. What's more, even this bit of pleasure will be forgotten before they've moved a few steps away.

There is nothing you can do with people like this; the only cure is to give them nothing to watch. There's no call for a briefly horrifying sacrifice; it's better to engage in protracted, tenacious struggle.

Unfortunately, it's too difficult to change China: blood will flow just by moving a table or mending a stove. And even if blood does flow, the table isn't necessarily going to be moved or the mending carried out. Unless a great whip lashes her back, China will never consider budging. I think such a whipping is bound to come. Whether for good or bad is another question, but it is bound to come. When it will come and how it will come, however, I cannot exactly tell.

I'll end my talk here.

TRANSLATED BY BONNIE S. MCDOUGALL

# On Photography and Related Matters

論照相之類

## I. Materials

During my childhood in S City—and by childhood I mean thirty years ago, which from the perspective of a progressive savant like myself seems like a century, and as for S City, I am not about to divulge its true name, nor will I say why I won't divulge it—in any case, one often heard in S City men and women of all ages discussing how the foreign devils would pluck out people's eyes. There was once a woman who was a servant in a foreign devil's household. After leaving their employ, it came out that her reason for quitting was that she had herself seen a jar of pickled eyes piled like carp fry, layer upon layer, right up to the edge of the jar. She fled quickly and far to avoid this peril.

It is the custom in S City that by winter's arrival families of means pickle in large jars enough cabbage to provide for the coming year's needs. Whether the cabbage is meant to be used in the same way as Sichuan pickled vegetables, I know not. The use foreign devils had for pickled eyes, of course, lay elsewhere, only the preparation was influenced by S City's pickling of cabbage, which is sure proof of the saying that China has great power of assimilation over the West. When people were asked what these things were that look like carp fry, their response was that these were indeed eyes of the residents of S City. In the temples of S City one often finds a Bodhisattva known

---

First published in issue 9 of *Threads of Talk* (Yusi) on January 12, 1925, and later anthologized in *Graves* (Fen, 1927). Lu Xun, *Lu Xun quanji* (Complete works of Lu Xun) (Beijing: Renmin wenxue, 2005), 1: 190–200.

as Our Lady of Sight. Those with eye ailments can pray to her, and if they are cured, they cut a pair of eyes out of cloth or silk and place it on the statue or to its side as gratitude for her holy protection. You need only look at how many eyes are hanging from the statue to get a sense of whether the Bodhisattva's powers are effective or not. And these hanging eyes are pointy at the ends, just like carp fry; you will look in vain for a pair of round-shaped eyeballs like those sketched in foreign biology drawings. The dialogues on medicine between the Yellow Emperor and Qi Bo belong to the mythical days of yore and deserve no mention![7] And we have no way of knowing whether drawings were made when the Han usurper Wang Mang killed Zhai Yi and had his body dissected for the inspection of his physicians (and even if they were, they are now long lost, so it is pointless to say "antiquity is the source of all things"). The Song dynasty *Classic of Dissection*, included in the *Shuofu*[8] (which I myself have read), relates eyewitness medical reports, but most are nonsense and likely spurious. When such eyewitness accounts are so confused, is it really any wonder that the people of S City would stylize eyeballs into the form of carp fry?

But still, did the foreign devils really eat pickled eyes in place of pickled vegetables? Surely not, although I understand they did put them to several practical uses. First, as wire. This is according to the account of a villager, who merely stated that they *were* used to make wire and didn't elaborate on just how they were so used. He did, however, say something about the intended use of the wire: every year wire was added to the fence the foreign devils were constructing to keep the Chinese from escaping when the devil-soldiers arrive. Second, for photography. Here the reason is clear enough, and there is no need to elaborate: one has only to be face-to-face with someone to see a little photograph of oneself appear in their pupils.

The foreign devils also had a practical use for the hearts they tore out of people. I once overheard an old devout Buddhist woman explain the rationale: after they tear them out, they boil them into oil, which they use to light lamps to shine underground. Since the heart of a man is a most greedy thing, when the lamp is shone on a place where treasure is buried, the flame leaps downward. They would then quickly dig it up and take the treasure away, thus explaining why foreign devils are all so wealthy.

The Neo-Confucian belief that "all the myriad things are within me" is known throughout the country, and in S City, at least, it is known even to those who can't tell B from a bull's foot. According to this belief, man is the "spirit of all things." Menstrual juices and semen can prolong one's life; hair and fingernails can thicken one's blood; excrement and urine can be used to treat an array of diseases; and a piece of flesh from the forearm can keep one's parents alive?[9] But all of this is beyond the scope of this essay, so let's leave it at that for now. Since the people of S City are very concerned about face, moreover, there are many things that cannot be spoken of, and those who utter such treachery will be severely punished.

## II. Forms

Photography was, in short, like witchcraft. During Emperor Wenzong's reign [1851–1861], it happened that in a certain province some peasants destroyed the property of a person who practiced photography. Yet when I was young (thirty years ago), S City already had a photography studio, and no one was particularly wary or terrified. During the Boxer Rebellion, twenty-five years ago, there were those in another province who believed that canned beef was the flesh of Chinese children killed by the foreign devils. But these are exceptions, and nothing is without exception.

In short, S City had long had a photography studio. Every time I passed by it, I couldn't resist lingering in enjoyment, although that was no more than four or five times a year. How I marveled at the glass bottles of every imaginable shape and color and the smooth and prickly ornamental cacti! Hanging on the wall were framed photographs of the great statesman Zeng Guofan, Minister Li Hongzhang, General Zuo Zongtang, and Commander Bao. A well-intentioned elder from my clan once used these photographs to offer me moral instruction. "These men," he said, "were all great officials of the day, distinguished public servants who had suppressed the Taiping 'Long Hairs' rebellion. You should emulate them." At that time I was keen to follow their example; yet I thought that for this to be possible, a quick reappearance of "Long Hairs" was also necessary.

At the time I knew only this: the people of S City did not seem very fond of having their photographs taken; since a person's spirit could be stolen by the camera, it was especially inappropriate to have one's photograph taken when one's luck was good (the spirit was also known as the "noble light").

Only recently have I learned that there are renowned scholars who never wash themselves for fear they will lose their "vital essence," the vital essence probably something equivalent to the noble light. How much wiser I am now: the Chinese spirit, otherwise known as the noble light or the vital essence, can be stolen by a camera or washed away with water.

And yet, though by no means many, there were people who did indeed patronize the photography studio. I am not clear who they were, however—perhaps some luckless souls or reformists. Portrait photographs of the upper half of the body were generally taboo, for this was like being chopped in half at the waist. Naturally, the Qing court had already abandoned this style of execution, but one can still see on the stage Judge Bao's execution of his nephew Bao Mian: one slice of the knife, and the body is rent in two. How terrifying! And even though this is part of our glorious "national essence," I "desire it not done unto me."[10] It is indeed most unfitting to have one's picture taken in this manner. Instead, they would take pictures of the entire body; to the side would be a tea table on which would lie a hat rack, teacups, a flower vase, and below which would be a spittoon (demonstrating that the subject's bronchial tubes were full of mucus and in need of continuous clearing). The subject would be sitting or standing, with a book or scroll in his hands or a very large timepiece hanging around his neck. If we look at the photograph with a magnifying glass, we can know what time the picture was taken, and since flash bulbs weren't used then, we needn't wonder about whether it was taken at night.

What age is without its Bohemians and dandies? Those of truly sophisticated taste had long been dissatisfied with the bland uniformity of the herd, and they would take off all their clothes and pretend to be the Jin dynasty eccentric Liu Ling or dress up in the traditional silk garb of someone from X dynasty, but there were not many of these.[11] What was rather more popular was to take two pictures of oneself, each with a different costume and expression, then put them together into a single photograph: two selves, like a guest and a host, or a master and a slave. This we called the "Picture of Two Selves." But a different name was used when one of the selves was seated imperiously above the other, who knelt before it depraved and pitiful: "Picture of Me Entreating Myself." After a print was developed, it was obligatory to write some poem or lyric on it (like "Melody for the Scented Garden" or

"Catching Fish") and then hang it up in one's study. Because they belonged to the herd, the wealthy elite could never in a million years imagine such refined designs. But they too had their particular pose, although it was little more than a "Family Togetherness" picture: oneself seated in the middle with a multitude of sons, grandsons, great grandsons (and so on) arranged at one's feet.

In his *Fundamental Issues of Ethics*, Th. Lipps makes the point that anyone who is a master can easily become a slave. Since the master recognizes that he is master, he naturally knows that he can also become a slave; so that as soon as he tumbles from power, he devotes himself heart and soul to serving the new master. Unfortunately I don't have the book with me, and I only remember the general idea. There is, fortunately, a Chinese translation, and although it contains only excerpts of the original, this passage is probably included. The most convincing example that proves with solid fact Lipps's theory is that of Sun Hao: when he conquered the state of Wu, he was an arrogant and cruel tyrant, but when he succumbed to the state of Jin, he became a depraved and shameless slave. In China there is a common saying that gets right to the heart of the matter: "He who is arrogant to his inferiors will be servile to those above." But nothing surpasses the "Picture of Me Entreating Myself" in fully expressing this idea. If in China we were to print an *Illustrated Fundamental Issues of Ethics*, this would truly be a perfect illustration, one that even the world's greatest satirical artist could never imagine or draw.

But what we see now are not photographs of the depraved and pitiful on bended knee. What we see are group commemoratives or an enlarged bust of someone grand and awe-inspiring. I wish it were the case that my frequent viewing of these as half of the "Entreating Self" photographs is just a vain preoccupation of mine, like the man from Qi who was obsessed with the fear that the sky was falling.

## III. Without Title

The custom of photography studios selecting enlargements of one or several important men and hanging them on their front doors for display is, it seems, either peculiar to Beijing or has only recently become more widespread in its popularity. The photographs I used to see of Zeng Guofan and his ilk in S City were only six or eight inches long, and it was always of Zeng Guofan and his ilk, not as in Beijing where the photographs changed from time to time, never the same from year to year. Perhaps after the revolution the pictures in S City were torn down, but I am not sure about this.

But I do know a little about what has been going on in Beijing over the past ten years. Those of wealth and power alone have their portraits enlarged and hung in this manner, and once they have left the halls of power, their portraits are nowhere to be found, as eternal as a flash of light. If one were to search Beijing day and night for a photo that was not one of these variously sized, ever-alternating photos of men of wealth and power, then, according to my humble knowledge, one would find only those of a single man: the Peking opera star Mei Lanfang. Portraits of him in the *Celestial Maiden Scatters Flowers* or *Daiyu Buries Flowers* (in the style of the fairy Magu) are more elegant indeed than those of men of wealth and power, and this is sufficient to prove that the Chinese do indeed have eyes with aesthetic sensibility. If photographs of pompous men sticking out their chests and stomachs continue to be enlarged and hung out for display, this is simply because it cannot be helped. I have read *Dream of the Red Chamber*, but before seeing these pictures of Daiyu burying flowers, I would never have imagined Daiyu's eyes to protrude so, nor her lips to be so thick. I had always thought she should have a thin, consumptive face. Now I know hers is a visage radiating health and good fortune, just like that of Magu. One need only look at photographs of the string of imitators of the Heavenly Maiden (whose faces are contorted with pain because they are tightly bundled up like little children wearing new clothes) to understand immediately Mei Lanfang's eternal appeal (his eyes and lips, of course, cannot be helped!). And this again is sufficient to prove that Chinese do indeed have eyes with aesthetic sensibility.

When the Indian saint of poetry, Tagore, visited China, he aromatized like sweet perfume several of our gentlemen of letters with his literariness and mysticism, but only Mei Lanfang earned the honor of sitting with Tagore to celebrate his birthday; it was a joining of hands of artists from the two nations. After this venerable poet changed his name to Zhu Cathay[12] and took leave of his all-but-ideal country of Cathay, the sage-poets of Cathay no longer much wore their Indian turbans, and the newspapers only very rarely reported news of Tagore. But what continued to adorn this all-but-ideal country of Cathay were those pictures, *Celestial Maiden Scatters Flowers* and *Daiyu Buries Flowers,* which hung so imposingly in the windows of the photography studios.

In China, only the art of this "artist" is eternal.

Although I have only seen a few photographs of famous foreign actors and beauties, I never saw one of a man playing the part of a woman. I have seen several of other famous people. Tolstoy, Ibsen, Rodin were all old; Nietzsche was fierce, and Schopenhauer appeared to be suffering; Oscar Wilde, decked out in his aesthete's frippery, looked rather doltish; Romain Rolland had an odd air about him, and Gorky simply looked like a hoodlum. And although I could see in all of these the traces of tragic suffering and bitter struggle, none were as manifestly "good" as the Celestial Maiden. If one thinks of the seal-carver Wu Changshi as a "sculptor" and recalls that his seals sell at the same price as some paintings, this should suffice to make him an "artist" in China, but nowhere do we see his photograph. Lin Shu's literary reputation is so well founded that the world does not appear keen on "bidding him a fond farewell." Although I once saw his photograph on some advertisement for a pharmacy, it was printed to express the gratitude of his "concubine" for the efficacy of the pharmacy's medicine and not for the excellence of his literary oeuvre. And what of those good sirs who use the "language of cart pullers and street hawkers" to write? Li Boyuan, Wu Woyao, and their ilk are now long gone, and we can forgo mentioning them. More recently there are the gentlemen of the Creation Society who have struggled valiantly and produced many literary works, but they have printed only one photograph of three of their members together, and it was but a copperplate photo.

The art that is the most noble and eternal in China is the art of men impersonating women.

Generally, it is members of the opposite sex who love one another. Eunuchs cause others no anxiety, absolutely no one loves them, because they are without sex—that is, assuming that I have not committed any error in using this word *without.* And yet we can see that it is the "man who plays the part of a woman" who causes the most anxiety and yet is the most prized. This is because each of the two sexes sees this role as the opposite sex: men see "a woman being impersonated," and women see "a man impersonating." Therefore, this type of photograph hangs eternally in the windows of our photography studios and in the minds of our citizens. Foreign countries do not have this kind of complete artist. All they can do is give free rein to the will of their rock chiselers, blenders of color, and ink masters.

The art that is the most noble, most eternal, and most universal in China is the art of men impersonating women.

November 11, 1924

TRANSLATED BY KIRK A. DENTON

# Modern History
## 現代史

Ever since I can remember, and even up to the present day, wherever I have been, wherever there's an open space, I've seen "conjuring tricks" performed, or what are sometimes called "magic shows."

There seem to be just two kinds of magic shows.

In one kind, a monkey wearing a mask and dressed up in uniform is made to brandish a spear and ride in circles on the back of a sheep. Then a bear, scarcely kept alive on a diet of gruel so that he's just skin and bones, does a few tricks as well. After that, everyone is asked for money.

In the other kind, a rock is placed in an empty box, and after a handkerchief is waved across the top, a dove emerges from inside; or someone's mouth is stuffed with paper and lit on fire, so that smoke and flames shoot out from his nose. Then everyone is asked for money. After the money has been demanded, one of the conjurors will complain that it's just not enough and will loudly pretend to refuse to do any more tricks, until someone else steps forward to plead with him, importuning the crowd for five more coins. In the end, someone tosses a coin, and then it's "four more," and then "three more" . . .

When there has been sufficient tossing of coins, the magic show starts anew. This time a child is squeezed into a big jug with a narrow opening, so that there's only a tuft of hair sticking out the top. If you want him to come

---

First published under the pen name He Jiagan in the "Free Talk" (Ziyou tan) column of *Shen bao* on April 8, 1933, and later anthologized in *Fake Liberty* (Wei ziyou shu, 1933). See Lu Xun, *Lu Xun quanji* (Complete works of Lu Xun) (Beijing: Renmin wenxue, 2005), 5: 95–96.

out again, you have to give more money. When enough money has been collected, the adult somehow contrives to stab the child to death with a long knife and covers him with a sheet. If you want him to come back to life, you have to give more money.

"At home, we depend on family . . . but out here in the world, we depend on the kindness of strangers . . . Huazaa! Huazaa!" The conjuror solemnly and sadly intones as he mimics the tossing of a coin.

If other children steal forward to take a closer look, he'll curse them; if they don't listen, he'll beat them back.

In the end, a lot of people "huazaa" their coins. When the amount matches expectations, the magician gathers the money and packs up his things, the dead child leaps up from off the ground, and they disappear together.

The befuddled spectators disperse as if on cue.

In this empty space, all is quiet for now. In a little while, the show will start once more. The proverb has it that "every magician has his own bag of tricks." Yet after all these years, it's still the same show, and there will always be those who watch and those who will "huazaa," just as long as there are a few days in between each show.

Now I have said all I set out to say, and there's not much to it—just that after everyone's finished with the "Huazaa! Huazaa!" things quiet down for a few days, until the same show starts all over again.

And it's only now that I remember I've written the title wrong—it has indeed turned into something "neither dead nor alive."

April 1, 1933

TRANSLATED BY ANDREW F. JONES

# Lessons from the Movies
電影的教訓

When I used to go to the village near my hometown to watch old-style Chinese operas, I had yet to be educated into an "intellectual"; my childhood friends were by and large peasants. We loved to watch the somersaults, the tiger dance, and demon spirits materializing onstage with a flash and a puff of smoke. The stories themselves seemed to have very little to do with us. The battles between the great "painted face" and the "old man" over cities and territories, the joys and sorrows of the young scholar and his lady love—that was their own business. As children of those who worked the plow, my friends knew very well that they would never be honored with military rank or travel to the capital to sit for the civil service examinations. Yet I recall one particular drama that had a stirring effect on us, titled, I think, "Beheading Mucheng."[13] A great official had been framed and was to be put to death to atone for a crime he didn't commit. A house servant in his employ happened to bear a striking resemblance to him, and thus stood forward to take his place and give himself up to the law. His solemn gestures and the sound of his arias truly touched the hearts of the audience. They found revealed in him a good model to which they could aspire, since many of the peasants in our region, once the busy season has ended, work as hired help in the great houses. As the moment of the execution drew near, the lady of the house, so as to keep up appearances, tried to fold him into a tearful embrace but was rebuffed in no uncertain terms, for even in extreme circumstances, one must keep to one's place and uphold proprieties. Such a loyal servant, such a righteous, good man!

But when I went to the movies in Shanghai, I found that I had already become one of the "lowly Chinese." In the galleries above were the white people and the rich people, and downstairs sat rows of middle- and lower-class "descendants of the Han," while on the screen white soldiers fought battles, white gentlemen made fortunes, white maidens got married, and

First published on September 11, 1933, in *Shen bao* and later anthologized in *Quasi Discourses on the Wind and Moon* (Zhun feng yue tan, 1934). Lu Xun, *Lu Xun quanji* (Complete works of Lu Xun) (Beijing: Renmin wenxue, 2005), 5: 309–311.

white heroes had adventures, all to the admiration, envy, and terror of the audience, who knew that they themselves could do none of these things. When the white hero goes adventuring in Africa, there's usually a loyal black servant who will clear the way for him, minister to his needs, fight fiercely for him, and die in his place so that the master may return safely home. And as he prepares to set out on his next adventure, the master recalls the dead man—a loyal servant is hard to find, after all—and a shadow flits across his features, the black face in his memory flickering across the screen; and across the yellow faces of the audience in the faint light of the theater a shadow would pass as well. They have been moved.

Fortunately, our domestic film industry is not giving up without a fight, and having made a tremendous leap up a high wall, it is raising its arms and tossing a volley of "flying daggers"—although like the 19th Route Army they too have left Shanghai behind, as they prepare to release new adaptations of Turgenev's *Spring Torrents* and Mao Dun's "Spring Silkworms."[14] That's all well and good and progressive. But what's arrived first on our screens, with a great deal of promotional fanfare, is a movie called *An Amorous History of the Yao Mountains*.[15]

The theme of the film is the civilizing of the Yao tribespeople, and the plot revolves around the courting of the chief's daughter, calling to mind old plays like *Fourth Son Visits His Mother*[16] and *Princess Shuangyang Pursues Di*.[17] These days we don't hear as much about the grand notion of Chinese spiritual civilization dominating the whole world. This great venture can only be achieved, first and foremost, through the establishment of matrimonial ties. The descendants of the Yellow Emperor, like black people, cannot marry the princesses of the great nations of Europe or Asia, and thus there's no way to disseminate our spiritual civilization. If we want to do some civilizing, one supposes it had better be among the likes of the Yao or the Miao. This is the lesson we can all learn from the movies.

TRANSLATED BY ANDREW F. JONES

# Shanghai Children

## 上海的兒童

The newly built section of North Sichuan Road just beyond the boundary of the concessions went quiet for the better part of a year because of the war, but this year it's as lively as ever. The stores have moved back from their safe haven in the French Concession, the cinemas have long since reopened, and you often see lovers walking hand in hand in the vicinity of the park. None of this was in sight last summer.

If you walk into the narrow residential alleys, you'll see public toilets, cooked rice sold from carrying poles, swarms of mosquitoes flying through the air, groups of children making mischief, dramatic disturbances, richly developed obscenities. It is truly a chaotic little world unto itself. Yet once you come back out to the boulevard, what projects itself into your vision are the spirited and lively foreign children playing and walking down the sidewalk. Somehow it is as if the Chinese children are no longer visible. It is not that they aren't there, just that with their shabby clothes and dispirited manner, they have been reduced to shadows by the others and hardly catch one's eye at all.

Middle-class households in China in the main have only two methods for raising children. The first is to indulge their mischief completely, with practically no restraints. They are allowed to curse and beat others with impunity; in the confines of the home, they are like little tyrants and despots. But once they go outside, they are like spiders who have lost their web, suddenly becoming utterly helpless. The second method is to treat them coldly and curse them all day long, even going as far as to slap and beat them, so that they shrink into themselves and recoil, like slaves or puppets. This is what parents call being "well behaved," which they attribute to the success of their educational practices. Yet once the children get outside, they

First published in volume 2, issue 9, of the *Shen bao Monthly* (Shen bao yuekan) on September 15, 1933, and later anthologized in *Southern Tunes in Northern Tones* (Nan qiang bei diao ji, 1934). Lu Xun, *Lu Xun quanji* (Complete works of Lu Xun) (Beijing: Renmin wenxue, 2005), 4: 580–581.

are like little birds released momentarily from a narrow cage, that not only don't know how to sing or to fly, but are unable to even hazard a little leap.

These days at least China is also printing picture books for children to read. The protagonists, naturally, are children, but the figures in the pictures all seem to have a savage and stupid look to them. If they are not mischievous pranksters, with an air of delinquency and even hooliganism about them, then they have the lifeless look of so-called good children, with bent heads and stooped shoulders, downcast eyes and blankly expressionless faces. Although this results in part from the artist's lack of skill, these pictures have used real children as their models, and real children, in turn, will model themselves after the pictures. When we take a look at illustrations of children from other nations, we see that the English are well-mannered, the Germans proud and forthright, the Russians generous and sturdy, the French good-looking, and the Japanese intelligent; none of them have the feeble and listless air of the Chinese. One can observe the state of a people not only through literature, but also through pictures, even the often-overlooked illustrations in children's books.

Stupidity and lethargy can lead people into decline or destruction. And the conditions that hold during childhood will determine one's future fate. Our moderns like to speak of romantic love, of smaller families, of independence and enjoyment, but few raise the question of how best to educate children at home and in our schools, or of how to reform our society. Our ancestors knew only how to "serve as horses and oxen for their children and grandchildren," which was no doubt a mistake. But if we think only of the present and fail to consider the future, letting "our children and grandchildren serve as horses and oxen," we will have committed an even graver error.

August 12

TRANSLATED BY ANDREW F. JONES

# How to Train Wild Animals

## 野獸訓練法

Another extremely beneficial lecture on "How to Train Wild Animals" was recently delivered to us by Sawade, manager of the Hagenbeck Circus, on the third floor of the China Society for the Arts.[18] What a shame I was unable to audit and merely saw some notes about the event transcribed in the newspaper. But that was already enough to give us pause:

> Some may think that wild animals can be handled by force or by the fist, but to oppress them is a mistake, for this is the way in which primitives used to do things, and today's training methods are altogether different. The method we use now is the power of love, with which we can gain their trust in humans, for only the power of love and a gentle disposition will move them. . . .

Although these words came from the mouth of a German, they are in fact completely in accord with the ancient teachings of our own sages. Handling by way of force or the fist is what they termed "tyranny." And "those who are convinced by force are not convinced in their hearts."[19] Which is why civilized peoples must adopt the "kingly way" in order to gain "trust": "if the people lack trust, the kingdom cannot stand."[20] Once there is "trust," the wild animals will perform tricks:

> When the trainers have gained their trust, they can begin to undertake the training. The first step is to teach them to distinguish between a sitting posture and a standing posture; next they can be taught to jump through hoops or stand on their hind legs. . . .

The method of training wild animals is much like the shepherding of the people, which is why our ancients referred to great men as "herders."[21] And yet animals such as cattle and sheep who allow themselves to be herded are

First published under the pen name Yu Ming in the "Free Talk" (Ziyou tan) column of *Shen bao* on October 10, 1933, and later anthologized in *Quasi Discourses on the Wind and Moon* (Zhun feng yue tan, 1934). See Lu Xun, *Lu Xun quanji* (Complete works of Lu Xun) (Beijing: Renmin wenxue, 2005), 5: 384–386.

more fearful than wild animals, which is why the ancients weren't always able to depend on "trust" alone and had to resort to the fist as well, or what is also known more grandly as "legitimacy."

Animals governed by "legitimacy" cannot expect simply to "jump through hoops or stand on their hind legs"; they must also contribute their pelts and horns and flesh and blood, or at the very least allow themselves to be milked each day, as with cows or sheep and the like.

Yet all of this was the way of old, and I don't imagine that it has any bearing on modern times.

After Sawade's lecture, there were apparently further excitements, such as "Oriental Music" and "Playing Shuttlecock," neither of which is elaborated on in the newspaper, so there's no way to know the details, which would also, I'm afraid, be of the greatest significance.

TRANSLATED BY ANDREW F. JONES

# Toys

## 玩具

This is the Year of the Child. I remember, and so I often keep an eye out for what toys are being made for our children.

The foreign goods shop by the roadside has a lot of little knickknacks hanging on display. The paper labels say that they are imported from France, but I saw the very same items in a Japanese toy store for an even better price. Peddlers with carrying poles and street-side stalls are all selling rubber balloons, with a mark printed on them saying "All Domestic Product," proving as they are inflated that they are indeed manufactured in China. But the balloons that the Japanese children are playing with have the same label, so I imagine those ones must have been made in *their* country.[22]

The department stores stock toy weapons: bayonets, machine guns, tanks. . . .

---

First published in the "Free Talk" (Ziyou tan) column of *Shen bao* on June 14, 1934, under the pen name Mi Zizhang and later anthologized in *Fringed Literature* (Huabian wenxue, 1936). Lu Xun, *Lu Xun quanji* (Complete works of Lu Xun) (Beijing: Renmin wenxue, 2005), 5: 523–524.

Yet even relatively well-off children are seldom seen playing with them. In the parks, foreign children will pile sand into a mound, and by sticking a couple of short twigs into it parallel to the ground, create what's clearly an armored vehicle. Yet the Chinese children, with their pallid and gaunt faces, hide behind the adults and look on timidly and with wonder, clad in their extremely refined long gowns.

In our China, it's the adults who have lots of toys: mistresses, opium pipes, mahjong tiles, popular songs like Li Jinhui's "Drizzle," séance tablets, Buddhist masses, and more, keeping us so busy that we barely have time to think of the children. Despite the fact that it's the Year of the Child and that we went through the cauldron of war the year before last, we have yet to make a toy that somehow commemorates all of this, and instead we merely copy others.[23] And one can only imagine how much less will be done next year when it's no longer the Year of the Child.

Yet the Jiangbei men[24] from north of the Yangzi are gifted toy makers. They fasten together two bamboo cylinders of unequal length, painted red and green, with a spring concealed inside and a lever to one side that rattles when you give it a shake. It's a machine gun! And it's the only newly invented toy I've come across. I bought one on the edge of the foreign concessions and kept rattling it with my son as we walked along the street. Most of the civilized Westerners and victorious Japanese who saw us threw disdainful or pitying smiles in our direction.

But as we rattled our way along the streets, we weren't ashamed, because this was something truly creative. Since the year before last, many people have had harsh words for Jiangbei people, as if just by denouncing them they could display their own integrity.[25] Now those voices have gone silent, and all of that unsullied integrity seems largely to have dissipated into the haze. And it's the Jiangbei people who with stubborn self-confidence and unaffected talent have created a crude toy machine-gun to compete against the toys of the civilized world. They are, I think, far more deserving of praise than those who have brought back the latest models of weaponry purchased in the West—even though I know saying that will perhaps elicit from some quarters a disdainful or pitying sneer.

June 11

TRANSLATED BY ANDREW F. JONES

# The Glory to Come

## 未来的光荣

Nowadays, foreign writers come to China almost every year. As soon as they arrive, they invariably stir up some trouble. First it was Bernard Shaw, then Dekobra.[26] It is only Vaillant-Couturier[27] that people either don't want to or can't talk about.

Dekobra didn't discuss politics, so he should have been able to avoid controversy altogether. But who would have guessed that he would earn the derogatory title "foreign literary bandit" on account of praising food and sex, giving our critics much fodder for discussion. He's probably off writing a work of fiction now.

Our noses are small and flat, unlike the tall and handsome noses of Europeans. There's nothing we can do about it, but if we happen to have a few dimes on hand, then at least we can, as the Europeans do, go watch movies. When we grow weary of detective movies, have memorized the plots of romantic movies, get tired of war movies, and become bored with comedies, there are always movies such as *Tarzan the Ape Man, Jungle Mystery, Adventures in Africa*,[28] etc.—movies that bring wild beasts and savages to the screen. Though set in uncivilized regions, they still have to include some subplot that involves a barbaric woman with ample curves. If we still love watching them, that just goes to show that no matter how ridiculous the plot, we are still drawn to it. "Sex" is very important for profiteers.

Literature from Western Europe has encountered problems no different from film. Some so-called littérateurs must also turn to the grotesque and erotic to satisfy their customers—this is how travel adventures came about.[29] Their motive lies not with showing the civility or banquets of the local hosts. Yet if you were to ask them bluntly about the places they visited, they would

First published in the "Free Talk" (Ziyou tan) column of *Shen bao* on January 11, 1934, under the pseudonym Zhang Chenglu and later anthologized in *Fringed Literature* (Huabian wenxue, 1936). Lu Xun, *Lu Xun quanji* (Complete works of Lu Xun) (Beijing: Renmin wenxue, 2005), 5: 443–445. The essay warns readers to be vigilant against the colonial narratives and pejorative representations of the Chinese transmitted in foreign texts and films.

simply laugh it off with a joke. They actually don't know these places and have no need to. Dekobra is simply one of these people.

But in the works of such littérateurs, the Chinese are invariably brought onto the scene with other so-called "natives." All you have to do is but glance at Dekobra's itinerary printed in the newspapers—China, Southeast Asia, South America. Places like England and Germany are just too ordinary. We have to become aware of how we are being represented by others and also how the "glory" of such representations will only grow with time. We must also be aware of how in the future some may find these things amusing.

January 8

TRANSLATED BY EILEEN J. CHENG

# The Decline of the Western Suit
洋服的沒落

For the past several decades, we have often lamented the lack of appropriate clothes to wear. In the last years of the Qing dynasty, heroes with an air of the revolutionary about them detested not only the queue, but also the riding jacket and the long robe, which were seen as Manchu attire. An elderly gentleman who traveled to Japan was so delighted after seeing the clothes worn there that he published in a journal an essay titled "On Unexpectedly Re-encountering Conventions of the Han."[30] He approved of reviving the old form of dress.

Yet after the revolution, we ended up wearing the Western suit, because people wanted reform, convenience, and their backbones to be erect. Eminently talented young lads not only insisted on wearing the Western suit, they detested those who donned the robe. I've heard it said that at the time someone even went so far as to reprimand the Elder Fan Shan,[31] questioning his choice to dress in Manchu garb. In response, Fan Shan asked: "Where do

First published in the "Free Talk" (Ziyou tan) column of *Shen bao* on April 25, 1934, under the pseudonym Wei Shiyao and later anthologized in *Fringed Literature* (Huabian wenxue, 1936). Lu Xun, *Lu Xun quanji* (Complete works of Lu Xun) (Beijing: Renmin wenxue, 2005), 5: 478–480.

the clothes you wear come from?" The young lad replied: "I'm wearing foreign clothes." To which Fan Shan rejoined: "I, too, am wearing foreign clothes."

This story was widely circulated for a time, and the advocates of the riding jacket and robe derived a sense of vindication from it. But for some of them, donning the robe reflected an antirevolutionary stance, quite a departure from more recent times when people wore it out of hygienic or economic considerations. Later on, the suit gradually fell out of favor with the Chinese. This was the case not only during the reign of Yuan Shikai, when the robe and riding jacket were designated the official garb; after the May Fourth movement, to instill campus-wide discipline, Peking University decided to adopt school uniforms, and students were invited to join the public discussion on the matter. And the decision arrived at after deliberation? The robe and riding jacket!

This time, the reason for not adopting the Western suit was precisely along the lines of what Mr. Lin Yutang had said—it was unhygienic.[32] The creator bestowed upon us hips and necks that were designed to bend, and flexible hips and curved backs are common sights in China. In the face of adversity, one is expected to go along without a fight; even more reason to expect that we would go with the flow when things take their natural course. And so it turns out that we are the race most capable of assessing the human body and making the most advantageous use of it. The neck is the most delicate part of the body, so we invented decapitation; the knee joint is capable of bending, so we invented the gesture of kneeling; since our buttocks are fleshy and because it's unlikely to result in fatalities, we invented spanking. The Western suit, which goes against the natural evolution of the body, then, naturally and gradually went into decline.

The remaining traces of the Western suit are now only to be found on a few fashionable men and women. Like the queue and bound feet, they are to be seen only occasionally on the body of the recalcitrant man or woman. But who would have imagined that yet another crushing blow would be dealt, this time from sulfuric acid splashed from behind?[33]

What can be done, then?

As for reviving old systems, it's hard to understand the logic behind the attire worn from the time of the Yellow Emperor to the Song and

Ming dynasties. One is bound to look ridiculous if one were to ride a motorcycle or dine on Western cuisine wearing black boots with thick white soles, the long robe embroidered with snakes, and a belt studded with jadestones—the costume worn by actors who play the role of the official in traditional dramas. So no matter what changes we adopt in dress, it seems that, in the end, it's the robe and the riding jacket that remain the safest bets. Though they are still forms of foreign dress, people are unlikely to be changing out of them soon—this really is something rather curious.

TRANSLATED BY EILEEN J. CHENG

# Take-ism
## 拿來主義

China has always adhered to "closed door-ism": we didn't leave, and others weren't allowed to enter. From the moment foreign guns and cannons pried open the gates to our country, ushering in a series of setbacks, it's always been about "give-ism." Setting aside all other examples for the moment, in the arts alone, we recently sent some antiques to Paris to be displayed, and lo and behold, we "don't know what happened to them." And then there were the few "great masters" who toured various countries in Europe carrying with them a few old-style and new-style paintings, exhibiting them in the name of "developing national glory." I've heard that in the near future Dr. Mei Lanfang will be sent to the Soviet Union to promote "symbolism," after which he can hop over to Europe to pass on his wisdom there. I don't want to discuss the relationship between Dr. Mei's art and symbolism here, but in brief, replacing an antique with a living person can, I dare say, be considered progress of sorts.

---

First published in *Tendency* (Dongxiang), a supplement to *China Daily* (Zhonghua ribao), on June 6, 1934, and later anthologized in *Essays from the Semi-Concessions* (Qiejie ting zawen, 1937). Lu Xun, *Lu Xun quanji* (Complete works of Lu Xun) (Beijing: Renmin wenxue, 2005), 6: 39–42.

The problem is, we don't have anyone who will declare aloud, following the notion that "courtesy is based on reciprocity": "Take it!"

Of course, it's not a bad thing to be giving. It lends the appearance of abundance, on the one hand, and generosity, on the other. Nietzsche boasted that he was the sun, an endless source of light and heat, only bestowing, never taking, but in the end, he turned out not to be the sun after all—he was just insane. China isn't the sun either, although there are people who say that if you dig up all the coal here, it would be enough for the entire world to use for the next several hundred years. But then what? After several hundred years, we'll all have turned into spirits, ascended to heaven or fallen to hell, but our descendants will be around, and we should therefore leave behind some gifts for them. Otherwise, when it's time for festivals and ceremonies, they won't have anything to display, and all they can do is kowtow in felicitation and ask for a little leftover porridge or cold meat as a reward.

Don't mistake these kinds of rewards as things "thrown at" us; they are things "thrown to" us or, phrased in a little more stately language, we can call it "given" to us. I don't feel like offering an example here.

And I really don't want to say anything more about "giving"; if I did, that wouldn't be very "modern" of me! I only want to encourage us to be a little stingier. In addition to "giving," there is also "taking" or what I call "take-ism."

The problem is, we've been scared by the things "given" to us. First there were British opium and useless discarded German guns and cannons; then there were French cosmetics, American movies, and the little knick-knacks from Japan with "Authentic National Product" printed on them. As a result, even enlightened youths have become terrified of foreign goods. Actually, it's precisely because they were "given" to us and not things we wanted to "take" for ourselves.

So, we need to rack our brains, set our sights high, and just take things for ourselves!

For example, if a poor youth from our midst acquired a large residence because of the good deeds (allow me, if you will, to use this term) of his ancestors but never asks if it was obtained by means of deception, confiscated, inherited legally, or in exchange for becoming a son-in-law, well, then what? In my opinion, no matter what the circumstances, just "take it!" If he was opposed to the original owner and was afraid of being tainted by his things and paced back and forth not daring to enter the residence, he would be a weakling; if he got angry and torched the place in order to preserve his purity, he would be an idiot. However, if out of envy of the original owner he took possession of everything and happily limped into the bedroom and smoked up all the leftover opium, he'd of course be even more of a good-for-nothing. The "take-ist" is not like this.

He takes possession of things and does it selectively. If he sees shark fin, he won't throw it on the road to show that he is a man of the common people; as long as it has nutritional value, he would eat it with his friends as if it were a turnip or a cabbage, but he would *not* use it to fete an honored guest. When he sees opium, he wouldn't make a show of dumping it in the toilet to display his thoroughly revolutionary ways; he would take it to a pharmacy to be used for curative purposes without playing the old clearance-sale trick of "everything must go!" Only our opium pipes and opium lamps, whose shapes may be different from those in India, Persia, and Arabia, can be considered a kind of national essence such that when taken around the world there are sure to be people who will come for a look. But in my opinion, apart from giving away a few to museums, the rest can very well be destroyed. There's also a group of concubines—it's best to have them go their own ways, otherwise "take-ism" might well experience a crisis.

In short, we should take things. We should use them, retain them, or destroy them. If we do, the master becomes a new master, and his residence can become a new residence. First of all, though, this person must be composed, courageous, discerning, and unselfish. If we don't take things, we won't be able to transform ourselves into new men, and literature won't be able to transform into new literature.

June 4

TRANSLATED BY KIRK A. DENTON

# Ah Jin

阿金

For some time now I have detested Ah Jin.

She is a domestic; in Shanghai they call them "aunties," whereas foreigners know them as "amahs": her employer was in fact a foreigner.

She had a lot of women friends. As soon as dusk fell, a succession of them would come and stand under her window and call up, "Ah Jin, Ah Jin!" in loud voices. This went on well into the night. She also seemed to have a string of paramours; she once proclaimed her philosophy from her back doorstep: what's the point of coming to Shanghai unless you're going to take a few lovers? . . .

But that did not concern me. The unfortunate thing was that the back door of her employer's house was kitty-corner from my front door, so when the cry of "Ah Jin, Ah Jin!" went up, I could not help but be affected: sometimes I could not get on with my writing; at others the word *Jin* would actually find its way into my manuscript. Even more unfortunate, in my comings and goings I had to pass under the balcony where she hung her washing; presumably she was averse to using the staircase, for bamboo poles, planks of wood, and other whatnots were liable to be just tossed over this balcony, which made me exercise extreme caution in passage. I would first look to see if the said Ah Jin was on the balcony; if she was, then I had to give the house a wide berth. Of course, this was mostly due to my own timidity, to my putting too high a price on my own life; but one had to take into consideration that her employer was a foreigner: if I got my head cut open, that of course would have been neither here nor there, but even if I had been killed, nothing could have come of calling meetings of my fellow townsmen and sending telegrams of protest—leaving aside my doubt that I would have merited a meeting of my fellow townsmen being called.

The world is a different place after midnight, one where the humors of the day do not pertain. One night I was still sitting up translating something

First published in issue 2 of *Storm Petrel* (Haiyan) on February 20, 1936, and later anthologized in *Essays from the Semi-Concessions* (Qiejie ting zawen, 1937). Lu Xun, *Lu Xun quanji* (Complete works of Lu Xun) (Beijing: Renmin wenxue, 2005), 6: 205–210.

at half past three when I heard someone in the street softly calling somebody's name. Though the sound was muffled, I could tell it was not Ah Jin's name they were calling, and naturally it was not mine either. I thought to myself, who could be calling anyone so late at night? With that, I got up and opened my upstairs window to take a look. In fact there was a man standing there, looking up at Ah Jin's lattice window. He had not noticed me. I regretted my impulsiveness and was about to close my window and withdraw when the upper half of Ah Jin's body appeared in the opening of the little window across the street. She spotted me immediately and, pointing in my direction, said something to the man I did not catch. Another gesture from her, and the man made off at some speed. I felt very uncomfortable, as if it were I myself who had done something wrong. After that I could not get on with my translation, and I told myself: in future just mind your own business; you have to harden yourself to the point that you would not turn a hair were Mount Tai to crumble in front of you and not flinch if bombs fell about your ears! . . .

But Ah Jin was apparently quite unperturbed, because she continued to laugh and joke as boisterously as before. However, I did not reach this conclusion until the next evening, so I suffered from my conscience for part of a night and a whole day. At that point I felt grateful to Ah Jin for her broadmindedness but at the same time no less detested her loud conferences and boisterous laughter. Ever since she appeared on the scene, the whole neighborhood had been thrown into a state of agitation, so great was her power. My warning intended to quell the disturbance proved entirely ineffectual: they did not even spare me a glance. Once a foreigner living nearby remonstrated with them in his own tongue, and they ignored him too; but he then rushed out and gave them all his boot, which did make them scatter and bring their conference to an end. The effect of his kicks lasted, as I remember, five or six nights.

Thereafter the former clamor was resumed, and the scope of the disturbance enlarged. Ah Jin got into a row with the old woman who kept a kiosk across the main road, and some men joined in on her side. Her voice was penetrating at the best of times; on this occasion it carried even further, being audible, I was sure, twenty houses away. In no time a crowd gathered. As the war of words drew to a close, inevitably there was reference to "taking lovers" and the like. I did not catch what the old woman said, but Ah Jin's reply was:

"Nobody fancies you, you old bag! But people do fancy me!"

I am afraid this was the truth, and the spectators on the whole seemed to find in her favor; the "unfancied old bag" was thus defeated. A foreign policeman strolled up, hands behind his back, looked on for a while, then began to disperse the spectators. Ah Jin rushed over to him and poured out a long story in his language. The foreign policeman heard her out attentively, then said with a smile:

"It seems to me you gave as good as you got!"

He made no move to arrest the "old bag," just crossed his hands behind his back again and strolled on. So this is how the backstreet battle can be said to have ended. But the altercations of this world are never so neatly settled: it seems that the "old bag" still had some forces in reserve. The next morning the "boy" who worked for another foreigner a few doors along from Ah Jin fled to her place for refuge. Three hulking men were pursuing him. His shirt was torn. It seems that he had been lured out of his house and then had his retreat blocked, so all he could do was to flee to his lover's. Men have always sought a safe haven at the side of their beloved: Peer Gynt, in Ibsen's play, was one great personage who in defeat ended up hiding under the skirts of his lover listening to her lullabies. But I fear Ah Jin could not match Norwegian girls: she had no heart and no spirit. She was alive only to her instincts. When the man was within a few strides of her back door, she slammed it in his face. With his escape cut off, he simply came to a halt. This turn of events seemed to take those hulking men by surprise too, for they visibly hesitated; but eventually they put up their fists, and two of them punched him about the body—only three blows in all, and apparently not very heavy ones—while the other gave him one in the face that did immediately leave a red mark. This backstreet battle was over in a flash, and as it was morning too, there were very few people on the sidelines. The victorious and the defeated left the field, and the world was temporarily at peace. Nevertheless, I was still uneasy, for I have heard it said: so-called peace is no more than a lull between two wars.

Yet a few days later Ah Jin disappeared, presumably discharged by her employer.

Her replacement is a fat maidservant whose countenance bears some marks of felicity and refinement. Twenty days have passed and all is yet peaceful; she has only hired a pair of poor balladeers to sing some rollicking songs like "The Eighteen Gropes."[34] No one could object to her taking such harmless pleasure after having "earned her keep." The only worrying thing was that it attracted a motley crowd, including even Ah Jin's lover, thus posing the threat that backstreet warfare might erupt again at any time. But for myself I was grateful, for it was a pleasure to listen to a natural baritone voice, so infinitely preferable to the strangled cat of "Drizzling Rain."[35]

Ah Jin was very ordinary in appearance. What I mean by ordinary is that she was like a multitude of others, quite unmemorable. After less than a month, I can no longer describe her looks. But I still detest her; the mere recollection of her name is repugnant to me. That she caused an uproar in the neighborhood is of course no reason for deep-seated malice; I detest her because in the space of a few days she shook the beliefs I have held and the stands I have taken for thirty years.

I have never credited the old stories about Wang Zhaojun bringing peace to the Han dynasty by marrying the barbarian khan, and the nomad girl Hua Mulan preserving the Sui by going to war; nor have I believed that the temptress Da Ji brought about the downfall of Yin, that the fabulous beauty Xi Shi ruined Wu, or that the emperor's concubine Yang Guifei plunged the Tang into chaos. In a male-dominated society, women could not exercise such power: the responsibilities for the fortunes of the state must rest on men's shoulders. All along, male authors had put the blame on the heads of women, but that just showed what worthless and pathetic men they were, I thought. I had not bargained for Ah Jin, a domestic nondescript in appearance and of no striking ability, turning our little neighborhood upside down in just a few weeks. If she had been a queen, an empress, or a dowager empress, one shudders to think what an effect she would have had: enough to wreak awful havoc, certainly.

In olden days, Confucius "on reaching the age of fifty understood the will of Heaven," yet I am thrown back on doubt and uncertainty even about human affairs, all because of a nobody like Ah Jin. Though one cannot rightly compare the sage with ordinary men, it shows the degree of her potency and my utter uselessness. I do not wish to blame the decline in my writing on Ah Jin's kicking up a row, and what is more, the above discussion verges on spitefulness, but it is a fact that lately I have detested Ah Jin for, as it were, blocking one of my pathways.

I just hope that Ah Jin does not rank as a specimen of Chinese womanhood.

1935

TRANSLATED BY DAVID E. POLLARD

# Written Deep into the Night

寫於深夜里

## III. A Fairy Tale

I saw published in the February 17 issue of DZZ[36] "A Fairy Tale" written by Willi Bredel in commemoration of the eightieth anniversary of the death of Heinrich Heine. I'm rather fond of this topic, so I thought I'd write a piece too.

Once upon a time, there was such a country: The rulers had subdued the people yet regarded them as formidable enemies; latinized words were viewed as machine guns, woodblock prints as tanks. Though the rulers had acquired the land, they felt they couldn't get off at designated transit stops; they couldn't move about on the ground anymore, so they had to fly to and fro by air. The immune response of their skin weakened; whenever important matters came up, one would catch a cold and spread it to the ministers, and they would get sick all at once.

More than one massive dictionary had been published, yet none of them had any practical use. To understand the actual circumstances, one had to

First published in volume 1, issue 3, of *Night Oriole* (Ye ying) in May 1936 and later anthologized in *Essays from the Semi-Concessions, Final Volume* (Qiejie ting zawen mo bian, 1937). Lu Xun, *Lu Xun quanji* (Complete works of Lu Xun) (Beijing: Renmin wenxue, 2005), 6: 521–525. Originally written for the English journal *Voice of China*, the essay was translated into English and published in volume 1, issue 6, of the journal on April 1, 1936. The "fairy tale" from the second part of section III to the end of section IV is Lu Xun's fictionalized rendition of the experiences of Cao Bai (pseudonym of Ren Fan), then a student at the National Arts Academy of Hangzhou and a member of the woodcut association. Section V of the essay contains an edited version of Ren Fan's letter to Lu Xun (not translated here).

consult a dictionary that had never been published. In it there are some novel and strange definitions. For example: *liberation* means "death by firing squad"; *Tolstoy-ism* means "escape"; under the character for *official* is the following annotation: "the relatives, friends, and slaves of high-ranking officials"; under the character for *city wall* is the following annotation: "a tall and solid brick wall built to prevent students from entering and exiting"; under the entry for *morality*, the annotation reads: "forbidding women from exposing their arms"; under the entry for *revolution*, the annotation reads: "flooding the fields and using planes to carry and release bombs on 'bandits and thieves.'"

A series of major legislation had been published, all compiled by scholars sent to observe the laws practiced in various countries, then adopting the most essential among them; so no other country had laws this complete and detailed. But on the first page was a blank sheet of paper, and only those who had seen the unpublished dictionary could decipher the words. The first three designations were the following: 1. Handle with leniency; 2. Handle with severity; 3. Completely inapplicable in some cases.

Naturally there were courts of law. But the suspects who could decipher the words written on the blank page would never appeal once the case went into proceedings, because only criminals are fond of appeals; as soon as one appeals, the case would inevitably be designated "handle with severity." Early one morning, a raft of soldiers and police surrounded an art school. Inside several people wearing Chinese and Western attire were jumping around, ransacking, and searching through things; following from behind were the police, who all bore arms. Not long after, our pal in a Western suit grabbed hold of the shoulders of an eighteen-year-old student in the dormitory.

"The government dispatched us here to conduct a search, can you please . . ."

"Go ahead and search!" the youth immediately dragged out his wicker suitcase from beneath the bed.

This youth had accumulated many years of experience and was quite clever; he dared not keep anything in his possession. Yet that student was, after all, only eighteen, and in the end they recovered a few letters from his drawer. Perhaps those letters mentioned how his mother had died of destitution, and he couldn't bear to burn them at the time. Our pal in a Western suit then carefully read each aloud word for word. When he got to the part that said: "The world is a banquet at which humans are eaten, your mother was eaten, countless mothers around the world will also be eaten," he lifted his brows, reached for a pencil, and drew a crooked line across the words, asking:

"How do you explain this?"

"..."

"Who ate your mother? Is there such a thing as people eating people in this world? We ate your mother? Fine then!" His eyes bulged as if they were transforming into bullets about to be fired.

"It isn't so! ... This ... It isn't so! ... This ..." The youth flew into a panic.

But he didn't fire his eyeballs, he just folded the letter and stuffed it in his pocket; then he placed the student's woodcuts, woodcutting knife, rubbings titled "The Iron Flows" and "And Quiet Flows the Don," and cut-out newspaper articles in one spot and said to one of the police officers: "I'm handing these over to you!"

"What's in these things that would make you confiscate them?" The youth knew that this was not a good thing.

But our Western-suit pal just gave him a glance and immediately pointed a finger and ordered another police officer:

"I'm handing this over to you!"

The police officer leapt like a tiger, grasped the back of the youth's clothing, and hauled him out from the dormitory to the main gate. Outside the gate were two more students about the same age, their backs each in the grip of a fearsome strong hand. On the side, a group of teaching staff and students had gathered around.

## IV. Another Fairy Tale

Early one morning twenty-one days later, a cross-examination was held at the detention center. In a small dark room, two old men were seated high above, one on the east, one on the west. The one on the east wore a Manchu riding jacket, the one on the west wore a Western suit. An optimist who didn't believe that people ate people recorded the confession. The police officer hollered as he dragged in an eighteen-year-old student with a pale face and dirty clothes, who stood below. After asking his name, age, and ancestral home, "Riding Jacket" continued the questioning:

"Are you a member of the Woodcut Association?"[37]

"Yes."

"Who is the head of the association?"

"Ch . . . is the head, H . . . is the vice-head."

"Where are they now?"

"They have both been expelled by the school. I don't know where they are."

"Why did you stir up protests on campus?"

"Oh!" . . . The youth cried out in surprise.

"Hmmph." Riding Jacket took out a woodblock portrait for him to look at. "Did you carve this?"

"Yes."

"Who is this carving of?"

"It's of a writer."

"What's his name?"

"His name is Lunacharsky."[38]

"He's a writer?——What country is he from?"

"I don't know!" The youth wanted his life spared and told a lie.

"You don't know? Don't lie to me! Isn't he Russian? Isn't he clearly an officer of the Russian Red Army? I've seen his photograph in the *Revolutionary History of Russia* with my own eyes! You still want to deny it?"

"It isn't so!" The youth cried out in desperation, as if he had been hit on the head with an iron hammer.

"This is as to be expected. You're a proletarian artist; if you carve, naturally you'll carve an officer of the Red Army!"

"It isn't so . . . This is completely not . . ."

"Stop denying it. You refuse to come to your senses! We know that your life in the detention center is very hard. But you need to fess up, so we can send your case off sooner to the court for sentencing. Life in prison is much better than it is here."

The youth didn't say anything—he clearly understood that saying something was the same as not saying anything.

"Say," Riding Jacket let out a cold laugh, "are you CP or CY?"[39]

"Neither, I don't understand any of this!"

"You know how to carve an officer of the Red Army but don't understand CP and CY? You are so young, yet so cunning! Off with you!" With a forward wave of Riding Jacket's hand, a police officer astutely and adeptly dragged the youth away.

I'm very sorry: what I've written up to this point no longer seems to be a fairy tale. But if I don't call it a fairy tale, then what would I call it? Especially in this day and age when I'm relaying this matter, which is the year 1932.

. . .

April 7

TRANSLATED BY EILEEN J. CHENG

Notes

Lu Xun's Oeuvre

Acknowledgments

Illustration Credits

Index

# Notes

1  Following the Meiji Restoration in 1868, Japan launched a radical modernization pro-gram that borrowed heavily from the West.

2  The New Culture movement (1915–1925) was led by a group of radical intellectuals af-filiated with the journal *New Youth* (Xin qingnian). They denounced the Confucian eth-ical system as oppressive and outdated and promoted in its stead Western cultural and social values.

3  For an examination of Lu Xun's engagement with the works of Sima Qian and Qu Yuan, see Eileen J. Cheng, *Literary Remains: Death, Trauma, and the Refusal to Mourn* (Hono-lulu: University of Hawaii Press, 2013), 37–78.

4  See "Jottings under Lamplight" and "Written Deep into the Night" in this volume.

5  This argument is explored in Cheng, *Literary Remains*, 219–233.

6  In "Preface to *Self-Selected Works*," Lu Xun wrote that only the works collected in these five volumes could pass as "creative" works.

7  It should be noted that Lu Xun profited handsomely from his writings, in particular his prose essays. According to Saiyin Sun, Lu Xun's total income from his writings between 1912 and 1936 was 120,000 yuan. In 1929 alone, he earned a "staggering" 15,128 yuan, 73 percent of which was from royalties. See Saiyin Sun, *Beyond the Iron House: Lu Xun and the Modern Chinese Literary Field* (New York: Routledge, 2017), 19–21.

8  Gloria Davies, *Lu Xun's Revolution: Writing in a Time of Violence* (Cambridge, MA: Har-vard University Press, 2013), 16.

9  For translations of Lu Xun's late Qing essays, see Jon Eugene von Kowallis, *Warriors of the Spirit: The Early Thought and Essays of Lu Xun* (Berkeley: University of California, Institute of East Asian Studies, China Research Monograph series), forthcoming.

10  David Pollard, "Lu Xun's *Zawen*," in *Lu Xun and His Legacy*, ed. Leo Ou-fan Lee (Berkeley: University of California Press, 1985), 54–89.

11  For a discussion of prose writing in the 1930s, see Charles Laughlin, *The Literature of Leisure and Chinese Modernity* (Honolulu: University of Hawaii Press, 2008).

12  See "Preface to *Essays from the Semi-Concessions*" in this volume.

13  See *Selected Works of Lu Xun*, 4 vols. (Beijing: Foreign Languages Press, 1980). Transla-tors of the essays in this volume have consulted previously published translations. Over-laps between the translations here and earlier renderings are inevitable.

14  The short stories collected in the volume have since seen multiple translations, but the essays have not. For translations of Lu Xun's fiction, see *The Real Story of Ah-Q and Other Tales of China: The Complete Fiction of Lu Xun*, trans. Julia Lovell (London: Penguin, 2009); and *Diary of a Madman and Other Stories*, trans. William Lyell (Honolulu: University of Hawaii Press, 1990).

15 In consideration of a broader readership, footnotes have been kept to a minimum. Translators consulted the footnotes of the 2005 edition of the *Complete Works of Lu Xun* (Lu Xun quanji) and cited them as appropriate in their individual translations.

16 On issues of representation in Lu Xun's writings, see Marston Anderson, *The Limits of Realism: Chinese Fiction in the Revolutionary Period* (Berkeley: University of California Press, 1990); and Theodore Huters, "Blossoms in the Snow: Lu Xun and the Dilemma of Modern Chinese Literature," *Modern China* 10, no. 1 (January 1984): 49–77.

17 "Mr. Fujino" (Tengye xiansheng) in *Morning Blossoms Plucked at Dusk* (Zhao hua xi shi, 1927). *Lu Xun quanji* (Complete works of Lu Xun) (Beijing: Renmin wenxue, 2005), 2: 317.

18 Leo Ou-fan Lee, *Voices from the Iron House: A Study of Lu Xun* (Bloomington: Indiana University Press, 1987), 18; David E. Pollard, *The True Story of Lu Xun* (Hong Kong: Chinese University Press, 2002), 31.

19 For Lu Xun's engagement with conventions of traditional biographies, see Cheng, *Literary Remains*, 58–78.

20 For an article on Lu Xun's relationship with Zhang Taiyan and his fashioning of Zhang Taiyan in the guise of a frustrated scholar, see Eileen J. Cheng, "Records of a Minor Historian: Lu Xun on Zhang Taiyan," special issue on Lu Xun and Zhang Taiyan, *Frontiers of Literary Studies in China* 7, no. 3 (September 2013): 367–395.

21 "Sudden Thoughts" (Huran xiang dao) in *Inauspicious Star* (Huagai ji, 1926), in Lu Xun, *Lu Xun quanji* (Complete works of Lu Xun) (Beijing: Renmin wenxue, 2005), 3: 18.

22 This term is borrowed from Jonathan Lear, *Radical Hope: Ethics in the Face of Cultural Devastation* (Cambridge, MA: Harvard University Press, 2008), 152. For a sustained analysis of Lu Xun's "radical hope," see Cheng, *Literary Remains*, 219–233.

## PREFACES AND AUTOBIOGRAPHICAL ESSAYS

1 A reference to the Jiangnan Naval Academy in Nanjing, the first Western-style school that the young Zhou Shuren attended.

2 In another account of this "slide incident" in the essay "Mr. Fujino" collected in Lu Xun's memoir, *Morning Blossoms Plucked at Dusk* (Zhao hua xi shi, 1928), the execution is described as by gunfire.

3 Jin Xinyi is a character based on Qian Xuantong in Lin Shu's (1852–1924) story "Jingsheng," which satirizes the New Culture movement. Qian Xuantong (1887–1939) was a linguist and professor at Peking University at the time and one of the founding editors of *New Youth* (Xin qingnian). The journal promoted a new literature written in the vernacular and played a central role in spreading the ideals of the New Culture movement. Lin Shu was the most prolific translator of the late Qing period. In collaboration with other translators, he rendered nearly two hundred novels into classical Chinese, in spite of having no knowledge of foreign languages, and opposed the New Culture movement's call to abolish classical Chinese.

4 The Buddhist term *tianyan tong* 天眼通, translated as "divine eye," refers to a line of sight that transcends time and space and penetrates the world of the visible and invisible.

5  "Estimable gentlemen" is Lu Xun's sarcastic epithet for his literary adversaries from the Crescent Moon Society and the Contemporary Review group, including Chen Xiying (also known as Chen Yuan, 1896–1970) and Xu Zhimo (1897–1931), most of whom had studied in England or America.

6  See "Must-Read Books for Young People" in this volume.

7  Lu Xun here continues the line of attack he launched against his literary adversaries, including Chen Xiying and Lin Yutang, in the essay "Why Fair Play Should Be Deferred" (in this volume), published two weeks prior.

8  A snide reference to Xu Zhimo. In an essay titled "Hamlet and Students Who Studied Abroad" (Hanmuleide yu liuxuesheng) published in the October 26, 1925, issue of *Supplement to the Morning Post* (Chenbao fukan), Xu claimed that only those who knew English and studied Shakespeare's plays while in England had the right to comment on Shakespeare.

9  A journal founded in 1907 by students in Tokyo. Lu Xun published his principal early essays in its pages.

10  *Min bao* was the organ of the Chinese revolutionary group Revolutionary Alliance (Tongmeng hui, predecessor of the Guomindang). Founded in 1905, it was edited from 1906 on by Zhang Taiyan, noted for his arcane and archaic prose.

11  Citation from the "Fundamentals of the Dao" (Yuan daoxun) chapter of the *Huainanzi*.

12  On March 18, 1926, a group of Beijing students marched from Tiananmen Square to the government offices to protest foreign interference in Chinese politics. Military guards opened fire on the crowd, killing and wounding several hundred people. For more details on the massacre and Lu Xun's commemoration of it, see "In Memory of Liu Hezhen" and "Roses without Blooms" in this volume.

13  See "Why 'Fair Play' Should Be Deferred" in this volume.

14  See "Must-Read Books for Young People" in this volume.

15  Lu Xun here cites the final lines of "Elegy for Cao Mengde" by the poet Lu Ji. Cao Mengde (155–220 CE), better known as Cao Cao, was chancellor in north China during the Three Kingdoms era at the end of the Han dynasty. Posthumously granted the title Emperor Wu of the Wei by the son who succeeded him, Cao Cao was a brilliant poet as well as a consummate statesman and military strategist. For all his achievements, however, he has been regarded as a crafty and evil man in subsequent Chinese historical writing and popular lore because of the perception that he played a large part in undermining the Han dynasty.

16  "C. T." is a reference to literary scholar and critic Zheng Zhenduo (1899–1959).

17  "Worker Shevyrev" is a satire of revolutionaries by Mikhail Artsybashev (1878–1927), a Russian writer who emigrated to Poland after the Russian Revolution. Lu Xun translated the work from German and had it serialized during the second half of 1921 in *Fiction Monthly* (Xiaoshuo yuebao). Gao Changhong wrote that meeting Lu Xun reminded him of Shevyrev's first meeting with the character Aladjev in the story.

18  A reference to Shi Youheng (1905–1982), who published an essay titled "In This Time and Season" in volumes 43 and 44 of the journal *Beixin*, dated August 16, 1927. He expressed his wish that Lu Xun would continue writing his blunt criticisms of society

because, as he quotes from the ending of Lu Xun's "Diary of a Madman," it's important to "save the children." See Lu Xun, *Lu Xun quanji* (Complete works of Lu Xun) (Beijing: Renmin wenxue, 2005), 3: 478n1.

19 "Destroying and exterminating all living things under heaven" is an idiom based on a citation from the section on "Accomplishment of War" (Wu cheng) in the *Book of Documents* (Shang shu): "Shou, the present King of Shang has behaved immorally, destroying and exterminating all living things under heaven and abusing and harming the people."

20 For more references to man-eating feasts, see "Jottings under Lamplight" in this volume.

21 Live shrimp steeped in wine.

22 Chen Yuan (also known as Chen Xiying, 1896–1970) was a noted literary adversary of Lu Xun's, and the two engaged in protracted "pen battles." The roots of their personal dispute stemmed from an incident at Women's Normal College in 1925, during which student activists protested against the restrictive policies of Yang Yinyu (1884–1938), their American-educated school principal. Lu Xun sided with the students, while Chen Yuan sided with the principal, who was supported by the minister of education, Zhang Shizhao (1881–1973). Many of Lu Xun's essays sarcastically refer to Chen Yuan and his ilk as "estimable gentlemen." For more on the Women's Normal College dispute, see "Why 'Fair Play' Should Be Deferred" in this volume.

23 Pseudonym of Zhang Shizhao.

24 The flag of the Nationalist Party.

25 *Spring and Autumn Annals* is a classic historical text recording the history of the state of Lu from 722–481 BCE. "The writing style of the *Spring and Autumn Annals*" refers to the text's use of particular words in the description of people or events to convey implicit criticism.

26 Gao Changhong (1898–1954), once a disciple of Lu Xun and then an adversary, used this phrase to describe Lu Xun in an essay titled "A Diagram of the State of Beijing Publishing in 1925," which was published in November 1926 in volume 5 of the journal *Hurricane* (Kuangbiao). He wrote that "Lu Xun, wearing his fake crown of paper authority, is in a state of being 'sick in body and mind.'" See Lu Xun, *Lu Xun quanji* (Complete works of Lu Xun) (Beijing: Renmin wenxue, 2005), 3: 411n6.

27 Chen Duxiu (1879–1942) founded *Youth Magazine* (Qingnian zazhi) in 1915, the title of which was changed to *New Youth* (Xin qingnian) in 1917. He was one of the founding members and first general secretary of the Chinese Communist Party established in 1921.

28 Lu Xun resigned from Sun Yat-sen University in April 1927 and departed from Guangzhou for Shanghai in September.

29 Tang Youren (1893–1935) was an economics professor at Peking University and a frequent contributor to the journal *Contemporary Review*, edited by Chen Yuan. In response to an article published in *Threads of Talk* that accused the *Review* of accepting bribes from the warlord Duan Qirui, Tang wrote a letter published in *Jing bao* on May 18, 1926, noting: "The source of the news that the *Contemporary Review* accepted bribes was Moscow. Last spring, I had a friend from Moscow who wrote to tell me that the story about Duan Qirui controlling the *Contemporary Review* and the monthly bribe of 3,000 *kuai* was transmitted through the hands of Zhang Shizhao and was widely spread by

the Chinese there at the time. I didn't feel it was strange when I heard this; this seemed to me just another one of the usual tactics of rumor-mongering adopted by the Communist Party." See Lu Xun, *Lu Xun quanji* (Complete works of Lu Xun) (Beijing: Renmin wenxue, 2005), 3: 479–480n15.

30   Wu Zhihui (1865–1953), a member of the Revolutionary Alliance and later the Nationalist Party, was an advocate of anarchism. Lu Xun's comment here refers to a letter Wu wrote claiming: "Becoming Red means becoming communist, something that might occur 300 years in the future. But there's something even more progressive, called anarchism, which might occur 3,000 years in the future." See Lu Xun, *Lu Xun quanji* (Complete works of Lu Xun) (Beijing: Renmin wenxue, 2005), 3: 480n17.

31   The warlord Duan Qirui (1865–1936) ordered the shooting of anti-Japanese protesters in Beijing in 1926 in the March 18 massacre. Lu Xun wrote a poem titled "Amid the Pale Blood Stains," collected in *Weeds* (Yecao, 1927), to commemorate the dead.

32   Intellectuals promoting the New Culture movement, such as Hu Shi (1891–1962), had been calling for a "new literature" written in the vernacular that would promote a new worldview in the pages of *New Youth* (Xin qingnian).

33   Launched in July 1913 by Sun Yat-sen and others to oppose Yuan Shikai's assumption of dictatorial powers, this movement was quickly suppressed by Yuan.

34   Nicknamed "the Pigtailed General," Zhang Xun (1854–1923), a northern Beiyang warlord, had styled himself a Qing loyalist and, with the cooperation of Kang Youwei, attempted to restore the last emperor Pu Yi to power on July 1, 1917. This coup was foiled by other warlord forces, and their regime ended on July 12.

35   This line is quoted in Lu Xun's prose poem "Hope" (Xiwang) in the collection *Weeds* (Yecao, 1927). The quotation is from a letter that Hungarian poet Sándor Petőfi (1823–1856) wrote to Frigyes Kerényi dated July 14, 1847: "But, my friend, despair is as deceptive as hope." Petőfi continues: "Do not judge by the exterior or you may be proved wrong." Translated from the Hungarian by Anton N. Nyerges, *Petőfi* (Buffalo, NY: Hungarian Cultural Foundation, 1973), 222.

36   Two of eight lines from Qu Yuan's (340–278 BCE) ancient elegy "Encountering Sorrow" (Li sao), which Lu Xun reproduced at the frontispiece of *Hesitation* (Panghuang, 1926).

37   A quote from the "Preface to *Outcry*," written ten years earlier and included in this volume.

38   The quotation is from "Huangyi" in the "Greater Odes" (Daya) section of the *Book of Songs* (Shi jing).

39   The allegory is from the "Autumn Water" (Qiu shui) section of *Zhuangzi*.

40   Chen Duxiu (1879–1942), a professor at Peking University, was founding editor of the journal *New Youth* (Xin qingnian).

41   Here Lu Xun uses the word *huazhi* (literally, "flowery papers"), a term from Shaoxing dialect to designate colorful woodblock prints, a type of folk art, sold during the lunar New Year.

42   Nüwa was a female mythological figure who is credited with creating humankind. In a struggle against another deity, she caused a crack in the sky but later repaired it with

colorful stones. Lu Xun later changed the title of his story "Broken Mountain" (Buzhou shan, 1922) to "Mending Heaven" (Bu tian) and anthologized it in *Old Tales Retold* (Gushi xin bian, 1936).

43 The younger critic Cheng Fangwu (1897–1984) was a member of the leftist Creation Society. Lu Xun considered Cheng one of his harshest critics.

44 For more on Lu Xun's views on Zhang Taiyan, see "A Few Matters regarding Zhang Taiyan" and "A Few Matters Recalled in Connection with Mr. Zhang Taiyan" in this volume.

45 "Long Hairs" refers to the Taiping rebels, who wore their hair long, flouting the Qing stipulation that men shave their foreheads and dress their hair in a queue according to Manchu practice.

46 "Short Hairs" refers to the Qing government troops; "Patterned Green Heads" refers to French and British troops. The former wrapped patterned cloths around their heads, while the latter wrapped green cloths around their heads. The terms as used here refer specifically to the troops that were involved in quelling the Taiping rebels.

47 A well-known phrase from Confucius's *Analects*, that at the age of thirty one would have established oneself and that at the age of forty one would understand the ways of the world.

48 A reference to the Manchu hairstyle for men.

49 A reference to the government's persecution of leftist intellectuals influenced by Russian thought at the time.

50 Qiu Jin (1879–1907), an anti-Qing revolutionary, poet, and feminist who was captured and killed by Qing forces in 1907.

51 Lu Xun began promoting woodcut art in the late 1920s, compiling and exhibiting works of eastern European artists and sponsoring workshops on the art of making woodcuts. Among his favorite works were those by the German artist Kaethe Kollwitz (1867–1945), twenty-one of which he collected and reprinted in *Selected Woodcuts of Kaethe Kollwitz* in 1936. For a more detailed examination of Lu Xun's involvement in the woodcut movement, see Xiaobing Tang, *Origins of the Avante-Garde: The Modern Woodcut Movement* (Berkeley: University of California Press, 2008), 82–89.

52 "Dr. S" refers to Sudo Iozo (1876–1959), a retired Japanese army doctor who opened his own clinic in Shanghai in 1917.

53 "Dr. D" refers to Thomas Balfour Dunn (1886–1948), an American introduced to Lu Xun by Agnes Smedley and who received his medical training at the University of California, Berkeley. In calling Dunn "European," Lu Xun may be referring to his ethnic heritage or that he had studied in Europe.

54 For more details on the debates on the "third type of person," see Lu Xun's "On the 'Third Type of Person'" in this volume.

55 The "preachers of death," a term from Friedrich Nietzsche's *Thus Spoke Zarathustra*, refers to people who retreat from life.

IN MEMORIAM

1    In 1925, a war broke out between the Nationalist army and the Japanese-backed northern warlord. On the grounds that the Nationalist army had violated the Boxer Protocol of 1900 by defending Tianjin from the Dagu Forts, on March 16, 1926, ambassadors representing eight signatory countries to the protocol sent an ultimatum to the Duan Qirui government demanding that all defense establishments on the Dagu Forts be destroyed. On March 18, in front of the Tiananmen Gate, students in Beijing organized a demonstration that was suppressed by the military police, resulting in the death of forty-seven protesters and the injuring of close to two hundred others. For more on the March 18 massacre, see "Why 'Fair Play' Should Be Deferred," "Roses without Blooms," and "In Memory of Liu Hezhen" in this volume.

2    On Sunday, January 22, 1905, unarmed demonstrators in Saint Petersburg were fired upon by soldiers of the Imperial Guard as they marched toward the Winter Palace to present a petition to Tsar Nicholas II of Russia, demanding improved working conditions, fair wages, and a reduction in working hours. The casualties on what has been referred to as "Bloody Sunday" were estimated to be more than one thousand dead or wounded.

3    Lu Xun quotes from "Yi," a poem from the "Greater Odes" (Daya) section of the *Book of Songs* (Shi jing).

4    For more of Lu Xun's views on the "March 18" incident, see "Roses without Blooms" and "Why 'Fair Play' Should Be Deferred" in this volume.

5    A reference to the eight-nation alliance of Austria-Hungary, France, Germany, Italy, Japan, Russia, the United Kingdom, and the United States, whose troops invaded Beijing during the Boxer Rebellion of 1900.

6    Translation of "Elegies" adapted from Tony Barnstone, in *The Anchor Book of Chinese Poetry*, ed. Tony Barnstone and Chou Ping (New York: Anchor Books, 2005), 83-84.

7    A reference to the "Five Martyrs of the League of Left-Wing Writers": Li Weisen (1903–1931), Rou Shi (1901–1931), Hu Yepin (1903–1931), Feng Keng (1907–1931), and Yin Fu (1909–1931).

8    "Three stripes" refers to the insignia on the uniform of the security police in the Shanghai concessions at the time, here serving as a flippant reference to the police themselves.

9    Fang Xiaoru (1357–1402) was a Ming Confucian scholar-bureaucrat who remained loyal to the Jianwen Emperor after the throne was usurped by the Yongle Emperor in 1402. When the Yongle Emperor commanded that he write an inaugural address, Fang refused. He was subjected to the extreme punishment of death and "extermination of the clan to the 10th degree," which extended to his kin, friends, and students as well.

10   Shanghai writer Ye Lingfeng (1905–1975) wrote popular romances and erotic stories, works that Lu Xun despised. Here Lu Xun is trying to wrest Fukiya Koji back from the hands of superficial imitators like Ye.

11   Ruan Lingyu (1910–1935) was one of the most prominent Chinese film stars of the 1930s.

12   The play Lu Xun refers to was performed in 1935 by the Shanghai Public Theatre (Shanghai gong wutai). Ai Xia (1912–1934) was a film actress and left-leaning writer who

committed suicide. The film *New Woman* (Xin nüxing, 1933), based on her life story, was one of Ruan's last starring roles.

13  Wu Zetian (624–705), Tang dynasty empress, was often portrayed in popular lore as having many lovers.

14  Zhang Taiyan and the Russian revolutionary Maxim Gorky (1868–1936) were born in the same year and died in the same year.

15  This phrase is an allusion to the line "ashamed to compete with goblins for light," which appears in a *Taiping guangji* anecdote on Ji Kang (223–262), one of the "Seven Sages of the Bamboo Grove." According to the anecdote, Ji Kang was playing his zither under the lamplight when a ghost appeared. He then blew out the flame, claiming that he would be "ashamed to compete with goblins for light," indicating that he was not afraid of ghosts. Zhang often likened those he admired to these "Seven Sages."

16  "Xx" and "xxx" appear in the original essay. For specific references to figures Lu Xun had in mind, see *Lu Xun quanji* (Complete works of Lu Xun) (Beijing: Renmin wenxue, 2005), 6: 569–570n12,13.

17  A ceremonial game of ancient Han origins in which arrows are pitched into a vat.

18  Awarded to Zhang by Yuan Shikai.

19  The warlord Zhang Xun (1854–1923), nicknamed "the Pigtailed General," styled himself as a Qing loyalist and, with the cooperation of Kang Youwei, attempted to restore the last Qing emperor Pu Yi to power on July 1, 1917. This coup was foiled by other warlord forces, and the restorationist regime ended on July 12.

20  Duan Qirui (1865–1936) served as commander of the army, chief of staff, and ultimately prime minister (1912–1916) under Yuan Shikai. From 1924 to 1926, he was chief executive when his troops perpetrated the March 18 (1926) massacre of student protestors, which Lu Xun excoriated in the press. See "Why 'Fair Play' Should Be Deferred" and "In Memory of Liu Hezhen" in this volume.

21  For women and children, the Liu Hai style was to have bangs hanging down over the forehead. Applying the term to men sounds slightly effeminate here because it would refer only to loose hair hanging aside the main queue. Liu Hai was the name of a "child immortal" who sported this style of hair.

22  In August 1902, nine Chinese students attempted to enroll in a military school but were prevented from doing so by the Qing diplomatic corps, which feared they wanted to learn military tactics to start a revolution. When Wu Zhihui went to the Qing mission with a group of over twenty students to deliver a protest, Cai Jun was unwilling to relent, and in the process of negotiations, Wu Zhihui got into a scuffle with him. Cai Jun later had the students arrested by the Japanese authorities as rioters and deported to China. For more details, see Lu Xun, *Lu Xun quanji* (Complete works of Lu Xun) (Beijing: Renmin wenxue, 2005), 6: 580n7.

23  The anecdote implies Wu acted as if he were intending to commit suicide rather than return to Qing-ruled China, but his choice of the imperial moat as a venue cast doubt on the sincerity of his intentions.

24  This would be the equivalent of 1900. As an indication of his nationalism and in order to show his contempt for the Manchu Qing dynasty, whom he considered barbarian in-

vaders, Zhang Taiyan eschewed the use of Qing reign–era dating, counting the years instead from 841 BCE when anciently the Zhou people drove out King Li and established a proto-republic.

25 Qi Bansun was a Ming loyalist from Shanyin (part of present-day Shaoxing), Zhejiang province, also Lu Xun's home. (Zhang Taiyan hailed from Yuhang, in the same province.) After his involvement in a plan to restore the fallen dynasty was discovered, Qi was exiled to Ninggu Pagoda, where he took refuge and became a Buddhist monk. Yinxuan may be the monk Yinyuan (Yinyuan Longqi, 1592–1673), who traveled to Japan circa 1655. There he eventually became the founder of a Buddhist sect. See *Rojin Zenshū* (Tokyo: Gakken, 1984), 8:634, notes 3 and 4.

26 The "Biography of Yan Zhu" can be found in juan 64, shang (first part) of the *History of the Han Dynasty* (Han shu).

27 Based on a passage from "Chronicles of the Line of Goujian, King of Yue" (Yue wang Goujian shijia) in the *Records of the Grand Historian* (Shi ji).

28 Huang Keqiang is the cognomen of Huang Xing (1874–1916), a revolutionary, poet, and later military commander who cooperated with Sun Yat-sen and Song Jiaoren to found the Revolutionary Alliance (Tongmeng hui) in Tokyo in July 1905. Huang came from Hunan, anciently part of the Chu kingdom.

## ON TRADITION

1 Kang Youwei (1858–1927), leader of the 1898 Reform movement and staunch supporter of the Qing emperors, argued in two January 1918 articles that China is better suited for constitutional monarchy than representative democracy. Chen Duxiu (1879–1942), a leading figure of the New Culture movement, wrote a long article in *New Youth* (Xin qingnian) lampooning Kang's views in March 1918.

2 In October 1917, Yu Fu (1856–1943), Lu Feikui (1886–1941), and others formed the Society for Psychical Research (Lingxue hui) in Shanghai, published their own journal, and held séances to consult the spirits on a diverse range of matters from social mores to the management of business to issues of life and death. Their views were criticized in the pages of *New Youth* (Xin qingnian) as superstition by Chen Bainian (1887–1983), Qian Xuantong (1887–1939), and Liu Bannong (1891–1934), leaders of the New Culture movement.

3 The term was coined by Liu Shipei, who wrote it to support the imperial ambitions of Yuan Shikai (1859–1916), president of the Republic of China. Starting in 1914, Yuan's government began "exalting chastity" by publicly rewarding chaste women and / or their families with public recognition.

4 Yosano Akiko, "My Views on Chastity" (Watakushi no teisō kan), in *A Miscellany Book* (Zakkicho, 1911), trans. Zhou Zuoren, *New Youth* (Xin qingnian) 4, no. 5 (May 1918).

5 Cheng Yi (1033–1107), *Surviving Work of the Chengs from Henan* (Henan Chengshi yishu), juan 22.

6 The Song dynasty was overthrown by the nomadic Mongols, who established the Yuan dynasty (1206–1368). Lu Xun uses transliterations of Mongolian here to highlight the distinctively non-Han nature of the Yuan ruling house.

7    There are many eulogies in local gazetteers that bear the title "Combined Biographies of Two Martyred Women." "Epitaph for Seven Concubines" refers to a widely known eulogy by Zhang Yu (1333–1385) that records the death of seven women in the household of Pan Yuanshao who lived at the end of the Yuan dynasty. Pan drove his seven concubines to take their own lives in anticipation of his own military defeat.

8    Qian Qianyi (1582–1664) is a famous literatus-official who switched his loyalty to the Qing when the Manchu conquerors overthrew the Ming dynasty in 1644.

9    The "etymological" connection between *fu* (woman) and *fu* (to submit) is "established" in the second-century dictionary *Analysis of Graphs and Explications of Characters* (Shuowen jiezi), juan 12.

10   The "etymological" connection between *ru* (Confucian scholar) and *rou* (to yield) is "established" in *Shuowen jiezi*, juan 8.

11   Lu Xun here alludes to Confucius, who famously said in the *Analects* that he does not make up anything new but only "transmits" the words of the ancient sages.

12   The most famous critics are Gui Youguang (1506–1571), Wang Zhong (1745–1794), and Yu Zhengqie (1775–1840), who argued against the custom of "chaste maidens" (unmarried young women who remain faithful to their dead fiancés).

13   The term *mob* appears in English in the original.

14   Here Lu Xun is making a mocking reference to the conservative and ethnocentric attitude of a letter written by Ren Hongjun to Hu Shi, who served on the editorial board of *New Youth*: "No matter how muddled our country's history, language, and thought, they have still been created by our people and bequeathed to us. These muddled seeds are not only in our language and our history, but exist now in our brains and will exist in our descendants' brains" (*Xin qingnian*, vol. 5, no. 2, August 15, 1918).

15   Quoted from Ibsen's *Gengangere* (1881); the English version is translated from Lu Xun's text.

16   This passage refers to four well-known examples of filial piety from the Yuan dynasty text *Twenty-Four Paragons of Filial Piety* (Ershisi xiao): a son unable to find bamboo for his mother to eat wept on the earth until bamboo shoots appeared; another son lay on ice in winter to catch a fish for his stepmother to eat; and another son took a mouthful of his father's feces, on his doctor's advice, to discover the nature of his illness. The fourth example is explained above.

17   A line from the late Qing poet Huang Zunxian (1848–1905).

18   A line from the *Book of Documents* (Shang shu) advocating the murder of the ancient tyrant Jie (1728–1675 BCE), last emperor of the Xia dynasty, who boasted that he was the sun.

19   Pen name of Xu Bingchang (1886–1976), professor of philosophy in Peking University and chief editor of the political weekly *Mengjin*, published in Beijing from March 1925 to March 1926.

20   Confucius, *Analects: Yanyuan*, 12.

21   *Mencius: Gaozi*, part 2.

22   *Mencius: Tengwang gong*, part 2.

23   Xu Zhonglin, *Investiture of the Gods* (Fengshen yanyi, sixteenth century). King Zhou's poem appears in chapter 1.

24 The expression comes from the Sima Qian (145–86 BCE), "Self-Preface" (Zi xu), *Records of the Grand Historian* (Shi ji).

25 Cao Xueqin, *Dream of the Red Chamber* (Honglou meng, eighteenth century).

26 Ernst Haeckel (1834–1919), German biologist and philosopher. Lu Xun quotes from chapter 4, "Our Embryonic Development," of his *Die Welträthsel* (Riddle of the universe).

27 "Instructions of Yi" (Yixun), *Book of Documents* (Shang shu).

28 "Epitaph of Yuan Zhan" (Yuan Zhan muzhi ming).

29 *Collected Documents of the Yuan Dynasty* (Yuan dianzhang), juan 57.

30 *Little Zhang Incinerates His Son to Save His Mother* (Xiao Zhang tu fen er jiu mu), an anonymous Yuan dynasty play, collected in *Gujin zaju* (Collected dramatic scripts, ancient and modern).

31 Feng Menglong, *Stories to Awaken the World* (Xing shi hengyan), juan 9.

32 Xuan Ding, *Notes Made on Rainy Nights Under Autumn Lamp* (Yeyu qiudeng lu), juan 3.

33 Yue Fei (1103–1142) was a general who defended the Song dynasty against the Jurchens but was put to death by the Song court. In the eighteenth-century *Biography of Yue Fei* (Shuo Yue quanzhuan), his death is attributed to unsettled accounts from previous incarnations.

34 Guan Yu (160?–219) was a general of Shu during the Three Kingdoms period. He became a symbol of loyalty and bravery and was deified by the late Song dynasty.

35 Here, Lu Xun refers to a massive public commemoration held on June 25 in Tiananmen Square in Beijing after the killing of labor demonstrators by British police in Shanghai on May 30, 1925. A giant wooden spirit tablet of about twenty-seven feet was erected together with a forty-foot banner praising the sacrifice of the dead.

36 Lin Yutang (1895–1976) was a prominent essayist and editor who went on to fame as an interpreter of China for Anglophone audiences with his best-selling *My Country and My People*. Lu Xun follows Lin in using a phonetic transliteration of the English "fair play" into Chinese characters, heightening its foreignness to notably comic effect. The article to which Lu Xun refers here was itself a reaction to the invective swirling around the Beijing Women's Normal College incident. Lin pointedly urges Lu Xun and others to moderate ad hominem attacks on political enemies in the name of "fair play." See "An Aside on Style in *Threads of Talk*: Moderation, Invective, and Fair Play" (Chalun Yusi de wenti: wenjian, maren, yu fei'e polai), *Yusi* 57 (December 14, 1925).

37 Here Lu Xun takes the first of many pokes at his political and personal nemesis, the prominent academic and editor of the liberal journal *Contemporary Review* (Xiandai pinglun), Chen Xiying (also known as Chen Yuan, 1896–1970), specifically referring to Chen's remarks in *Contemporary Review* satirizing Lu Xun's tendency toward sharp polemic.

38 Qiu Jin (1879–1907), an anti-Qing revolutionary, poet, feminist, and would-be assassin from Lu Xun's own hometown, was captured and killed by Qing forces in 1907.

39 Here Lu Xun takes another swipe at Chen Xiying, implying that his support for Yang had something to do with their common origin in Wuxi and its local patronage networks.

40  The first phrase is from the Confucian *Analects*; the second from the Old Testament.

41  "Throwing stones down a well" refers back to a Tang dynasty text by Han Yu, but the more immediate and sardonic reference is to Lin Yutang's advocacy for "fair play" in the pages of *Threads of Talk* (Yusi), such that authors would refrain from "throwing stones down a well" at their adversaries.

42  The quotation derives from the *History of the Later Han* (Hou han shu), but it appears here because it was marshaled against Lu Xun's lack of impartiality in the pages of *Contemporary Review* by Chen Xiying, who wrote, "Chinese people have no sense of right and wrong . . . everything about their own party is right, while everything about the opposing party is always wrong." Chen goes on to defend his own impartiality by asserting that, "in a society in which 'people ally with the like-minded, and attack those who are different from themselves,' there are those who will not only attack an avowed enemy, but also bravely criticize their own friends." See Chen Xiying, "Idle Chat" (Xian hua), *Xiandai pinglun* 3, no. 53 (December 12, 1925).

43  Liu Baizhao (1893–?) was an educational official charged with dispersing the student protests.

44  The eventual sacking of Yang Yinyu was the whiff of "fairness" to which Lu Xun refers, but she and her associates, he implies, rather than "drowning," remained very much in power, despite the temporary setback.

45  Han Yu (768–825) and Su Shi (1037–1101) were two of the eight great masters of archaic prose *(guwen)*, often taken as models by those writing in the Ming and Qing periods. Liu Zongyuan (773–819), mentioned below, was another of the eight.

46  Quoted from an essay by F. J. Goodnow, published during Yuan Shikai's resumption of the imperium in 1915, which argued that China was uniquely predisposed toward autocracy and should therefore abandon republican government.

47  From the *Analects*, 11.14, in which Confucius praises a disciple who suggests rebuilding a treasury without updating or changing its style.

48  King Zhou was the last king of the Shang dynasty, famous for his decadence and cruelty. His posthumous name Zhou means "horse crupper," which is a leather strap that is fixed under a horse's tail and is often soiled by feces.

49  King Zhou's decapitated head was displayed in the capital on a white piece of cloth.

50  From part 2 of the essay "More Roses without Blooms" (Wu hua de qiangwei zhi er), in Lu Xun, *Lu Xun quanji* (Complete works of Lu Xun) (Beijing: Renmin wenxue, 2005), 3: 279–280.

51  Adapted from Matthew 5:27: "I tell you that anyone who looks at a woman lustfully has already committed adultery with her in his heart."

52  The source of this phrase is unknown, but Lu Xun's scorn is clearly directed at modernity's (science's) complicity in propagating traditional social values.

53  The writer Ye Shengtao (1894–1988) used this term in 1921 to criticize those who advocated the modern vernacular but still also composed classical prose and poetry.

54  A reference to the 1898 reformers such as Liang Qichao (1873–1929) and Kang Youwei (1858–1927).

55  A reference to the Sino-Japanese War of 1894–1895.

56 *On Learning Mathematics* (Xuesuan bitan) is a multivolume mathematics textbook by Hua Hengfang (1833–1902), first published in 1882; *Principles of Chemistry* (Huaxue jianyuan) was translated from *Well's Principles of Chemistry* by John Fryer and Xu Shou in 1871.

57 Zhang Zhidong (1837–1909), a major Qing statesman and advocate of the Self-Strengthening movement in the late Qing, published *Guidebook to Bibliography* (Shumu wenda) during his stint as the educational minister in Sichuan in 1875. It contained more than 2,300 titles in classical education. Miao Quansun (1844–1919) is a noted late Qing bibliophile.

58 *Zhuangzi* was composed in the third century BCE, reputedly the work of the philosopher Zhuang Zhou. *Selections of Refined Literature* is a literary anthology containing works from 300 BCE to 500 AD, commissioned by the crown prince Xiao Tong (501–531). This is a snide reference to Shi Zhecun who, when asked by the editors of *Da wan bao* to recommend books for youths, advised that in order to write well in the vernacular, young people had to read *Zhuangzi* and *Selections of Refined Literature*.

59 Modern verse that is arranged typographically to look like classical regulated poetry.

60 Matthew 9:17. During the May Fourth movement, advocates of the vernacular often invoked it to argue that the classical styles cannot express modern experience and sentiments.

61 Traditional Chinese liquor with an herbal infusion.

62 Traditional folk tune patterns.

63 "Tongcheng lackeys" (*Tongcheng miuzhong*) and "Metaphysics evildoers" (*xuanxue yaonie*) are quoted from Qian Xuantong (1887–1939), whose wording became popular disparagement of the two traditional schools of prose.

64 Lu Xun is citing a quotation from the *Book of Rites* (Li ji), one of the Five Classics.

65 A slogan coined by the Qing reformist politician Zhang Zhidong (1837–1909), who promoted the adoption of Western learning in order to further national strength.

66 All these examples are based on actual news accounts of events tacitly or openly supported by KMT authorities. The "fat lady" refers to "Jolly Nellie" Terrell (1894–1955), a 700-plus pound circus sideshow performer and actress. In 1934, a Shanghai branch of the Hong Kong–based department store Sincere invited Terrell to perform as a promotion.

67 In August 1934 performers staged a recreation of an ancient Confucian ritual dance in Shanghai. In June of the same year, Chiang Kai-shek personally approved an ordinance in Jiangxi province that mandated all skirts must pass the knees by no less than four inches, and forbade the exposure of bare feet. For more details, see Lu Xun, *Lu Xun quanji* (Complete works of Lu Xun) (Beijing: Renmin wenxue, 2005), 5: 573n9.

68 The Yushima Temple in Tokyo burned down in 1923. Rebuilding was completed in April 1935.

69 *Sayings of the Kong Family* (Kongzi jiayu), a collection of writings on Confucius's deeds and sayings compiled and annotated during the Three Kingdoms period (220–265).

70 Liang Qichao (1873–1929) fled to Japan after the failure of the Hundred Days Reform in 1898. *The China Discussion* (Qingyi bao) advocated constitutional monarchy.

71 The Kobun Academy was a Japanese-language preparatory school set up in Tokyo for Chinese students.

72 "Ochanomizu" refers to the Yushima Temple discussed in note 68.

73 Quotation from *Mencius*, book 5B. The translation is from D. C. Lau, *Mencius* (Penguin, 1970), 150.

74 The quotation is from the Confucian *Analects*, book 4.

75 The quotation is from "Duke Ai 15th Year," *Zuozhuan*.

76 This anecdote appears in "Zigong Asks" (Zigong wen) in *Kongzi jiayu*.

77 *Mencius*, book 3B.

78 Yuan Shikai (1859–1916) was the first president of the Republic; he proclaimed himself Hongxia Emperor in January 1916 but was forced to abdicate in March. He died the same year, in June.

79 Sun Chuanfang (1885–1935) revived the ceremony of tossing arrows into a pot—originally a drinking game (Cf. Ouyang Xiu, "The Old Toper's Pavilion" [Zui weng ting ji])—in Nanjing in 1926.

80 Zhang Zongchang (1881–1932) led a campaign to promote Confucianism in Shandong in 1925.

81 *Zi jian Nanzi*, by Lin Yutang (1895–1976), was published in 1928 in *Torrent* (Benliu). While the play was in rehearsal at the Qufu Second Normal School, the Kong clan objected to the Ministry of Education that it was a "public insult" to Confucius. Lu Xun published documents relating to the case in 1929.

82 The quotation is from "Quli," *Book of Rites* (Li ji).

## ON ART AND LITERATURE

1 *Gongmin tuan* refers to the ruffians hired by Yuan Shikai (1859–1916) to intimidate members of the National Assembly to vote for him as president during the October 6, 1913 elections.

2 The original uses the incorrect character *er* (而) in the compound that should be *erzi* (兒子), which means "son."

3 Lu Xun recommended that readers read fewer Chinese books in "Must-Read Books for Young People" in this volume.

4 See "Warriors and Flies" in this volume.

5 Refers to Zhang Shizhao (1881–1973), an early revolutionary who, by the 1920s, had turned into a cultural conservative. He was appointed minister of education by the Beiyang warlord regime in 1925, and Lu Xun excoriated his policies. See "Why 'Fair Play' Should Be Deferred" in this volume.

6 A reference to the March 18, 1926, massacre in which the northern warlord Duan Qirui's (1865–1936) forces attacked antiwarlord and anti-imperialist student protesters in Beijing. See "In Memory of Liu Hezhen" and "Why 'Fair Play' Should Be Deferred" in this volume.

7 Sun Chuanfang (1885–1935) was a warlord who controlled Shanghai as well as the provinces surrounding the city. He was defeated in 1927 by the Nationalist-led Northern Expedition.

8 The onomatopoeic original, *geming, ge geming, ge ge geming, ge ge* . . . , is intended to simulate the sound of machine-gun fire. The line plays on the characters *ge* (to get rid of) and *ming* (life) in *geming* (revolution).

9 Thereby simplifying the complicated Qin system of rules and regulations, which the elders had been displeased with, to the following three: that homicide would be punished by death and that injuring others or theft would incur commensurate punishment. Recorded in the "Annals on Emperor Gaozu" (Gaozu benji), *Records of the Grand Historian* (Shi ji).

10 A reference to the proletariat (the other three estates being the clergy, nobility, and bourgeoisie in classic European political science), not the current usage meaning news media.

11 Huang Chao (?–884) was the leader of a rebellion during the Tang dynasty.

12 Fragrant Rice Village (Dao xiang cun) and Lu's Straw Mat (Lu gao jian) are formerly popular brands of food in Shanghai.

13 This quotation is from the "Author's Note" of Feng Naichao's published script *Walking Together along the Dark Road* (Tong zai hei'an de lu shang zou, 1928). The full line reads: "The essence of drama should be sought in the actions of the characters. Let yesterday's littérateurs work at refined dialogue and discovering the profundity of reality" (see Feng Naichao, *Collected Works*, p. 224, http://book.ss.xuexi365.com/ebook/detail.jhtml?id=10123482&page=217, accessed August 6, 2014). Feng Naichao (1901–1983), known principally for his poetry, was an important figure in the later period of the Creation Society. As a member of the Chinese Communist Party, he also played a role in the formation of the League of Left-Wing Writers in the 1930s.

14 From the same play referenced earlier (see note 13). Lu Xun offers this quotation as an example of what he sees as the poor writing found in many revolutionary publications.

15 The foreigner's speech ("yes" and "no") and the title of the poem "Pong Pong Pong," referred to later, appear in English in the original essay.

16 Xu Zhimo was an admirer of Mansfield, met her briefly when he studied at Cambridge, and later translated her fiction into Chinese.

17 The Nanshe, or Southern Society, was a literary society founded in 1909 that also engaged in anti-Qing political activities.

18 This quotation refers to the *History of the Later Han* (Hou han shu) compiled in the fifth century CE.

19 A reference to the sumptuary clothes literati wore in imperial times.

20 Guo Moruo, "Only One Hand" (Yi zhi shou, 1927). Serialized in *Creation Monthly* (Chuangzao yuekan) in 1928, volume 1, numbers 9–11.

21 *Kumon no shōchō*, a collection of essays on literature by the Japanese scholar Kuriyagawa Hakuson that Lu Xun had translated into Chinese as *Kumen de xiangzheng* in 1924.

22 Cheng Fangwu (1897–1984) was a founding member of the Creation Society and a leader in the leftist transformation of its members.

23 See "Must-Read Books for Young People" in this volume.

24 One of China's earliest and longest-running newspapers (from 1872 to 1949), published in Shanghai.

25  The 1858 Treaty of Tianjin forbade the use of the character *yi* (barbarian) to refer to the British Empire and its subjects.

26  *Analects* (Lunyu) 5.7. See Confucius, *Analects: With Selections from Traditional Commentaries*, trans. Edward Slingerland (Indianapolis: Hackett, 2003), 41.

27  *The Scholars* (Rulin waishi) is a Qing dynasty novel by Wu Jingzi that satirized the world of civil examinations. *Eunuch Sanbao's Voyage to the West* (Sanbao taijian xiyang ji) is a Ming dynasty novel that fictionalized the journeys of Zheng He (1371–?), a palace eunuch who led exploratory and trade expeditions from Southeast Asia to Africa. *Stories to Delight the Heart* (Kuaixin bian) is a Qing dynasty romantic novel.

28  *Greatest Event in Life* (Zhongshen dashi) is a 1919 play by Hu Shi that dealt with the marriage question. "Nora" refers to the heroine of Ibsen's *A Doll's House.*

29  The scholar Wu Mi (1894–1978) was a proponent of archaism.

30  *Fiction Monthly* ran from 1910 to 1931 and was published by Commercial Press. It initially featured mostly fiction from the Saturday School. In 1921 Mao Dun became editor and tried to push the magazine in a more critical direction, arousing the anger of Saturday School proponents. Under pressure from such critics, the Commercial Press removed Mao Dun from the editor's post in 1923. Commercial Press established *Fiction World*, a venue for Mandarin Ducks and Butterflies fiction, as a counterweight to *Fiction Monthly* in 1923. For more details, see Lu Xun, *Lu Xun quanji* (Complete works of Lu Xun) (Beijing: Renmin wenxue, 2005), 4: 314n25–26.

31  Ivan Goncharov (1812–1891) was a Russian writer, best known for the novel *Oblomov* (1859), a portrait of a slovenly, aimless aristocrat. Lu Xun mocks counterrevolutionary critics who pointed to Lenin's reading of the novel as evidence of a tempering of Lenin's revolutionary fervor. In fact, Lenin diagnosed the character Oblomov as symptomatic of a corrupt and dying feudal class.

32  In Ye Lingfeng's 1929 novel, *Autobiography of a Desperate Man* (Qiongchou de zizhuan), the protagonist tears out pages from Lu Xun's *Call to Arms* before heading to the toilet as part of his morning routine.

33  Xiang Peiliang (1905–1959) was one of the founders of the Sturm und Drang Society (Kuangbiao she) and a contributor to its journal *Sturm und Drang* (Kuangbiao). In a 1926 issue of the journal, Xiang called upon the youth to emulate wolves and rebel against society. By 1929 he had become an advocate for Guomindang literary policy. For more details, see Lu Xun, *Lu Xun quanji* (Complete works of Lu Xun) (Beijing: Renmin wenxue, 2005), 4: 314n30.

34  The journal of the Chinese Communist Party's Youth League, published from 1923 to 1932.

35  Here Lu Xun is playing with the term *revolution* (geming), a compound made up of two words, *ge* (to change, get rid of) and *ming* (mandate, destiny, life), in order to critique these literary journals' antirevolutionary attitude.

36  Movement launched by the Guomindang in 1930 to promote literature that supported its policies and acted as a rebuff to left-wing literary movements.

37  A snide reference to Buddhist head shaving on the path to transcendence.

38 Here, Lu Xun sarcastically refers to Beijing opera, an art form that he abhorred, and alludes to the popularity of the most famous female impersonator of his time, Mei Lanfang (1894–1961).

39 The term *zhongyong*, sometimes translated as "doctrine of the mean," appears in the *Analects* (Lunyu) and is the name of one of the other Confucian Four Books. It refers to the conduct of superior men who display probity, moderation, and objectivity in their course of action. The essay uses "middle way" pejoratively, alluding to the use of ambiguous words and action to deceive the unwitting masses.

40 *Juren* refers to the title conferred on candidates who passed the provincial-level exam in the examination system. Here Lu Xun is engaging in some word play, showing how the new election system did not differ much from the examination system, whether in use of language or in practice.

41 Title conferred on candidates who passed the prefectural exam.

42 Title conferred on candidates who passed the court exam.

43 A phrase Chiang Kai-shek used in 1932 to describe the Nationalist government's policy toward the Japanese.

44 "Modestly poor" is a phrase Sun Yat-sen used in *The Three Principles of the People*. He wrote: "What the Chinese refer to as the disparity between the wealthy and poor is merely a distinction between the really poor and the slightly poor. Actually, the foremost capitalists in China, when compared to foreign capitalists, are merely the slightly poor."

45 Shanghai businessmen declared 1933 "national products year." Lu Xun here is alluding to the fact that imported Japanese goods were sometimes stamped with a "national products" label. In "The True or False Don Quixote" (Zhen jia Tangjihede), Lu Xun describes the "national products" movement as a marketing ploy disguised as patriotism. See Lu Xun, *Lu Xun quanji* (Complete works of Lu Xun) (Beijing: Renmin wenxue, 2005), 4: 434–437.

## ON MODERN CULTURE

1 The temple fair is a religious festival held to seek blessings from the gods, during which idols on stilts and various performers parade around town. Lu Xun writes specifically of such festivals in "Festival of the Five Ghosts" in his memoir *Morning Blossoms Plucked at Dusk* (Zhao hua xi shi, 1928).

2 Motto of the eponymous character in *Brand*, by the Norwegian playwright Henrik Ibsen (1828–1906), reflecting the character's distaste for compromise.

3 The first translation into Chinese of *Et Dukkehjem*, by Luo Jialun and Hu Shi, was published in volume 4, issue 6, of *New Youth* in June 1918 under the title *Nuola*.

4 Lu Xun did not know the Dano-Norwegian in which Ibsen wrote, but he was fluent in German and refers to Ibsen's plays by their German titles.

5 From a published speech Ibsen gave in 1898 in Christiania (an earlier name for Oslo). It is unclear whether Lu Xun is referring to the English or German translation, but there may be some confusion about the meaning of the Norwegian word *dikt* (equivalent to German *Dichtung*), which refers both to "poetry" and to "fiction" (i.e., as opposed to fact).

6  Ahasvar is rendered in Latin letters in the original. Ahasvar, sometimes rendered Ahasver, may be a bastardization of the name Ahasuerus, an ancient king of Persia. All three renderings have been used to refer to the Wandering Jew.

7  Lu Xun is referring to the Chinese classic *Yellow Emperor's Classic of Internal Medicine* (Huangdi neijing) attributed to Huangdi (the mythical Yellow Emperor) and his minister Qi Bo.

8  *Classic of Dissection* (Zhegufen jing) is erroneously ascribed by Lu Xun to the Song collection *Shuofu*. It is actually a Ming text found in the *Xu Shuofu*, a Qing addendum to the *Shuofu*.

9  This is a reference to one of the twenty-four paragons of filial piety, Du Shishou, who is said to have cut off a piece of his own flesh to feed his starving parents.

10  See *Analects* 5.11: "Zigong said, What I do not want others to do to me, I have no desire to do to others"; in Arthur Waley, trans., *The Analects of Confucius* (New York: Vintage Books, 1938), 110.

11  From *A New Account of the Tales of the World* (Shishuo xinyu): "Liu Ling often indulged in wine and caroused. Sometimes he would take off his clothes and stand stark naked in his house. When people mocked him, he replied: 'Heaven and Earth are my house, my house is my pants. What are you doing in my pants?'" (my translation).

12  The Chinese is *Zhu Zhendan*. *Zhu* is a classical designation for India and was often adopted as a Chinese surname by Indian monks who came to China. *Zhendan* is the Chinese rendering of the term for China in ancient Indian Buddhist texts. Tagore's adopted name thus symbolized the unity of the two cultures. I have rendered Zhendan as Cathay to give the sense of an obsolete designation for China.

13  A story based on a Qing dynasty *chuanqi* drama by Li Yu entitled "A Handful of Snow" (Yi peng xue).

14  The 19th Route Army was famed for its fierce resistance to the Japanese attack on Shanghai that commenced on January 28, 1932.

15  The film *Yao shan yanshi*, released in September 1933, featured a romantic entanglement between a Han Chinese explorer and the princess of the Yao people, an ethnic minority in the southwest regions bordering Vietnam, Burma, and Laos.

16  *Fourth Son Visits His Mother* (Silang tan mu) is a classic Peking opera concerning the captivity of the Northern Song general Yang Silang by the nomadic Liao people beyond the Great Wall. Yang ends up marrying a Liao princess; the plot revolves around his surreptitious journey back to the northern Song to visit his beloved mother for the last time.

17  *Princess Shuangyang Pursues Di* (Shuangyang gongzhu zhui Di) is also from the Peking opera repertoire, concerning a dashing Northern Song general, Di Qing, who is tricked into marrying the "barbarian" Princess Shuangyang of Shanshan, and then leaves her to continue his military campaign to pacify the regions to the west of China. She chases after him in an effort to compel him to remain true to his vows.

18  Hagenbeck's world-famous traveling circus visited Shanghai in October 1933. Richard Sawade (1869–1947) was the circus's general manager and trainer.

19  Lu Xun cites the "Gongsun Chou" chapter of the *Mencius* (Mengzi).

20  See the "Yanyuan" chapter of the *Analects* (Lunyu).

21  See the "Quli" chapter of the *Book of Rites* (Li ji).

22  Lu Xun is puncturing the illusions of the "national products" movement of the early 1930s that promoted the consumption of domestically manufactured Chinese goods.

23  The war here refers to the Battle of Shanghai (begun on January 28, 1932), during which Japanese forces devastated Shanghai's Zhabei district before meeting staunch resistance from the Chinese 19th Route Army.

24  A reference to rural migrants from a region in Jiangsu province located between the Yangzi River to the south and the Huai River to the north who have traditionally been looked down on by Shanghai residents.

25  The allusion here is to widely circulated reports that a Jiangbei neighborhood association in Zhabei had collaborated with the Japanese during the Battle of Shanghai.

26  French writer and journalist Maurice Dekobra (1885–1973).

27  French writer, journalist, and politician Paul Vaillant-Couturier (1892–1937). Presumably people were unwilling to talk about Vaillant-Couturier because of his leftist political sympathies.

28  This is a literal translation of the title *Feizhou Tanxian*, which might refer to the film *Hunting Big Game in Africa with Gun and Camera* (Universal, 1922).

29  The English terms *grotesque* and *erotic* appear in parentheses in the original.

30  An essay written by Ying Bo published in the September 1903 issue of the *Zhejiang Tide* (Zhejiang chao), recounting the author's delight upon seeing the Han robe worn in Japan.

31  A reference to Fan Zengxiang (1846–1931), a renowned classical-style poet.

32  In his essay titled "On Western Dress" (Lun xizhuang, 1933), published in issue 39 of *Analects* (Lunyu), Lin Yutang wrote: "The only reason why Western dress was all the rage for a time and modern women were keen to follow its fashions was because people were so taken with Western customs and fond of imitating them. There is absolutely no ethical, aesthetic, or hygienic basis for its adoption."

33  A report dated April 14, 1934, in volume 1, issue 10, of the monthly *New Life* (Xin sheng) reads: "In the city of Hangzhou, there was the appearance of a stalwart group dedicated to destroying things modern. They used sulfuric acid to ruin people's modern-style clothes. This is a warning written to the modern women who use Western goods." For more details, see Lu Xun, *Lu Xun quanji* (Complete works of Lu Xun) (Beijing: Renmin wenxue, 2005), 5: 480n6.

34  "Eighteen Gropes" (Shiba mo) is a vulgar song sung by blind balladeers. It must have been very popular in the 1930s, as it figured in the repertory of the vulgar boatman in Shen Congwen's story "Baizi," set in far-off West Hunan.

35  "Drizzling Rain" (Maomao yu) is a song composed by Li Jinhui, popular around 1930.

36  A reference to the *Deutsche Zentral Zeitung* (German central newspaper), a German-language Communist newspaper published in Moscow.

37  The Association for the Study of Woodcuts was founded in Hangzhou in 1933. For more on Lu Xun's association with the woodcut movement, see Xiaobing Tang, *Origins of the*

*Chinese Avant-Garde: The Modern Woodcut Movement* (Berkeley: University of California Press, 2008).

38 Anatoly Vasilyevich Lunacharsky (1875–1933) was a Russian Marxist revolutionary, writer, and critic.

39 CP is an abbreviation for Communist Party. CY is an abbreviation for Communist Youth.

# Lu Xun's Oeuvre

## Creative Writing

*Nahan* 吶喊 (Outcry). Beijing: Xinchao she, 1923.

*Panghuang* 彷徨 (Hesitation). Beijing: Beixin shuju, 1926.

*Yecao* 野草 (Weeds). Beijing: Beixin shuju, 1927.

*Zhao hua xi shi* 朝花夕拾 (Morning blossoms plucked at dusk). Beijing: Weiming she, 1928.

*Gushi xin bian* 故事新編 (Old tales retold). Shanghai: Wenhua shenghuo, 1936.

## Essay Collections

*Re feng* 熱風 (Hot wind). Beijing: Beixin shudian, 1925.

*Huagai ji* 華蓋集 (Inauspicious star). Beijing: Beixin shuju, 1926.

*Huagai ji xubian* 華蓋集續編 (Sequel to inauspicious star). Beijing: Beixin shuju, 1927.

*Fen* 墳 (Graves). Shanghai: Weiming she, 1927.

*Eryi ji* 而已集 (And that's all). Shanghai: Beixin shuju, 1928.

*San xian ji* 三閒集 (Three leisures). Shanghai: Beixin shuju, 1932.

*Er xin ji* 二心集 (Two hearts). Shanghai: Hezhong shudian, 1932.

*Wei ziyou shu* 偽自由書 (Fake liberty). Shanghai: Beixin shuju, 1933.

*Nan qiang bei diao ji* 南腔北調集 (Southern tunes in northern tones). Shanghai: Tongwen shudian, 1934.

*Zhun feng yue tan* 准風月談 (Quasi discourses on the wind and moon). Shanghai: Lianhuan shuju, 1934.

*Ji wai ji* 集外集 (Collection of the uncollected). Shanghai: Qunzhong tushu gongsi, 1935.

*Huabian wenxue* 花邊文學 (Fringed literature). Shanghai: Lianhua shuju, 1936.

*Qiejie ting zawen* 且介亭雜文 (Essays from the semi-concessions). Shanghai: San xian shuwu, 1937.

*Qiejie ting zawen er ji* 且介亭雜文二集 (Essays from the semi-concessions, volume 2). Shanghai: San xian shuwu, 1937.

*Qiejie ting zawen mo bian* 且介亭雜文末編 (Essays from the semi-concessions, final volume). Shanghai: San xian shuwu, 1937.

*Ji wai ji shiyi* 集外集拾遺 (Supplement to the collection of the uncollected). In *Lu Xun quanji* (Complete works of Lu Xun). Hankou: Shanghai fushe, 1938.

# Acknowledgments

Yang Xianyi and Gladys Yang, whose translations of Lu Xun's works have been invaluable to the field of modern Chinese literature, were an inspiration for this volume. First and foremost, we are grateful to all the translators who participated in this project. Their skill and artistry in rendering Lu Xun's language, which can sometimes be dense and abstruse, has made this collection what it is. In addition to contributing translations, Hu Ying and Theodore Huters also served as sounding boards and consultants. Peter Flueckiger, Christopher Rea, Tan Chang, Nicolai Volland, and Yao Ping gave invaluable advice along the way. The incisive comments of four anonymous reviewers helped us refine our thoughts and shape the manuscript into its current form.

The Ohio State University College of Arts and Sciences and Pomona College provided funds for a subvention and for research assistants. The volume would not have come to fruition without the help of Ji Zhiqiang, who took care of much of the nitty gritty work of the project—meticulously organizing files, tracking down answers to random queries, and locating and configuring illustrations. Xu Yichun offered valuable assistance with formatting the manuscript.

At Harvard University Press, we found enthusiastic support from Lindsay Waters and his team, including Joy Deng, Amanda Peery, and a host of others who seamlessly navigated us through the publishing waters.

For Eileen, the project coincided with the arrival of two little bundles, Ari and Melanie, sources of ceaseless wonder and delight. With gratitude to the village of family, friends, and caretakers who made it all possible and to Ko, for sharing the burdens and joys of everyday life.

For Kirk, the project coincided with the deaths of his beloved parents, who always encouraged him to follow his passions. He would like to dedicate this book to their memory.

The following presses granted permission for the inclusion of previously published translations:

"Ah Jin" and "Confucius in Modern China," in *The Chinese Essay*, translated and edited by David Pollard. Hong Kong: Research Centre for Translation, The Chinese University of Hong Kong, 1999; New York: Columbia University Press, 2000; London: C. Hurst & Co. (Publishers) Ltd., 2000, pp. 116–128. Copyright © 2000 by David Pollard. Reprinted with permission of Research Centre for Translation, The Chinese University of Hong Kong, in Asia and Australia, Columbia University Press, in North America, and C. Hurst & Co. (Publishers) Ltd., in the United Kingdom and Commonwealth.

"Divergence of Art and Politics," translated by Donald Holoch and Shu-ying Tsau, in *Modern Chinese Literary Thought: Writings on Literature, 1893–1945*, edited by Kirk A. Denton. Stanford, CA: Stanford University Press, pp. 328–334. Copyright © 1996 by the Board of Trustees of the Leland Stanford Jr. University. All rights reserved. Reprinted by permission of the publisher, Stanford University Press, sup.org.

"Impromptu Reflections No. 38: On Conceitedness and Inheritance," translated by Kirk A. Denton, in *Republican China* 16, no. 1 (November 1991): 89–97. Reprinted with permission of the publisher.

"On Photography," translated by Kirk A. Denton, in *Modern Chinese Literary Thought: Writings on Literature, 1893–1945*, edited by Kirk A. Denton. Stanford, CA: Stanford University Press, pp. 196–203. Copyright © 1996 by the Board of Trustees of the Leland Stanford Jr. University. All rights reserved. Reprinted by permission of the publisher, Stanford University Press, sup.org.

"Modern History" and "How to Train Wild Animals," translated by Andrew F. Jones, in *Developmental Fairy Tales: Evolutionary Thinking and Modern Chinese Culture*, by Andrew F. Jones. Cambridge, MA: Harvard University Press, pp. 1–2, 22–23. Copyright © 2011 by the President and Fellows of Harvard College.

# Illustration Credits

PAGE 14

Lu Xun in Japan, 1903. Reproduced from Zhou Haiying, *Lu Xun jiating da xiangpu* (Lu Xun family album) (Beijing: Tongxin, 2005), p. 10.

PAGE 28

Owl illustration by Lu Xun. From Lu Xun, *Fen* (Graves) (Shanghai: Qingguang shuju, 1933).

PAGE 38

Image of Ah Q, by Feng Zikai. From Feng Zikai and Lu Xun, *Manhua Ah Q zheng-zhuan* (Comic illustrated "True Story of Ah Q") (Shanghai: Kaiming shudian, Minguo 38, 1949), p. 3.

PAGE 88

*The Sacrifice*, by Käthe Kollwitz. From Käthe Kollwitz, *War (Krieg)* (1922; Dresden: Emil Richter, 1923), Plate 1. Reproduced from Käthe Kollwitz and Carl Zigrosser, *Kaethe Kollwitz* (New York: H. Bittner and Company, 1946), p. 69.

PAGE 194

"The Harvest Moon," by L. D. Bradley, *Chicago Daily News* (August 31, 1914). From L. D. Bradley and H. J. Smith, *Cartoons by Bradley: Cartoonist of the Chicago Daily News* (Chicago: Rand McNally & Co., 1917), p. 61. Reproduction courtesy of Frances Mulhall Achilles Library, Whitney Museum of American Art, New York, NY / Internet Archive.

PAGE 242

Speech at Beijing Normal University. Reproduced from *Lu Xun wenxian tu zhuan* (A pictorial biography of materials on Lu Xun) (Zhengzhou: Daxiang, 1998), p. 183.

PAGE 250

Portrait of Lu Xun, May 1, 1933. Reproduced from Zhou Haiying, *Lu Xun jiating da xiangpu* (Lu Xun family album) (Beijing: Tongxin, 2005), p. 69.

# Index

Note: Page ranges in boldface refer to essays in the volume.